MasterLife

Student Edition

Avery T. Willis, Jr.

LifeWay Press®
Nashville, Tennessee

© 1998 LifeWay Press®
Reprinted 2000, 2002, 2004, 2005, August 2006

No part of this work may be reproduced or transmitted in any form or by any means, electronic
or mechanical, including photocopying and recording, or by any information storage or retrieval system,
except as may be expressly permitted in writing by the publisher. Requests for permission should
be addressed in writing to LifeWay Press®, One LifeWay Plaza, Nashville, TN 37234-0174.

ISBN 0-7673-3495-7

This book is a resource in the Personal Life
category of the Christian Growth Study Plan.
Course CG-0438
Dewey Decimal Classification Number: 248.83
Subject Heading: YOUTH—RELIGIOUS LIFE/CHRISTIAN LIFE

Printed in the United States of America

Student Ministry Publishing
LifeWay Church Resources
One LifeWay Plaza
Nashville, TN 37234-0174

We believe the Bible has God for its author; salvation for its end; and truth,
without any mixture of error, for its matter and that all Scripture is totally true and trustworthy.
The 2000 statement of *The Baptist Faith and Message* is our doctrinal guideline.

Unless otherwise noted, Scripture quotations are from the Holy Bible,
New International Version,
copyright © 1973, 1978, 1984 by International Bible Society.
Used by permission.

Scripture quotations marked AMP are from The Amplified Bible © The Lockman Foundation 1954, 1958, 1987.
Used by permission.

Scripture quotations marked GNB are from the Good News Bible, the Bible in Today's English Version.
Copyright © American Bible Society 1976. Used by permission.

To order additional copies of this resource: WRITE LifeWay Church Resources Customer Service,
One LifeWay Plaza, Nashville, TN 37234-0113; FAX order to (615) 251-5933; PHONE 1-800-458-2772;
E-MAIL to *CustomerService@lifeway.com;* ONLINE at *www.lifeway.com;*
or visit the LifeWay Christian Store serving you.

CONTENTS

THE AUTHORS

AVERY T. WILLIS, JR., the author and developer of *MasterLife,* is the executive director of the International Orality Network. The original *MasterLife: Discipleship Training for Leaders,* published in 1980, has been used by more than 350,000 people in the United States and has been translated into more than 50 different languages. Willis is also the author of *Indonesian Revival: Why Two Million Came to Christ, The Biblical Basis of Missions, MasterBuilder: Multiplying Leaders, BibleGuide to Discipleship and Doctrine,* and coauthor with Henry Blackaby of *On Mission With God.* He also wrote Lead Like Jesus with Ken Blanchard and others, plus several books in Indonesian.

Avery served for 10 years as a pastor in Oklahoma and Texas and for 14 years as a missionary to Indonesia, during which he served for 6 years as the president of the Indonesian Baptist Theological Seminary. He served as the director of the Adult Department of the Discipleship and Family Development Division, the Sunday School Board of the Southern Baptist Convention for 15 years and as the senior vice-president of overseas operations at the International Mission Board of the Southern Baptist Convention for 10 years. He and his wife, Shirley, have five grown children. They experienced 19 straight years of having teenagers in the home and now are relating to their 15 grandchildren.

KAY MOORE is a veteran church curriculum writer and former senior editor for LifeWay Christian Resources. She and her husband, Louis, live in Garland, Texas, and have two grown children.

INTRODUCTION

MasterLife, Student Edition, is a developmental, small-group discipleship process that will help you develop a lifelong, obedient relationship with Christ. Through this study you will experience a deeper relationship with Jesus Christ as He leads you to develop six biblical disciplines of a disciple. This study will enable you to acknowledge Christ as your Master and to master life in Him.

WHAT'S IN IT FOR YOU

The goal of *MasterLife* is your discipleship—for you to become like Christ. To do that, you must follow Jesus, learn to do the things He instructed His followers to do, and help others become His disciples. *MasterLife* was designed to help you make the following definition of *discipleship* a way of life:

> Christian discipleship is a personal relationship with Jesus Christ experienced in a lifelong journey of obedience. As you follow Christ He transforms you to be like Him, He changes your values to His kingdom values, and He involves you in His mission in your home, church and world.

As you study the MasterLife process and learn to follow Christ as His disciple, you'll experience the thrill of growing spiritually. Several ways you'll grow are:

- Discovering that denying yourself, taking up your cross, and following Christ is such an exciting and challenging adventure that it will become the top priority of your life.
- Understanding what it means to abide, or live, in Christ, and you will experience the peace, security, and purpose that abiding in Christ brings.
- Experiencing the assurance and confidence that come from living in the Word. You'll develop new skills for studying and understanding the Bible. The Holy Spirit will use those skills to help you understand God's will for your life.
- Experiencing new power in prayer as you learn to pray in faith.
- Deepening fellowship with believers.
- Discovering the joy of sharing Christ with others—both by your words and actions.
- Experiencing the fulfillment of investing yourself in others by ministering to their needs.

- Observing that Christlike attitudes develop naturally and spontaneously in your life. These include—
  - —humility and servanthood;
  - —dependence on God;
  - —love for people, especially fellow Christians;
  - —confidence in yourself and in God;
  - —a sense of God's presence through His direct guidance;
  - —a desire to serve God and people;
  - —concern for unsaved people;
  - —deepening faith;
  - —overflowing joy;
  - —perseverance in faithfulness;
  - —appreciation of God's work through the church;
  - —companionship with family members;
  - —a prayerful spirit.

In weeks 1-6 you will explore your personal relationship with Jesus Christ. You'll learn how to draw the Disciple's Cross to illustrate the balanced life Christ wants His disciples to have. You'll learn that Christ wants to be at the center of your life so that everything you do is because of your relationship with Him.

Then in weeks 7-12 you'll focus on Christ's transforming your character into Christlikeness through the work of the Holy Spirit. Although you are a Christian, you may wonder why you continue to sin despite your best intentions, as if two people are at war inside you—one controlled by the Spirit and one controlled by the flesh. Jesus' disciples were not yet Christlike when they were born again, and neither were you. In this study you'll learn how the Holy Spirit can change your character and behavior into Christlikeness so that He can work through your will and your life. If you deny yourself and open yourself to the leading of the Holy Spirit, who lives in you, your character can grow more like that of Christ. The outgrowth of having Christ at the center of your personality is life in the Spirit. He will build Christlike character in you as you practice the following six disciplines:

- Spend time with the Master
- Live in the Word
- Pray in faith
- Fellowship with believers
- Witness to the world
- Minister to others

THE *MASTERLIFE* PROCESS

This study is designed to be individually studied and then processed in group sessions. Discipleship is experiential. Your experiences in studying *MasterLife* will be life-changing, and it's important that you discuss these experiences with your group.

HOW TO STUDY THIS BOOK

Each day, five days a week, you'll be expected to study a part of the material in this workbook and the related activities. You may need 20 to 30 minutes of study time each day. Even if you find that you can study the material in less time, spreading the study over five days will give you time to apply the truths to your life.

You will notice that discipline logos appear before various assignments:

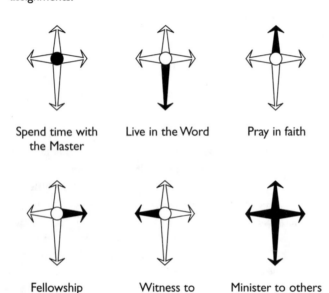

Spend time with   Live in the Word   Pray in faith
the Master

Fellowship   Witness to   Minister to others
with believers   the world

These logos link certain activities to the six disciplines you are learning to incorporate into your life as a disciple. These activities are part of your weekly assignments, which are outlined in "My Walk with the Master This Week" at the beginning of each week's material. The discipline logos differentiate your weekly assignments from the activities related to your study for that particular day.

Set a definite time and select a quiet place to study with little or no interruption. Keep a Bible handy to find Scriptures as directed in the material. Follow a systematic plan to read your Bible. This course suggests passages of Scripture for you to read each day. Later, you may want to follow the one provided in *DiscipleHelps: A Daily Quiet Time and Guide and Journal,* which can be ordered by calling 1-800-458-2772.

Memorizing Scripture is an important part of your work. You will be asked to memorize one Scripture each week. Set aside a portion of your study period for memory work. Unless I have deliberately chosen another version for a specific emphasis, all Scriptures in *MasterLife* are quoted from the *New International Version* of the Bible. However, feel free to memorize Scripture from any version of the Bible you prefer. I suggest that you write each memory verse on a card that you can review often during the week.

After completing each day's assignments, turn to the beginning of the week's material. If you completed an activity that corresponds to one listed under "My Walk with the Master This Week," place a vertical line in the diamond beside the activity. During the following group session a member of the group will verify your work and will add a horizontal line in the diamond, forming a cross in each diamond. This process will confirm that you have completed each weekly assignment before you continue. You may do the assignments at your own pace, but be sure to complete all of them before the next group session.

THE DISCIPLE'S CROSS

On page 204 you will find a diagram of the Disciple's Cross which illustrates the six Christian disciplines that you'll learn in this book. In weeks 1-6, you'll study an additional portion of the Disciple's Cross and will learn the Scripture that accompanies it. By the end of the study you will be able to explain the cross in your own words and to say all of the verses that go with it. You can learn to live the Disciple's Cross so that it embodies the way you show that you are Christ's follower.

THE DISCIPLE'S PERSONALITY

On pages 213-19 you will find the Disciple's Personality presentation. The Disciple's Personality, explains how to become more Christlike in character and behavior. In weeks 7-12 you'll study an additional part of the Disciple's Personality and will learn the Scripture that accompanies it. By the end of the study you will be able to explain the Disciple's Personality in your own words and to say all of the verses that go with it.

ABIDING IN CHRIST

This Bible study will help you understand what it means to abide in Christ and will allow you to commit to abide in Christ. Read *John 15:1-17*. Then complete the following questionnaire. Later, you will share phase 1 with another person, phase 2 with three other persons, and phase 3 with your entire group.

Phase 1
I find *John 15:1-17* (check one)—
❑ challenging; ❑ confusing;
❑ comforting; ❑ scary;
❑ refreshing; ☑ restrictive;
❑ other: _____

Imagine that Jesus is speaking directly to you as you read *John 15:1-17*. He says (check the statements that apply)—
❑ "I love you" *(v. 9);*
❑ "You are My friend" *(v. 15);*
☑ "I have chosen you" *(v. 16);*
❑ "I have ordained you to bring forth fruit" *(v. 16);*
❑ "I am speaking to you so that you may have fullness of joy" *(v. 11).*

How do you feel when Jesus makes the previous statements about you? Check one:
❑ Way to go, God!
❑ You couldn't mean me, Lord.
❑ I don't deserve this.
❑ Great; let's get going.
☑ What's the catch?

Phase 2
Christ says that if I am to abide in His love, I must keep His commandments. That makes me feel like (check one)—
❑ He is trying to bribe me into being obedient;
❑ He is sharing His secret for the way He abides in the Father's love;
❑ He is asking too much;
❑ He does not love me;
❑ He really wants me as a friend;
☑ Keeping His commandments is a great way to show my love for Him.

As I read that Christ has ordained me to bear fruit and that my fruit will last, I feel (check two)—
☑ thankful;
❑ inadequate;
❑ overjoyed;
❑ strengthened;
❑ defeated;
❑ confident;
☑ enthusiastic;
❑ indifferent.

Phase 3
To abide in Christ, I need to—

_____

_____

_____

_____

_____

In response to Jesus' speaking to me through *John 15:1-17*, for the next week I will concentrate on abiding in Christ by—

_____

_____

_____

_____

_____

AUTOBIOGRAPHY WORKSHEET

Session 1 provides an opportunity for you and other *MasterLife* participants to get to know one another. You will be asked to share your responses to the questions below. Jot down brief thoughts you want to share. Your response to each question should be no longer than one minute.

1. How have I become the person I am? What person(s) or event(s) have most influenced by values?

_____

_____

_____

_____

_____

_____

_____

_____

_____

_____

2. What motivated me to take MasterLife? Why do I want to be in this MasterLife group?

_____

_____

_____

_____

_____

_____

_____

_____

3. What may be my greatest weakness or difficulty in completing the 12 weeks?

_____

_____

_____

_____

_____

_____

DISCIPLESHIP COVENANT

To participate in *MasterLife*, you are asked to dedicate yourself to God and to your *MasterLife* group by making the following commitments. You may not currently be able to do everything listed, but by signing this covenant, you pledge to adopt these practices as you progress through the study.

As a disciple of Jesus Christ, I commit myself to—
- *acknowledge Jesus Christ as Lord of my life each day;*
- *attend all group sessions unless an emergency prevents it;*
- *spend enough time each day to complete all assignments;*
- *have a daily quiet time;*
- *keep a Daily Master Communication Guide about the way God speaks to me and I speak to Him;*
- *be faithful to my church in attendance and stewardship;*
- *love and encourage each group member;*
- *share my faith with others;*
- *keep in confidence anything that others share in the group sessions;*
- *be accountable to others in the group;*
- *become a discipler of others as God gives opportunities;*
- *pray daily for group members.*

List names and phone numbers of group members here.

Name	Phone #	Name	Phone #
Kiante Robinson			

Signed _Kiante Robinson_ Date _2-16-12_

WEEK 1

Spend Time with the Master

This Week's Goal

You will evaluate your discipleship and will focus on Christ as the center of your life.

My Walk with the Master This Week

You will complete the following activities to develop the six biblical disciplines. When you have completed each activity, draw a vertical line in the diamond beside it.

SPEND TIME WITH THE MASTER
◊ Tell how to have a daily quiet time and begin to have one regularly.

LIVE IN THE WORD
◊ Read your Bible every day. Write what God says to you and what you say to God.
◊ Memorize *John 15:5*.
◊ Review *Luke 9:23*.

PRAY IN FAITH
◊ Pray for each member of your *MasterLife* group by name at least twice this week.
◊ Find a prayer partner with whom you will pray each week.
◊ Use a map to pray for people throughout the world.

FELLOWSHIP WITH BELIEVERS
◊ Get better acquainted with a group member.

WITNESS TO THE WORLD
◊ Demonstrate how others know that you are a Christian.

MINISTER TO OTHERS
◊ Explain the center of the Disciple's Cross.

This Week's Scripture-Memory Verse

"I am the vine; you are the branches. If a man remains in me and I in him, he will bear much fruit; apart from me you can do nothing" (John 15:5).

The First Priority

When I went to college, I had been a Christian for several years. I had done almost everything my church had asked me to do. I tithed, attended church five times a week, occasionally visited prospects, and read my Bible daily. But when the influences of home and church were removed, I came face to face with who I really was. I realized that I possessed Christ as my Savior but that He did not possess me. I faced the decision, Am I going to be a disciple who gives everything to Christ? I spent many nights walking through the fields near the college, talking to God, and thinking about whether I really meant business about being a Christian.

Then I started looking at the Scriptures to see what being a disciple involves. The Bible told me that a disciple of Christ is someone who makes Christ the Lord of his or her life. As you learned during your introductory group session, *Luke 9:23* says, *"If anyone would come after me, he must deny himself and take up his cross daily and follow me."*

I realized that I would be either a real disciple of Christ or a luke warm Christian for the rest of my life. As people often do when they arrive at a crossroads in their walk with Christ, I began to make excuses. I told God that I wasn't capable of doing all He wanted me to do, that I had failed many times, and that I was not even sure He would want me to be His disciple.

In answer to my excuses, God showed me *2 Chronicles 16:9: "The eyes of the Lord range throughout the earth to strengthen those whose hearts are fully committed to him."* I remembered that evangelist D. L. Moody had heard his friend Henry Varley say, "It remains to be seen what God will do with a man who gives himself up completely to Him." In response Moody said, "I will be that man."[1] If anyone gave himself up wholly to God, it was D. L. Moody. With only a third-grade education he led hundreds of thousands of people in England and America to God. My response was "Lord, I want to be like that. I want to have a heart committed to You. Then if You do anything with my life, everyone will know it was because You did it and not because of my abilities."

My heart hasn't always been right toward God since that time. However, because of the commitment I made, the Holy Spirit shows me when my heart isn't right. I immediately confess and ask God to forgive me and to restore my heart.

That's how I decided to be a true disciple of Christ and to commit to a lifelong, obedient relationship with Him. I began by saying "I will obey and do whatever God tells me to do, and I will depend on Him to accomplish whatever He wants to accomplish through my life." The commitments I made during the following year set the course for my entire life. God began to reveal Himself to me and to teach me how to walk with Him. Looking back, I can say that everything that has been accomplished in my life has been because God did it.

This study is an opportunity for you to see where you stand in your relationship with Christ. It will help you evaluate yourself as a disciple and take steps to follow Him. Throughout your study of *MasterLife* I will share with you how Christ

Am I going to be a disciple who gives everything to Christ?

"Lord, I want to have a heart committed to You."

This study is an opportunity to see where you stand in your relationship with Christ.

[1]R. A. Torrey, *Why God Used D. L. Moody* (Chicago: Moody Press, 1923), 10.

continued to reveal to me what it means to be His disciple. As I share with you how Christ helped me through my journey as a student, a pastor, and a missionary and as I share other believers' testimonies, I hope that you'll learn the concepts of truly mastering life as Christ lives through you—that you'll learn what life in Christ is all about.

WHAT IS A DISCIPLE?

We begin this study by looking at who a disciple is and what a disciple does. The New Testament uses the term *disciple* three ways. First, it is a general term used to describe a committed follower of a teacher or a group.

Read *Mark 2:18* in the margin. The verse mentions three groups or individuals who have disciples. Who are they?

John's disciples and the Pharisees were fasting. Some people came and asked Jesus, "How is it that John's disciples and the disciples of the Pharisees are fasting, but yours are not?" (Mark 2:18).

1. _____

2. _____

3. _____

The persons or groups who had disciples are John, the Pharisees, and Jesus. These disciples were committed followers of these teachers or groups.

Second, the New Testament uses the term *disciple* to refer to the twelve apostles Jesus called. *Mark 3:14*, in the margin, is very specific about why Jesus called these apostles.

He appointed twelve—designating them apostles—that they might be with him and that he might send them out to preach and to have authority to drive out demons (Mark 3:14-15).

In *Mark 3:14* underline the phrases that show two purposes for which Jesus chose the twelve.

You probably underlined the words *that they might be with him* and *that he might send them out to preach.*

Jesus also used *disciple* to describe a follower who meets His requirements. For example, He said that His disciples must forsake families, possessions, or anything else that keeps them from following Him.

Read these verses: *Large crowds were traveling with Jesus, and turning to them he said: "If anyone comes to me and does not hate his father and mother, his wife and children, his brothers and sisters—yes, even his own life—he cannot be my disciple. And anyone who does not carry his cross and follow me cannot be my disciple" (Luke 14:26-27). Write in your own words what Jesus did when people began to follow Him.

Did you write something like this? He told them that to follow Him they must be His disciples. He then explained what it meant to be a disciple. *Luke 9:23*, the verse I hope you memorized in your introductory group session, also states what it means to be a disciple.

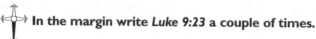 **In the margin write *Luke 9:23* a couple of times.**

So, now you know the term *disciple* is a general term for a committed follower of a teacher or a group, one of Jesus' twelve apostles, or a follower who meets Jesus' requirements.

LEARNING THE DISCIPLE'S CROSS

One way you can learn more about what Jesus had in mind for His disciples is to learn the Disciple's Cross—the foundation of this study. You can see the complete cross on page 204 and can read the presentation of the Disciple's Cross on pages 202–04. When you learn the cross thoroughly, you can use it in a variety of ways: it can help you to witness, to evaluate your church, and to reflect on where you stand in your discipleship.

As you complete this book, you'll study the various elements of the Disciple's Cross. Each week you will learn additional information. By the end of six weeks you'll be able to explain the cross in your own words and to quote all of the Scriptures that go with it.

Begin learning the Disciple's Cross by drawing a circle, representing you, in the margin. Write *Christ* in the center of the circle. This circle will help you focus on ways Christ is to be at the center of your life.

The empty circle you drew represents your life. It pictures denying all of self for Christ. This means that you lose your self-centeredness, not your identity. No one can become a disciple who is not willing to deny himself or herself. Christ must be the number one priority in your life.

PUTTING CHRIST FIRST

If someone asked you about your priorities, what would be on your list? Do you have a priority above Christ? For some that top priority might be a commitment to a sport. For others that priority might be acquiring material possessions. For still others that priority might be participating in religious activities. Religious activities? you may ask. Doesn't that mean I'm putting Christ first? Not always. Some people can be so involved in "doing church" that they forget the real reason for the activity. Their relationship with Christ may take a back seat to their desire to be recognized for their works or to meet an inner drive to achieve.

List the three highest priorities in your life.

1. _School_
2. _Golf_
3. _Sports_

You can't become a disciple of Christ if you're not willing to make Him number one on your priority list. Stop and pray, asking God to help you remove anything that keeps Him from having first place in your life. What do you need to do to give Him first place? List one action you will take to remove whatever stands in the way of placing Him first in your life.

Begin the practice of reading your Bible daily. Today read *Matthew 6:25-34*. After you have read this passage about priorities, complete the Daily Master Communication Guide in the margin.

Daily Master Communication Guide

Matthew 6:25-34

What God said to me:

What I said to God:

Under Christ's Control

JJesus' followers must love Him more than any other person, possession, or purpose.

You may believe that you are unusual if you struggle with the issue of priorities. Your friends, family, school, job, and other responsibilities demand a great deal of your time. Maybe you think that because previous generations had simpler lives, it was easier for them to focus on Christ and to meet the requirements for discipleship.

If that was true, then why was it necessary for Jesus to remind His disciples, who lived two thousand years ago, that they must give Him total loyalty? *Luke 14:26-33,* in the margin, states that His followers must love Him more than any other person, possession, or purpose.

"If anyone comes to me and does not hate his father and mother, his wife and children, his brothers and sisters—yes, even his own life—he cannot be my disciple. And anyone who does not carry his cross and follow me cannot be my disciple.
…In the same way, any of you who does not give up everything he has cannot be my disciple" (Luke 14:26-33).

Read the Scripture passage in the margin. Circle the parts teaching that Christ must have priority over the following areas of life. Draw a line from the part of the passage to its corresponding area. I have drawn the first line for you.

Person
Possession
Purpose

Clearly, these areas were concerns in Jesus' day just as they are in ours. In the previous exercise the correct answers are: Possession: *"Any of you who does not give up everything he has cannot be my disciple."* Purpose: *"And anyone who does not carry his cross and follow me cannot be my disciple."* The highest purpose is to bear one's cross, which glorifies God. One of the best ways to express cross bearing is by voluntary commitment to Kingdom work that you know is costly.

A DISCIPLE'S PRIORITIES

Christ's disciples had to learn gradually, just as we do. His followers sometimes put their own selfish needs and concerns above Him. Two of them chose sleep over honoring His request to stay awake and pray with Him in the garden of Gethsemane. They argued about who would be chief in His kingdom. When Jesus was arrested, His followers fled, and one of the closest to Him denied Him. Who was the disciples' first priority on such occasions?

But Jesus never gave up on the disciples, and after His death and resurrection their lives changed dramatically. *Acts 4:18-37* shows that His disciples loved Him more than any other person, possession, or purpose in their lives. Jesus never stopped working with them to transform them into His own character. Like them, you can begin to grow now, no matter how old or in what stage of discipleship you find yourself.

✝ **Continue the practice of reading your Bible daily. Read *Acts 4:18-37* today and ask God to speak to you. Then complete the Daily Master Communication Guide in the margin. Pray about how you will respond to Him. Under "What I said to God" write a summary of your prayer.**

The passage you just read indicates that the disciples loved Christ more than any other person, possession, or purpose. Can you say this about your relationship with Christ? Apply this passage to your life. List anyone or anything that presently takes priority over Christ in your life.

Person: _____

Possession: _____

Purpose: _____

As you began to draw the Disciple's Cross in day 1, you learned that Christ should have the main priority in your life, filling up the entire circle of your life as you focus on Him. This priority is necessary for a lifelong, obedient relationship with Him.

CHRIST AT THE CENTER

Randy prided himself on the work he did at church. Each Saturday he set up chairs for youth Sunday School. He served on the student council, taught a weekly Bible study, and helped at all student events. At least four nights a week he was involved in a project at church. Randy thought that if he did enough at church, people would appreciate and compliment him. When people told Randy that they admired him for his work, he beamed with pride. Soon Randy depended so much on others' praise of him that he forgot the real reason for his service. Randy thought that he was being obedient to Christ by his faithful church service, but his priorities had become misplaced, making his relationship with Christ second place.

If Randy drew a circle representing his life, whose name would likely be in the center of the circle?

What seems to be the motivation behind Randy's acts of service?

In the case study about Randy, what looked like service from obedience to Christ was actually service for self. Instead of doing good deeds in Christ's name to serve others, Randy served to gain the approval of others. It could be said that Randy, instead of Christ, was at the center of his circle. Realizing that the focus of our lives is on self instead of on Christ can be a startling revelation, but it is very important to be honest with yourself and with God about this matter.

Stop and pray, asking God to show you ways other persons, possessions, or purposes motivate you instead of your love for Him.

Who or what motivates you?

Daily Master Communication Guide

Acts 4:18-37

What God said to me:

What I said to God:

If you listed anything or anyone besides your love for Jesus Christ, confess in prayer that your life is controlled by impure desires. Then list the steps you will take to give Christ control of your life.

To be Christ's disciple, you need to surrender control to Him in every area of life.

To be Christ's disciple, you need to surrender control to Him in every area of life. Through MasterLife, the Holy Spirit will help you with this process.

 Pray for each member of your MasterLife group. Refer to your Discipleship Covenant on page 9 to recall group members' names.

DAY 3

Connected to the Vine

So far, so good, you may think. I want to have Jesus at the center of my life. I want to adjust my relationship with anyone, anything, or any purpose that takes priority over Him. But I get distracted. I get busy. I forget about Him. I sometimes wait to call on Him until I'm at the end of my rope. How can I allow Him to be the first priority in my life so that I turn to Him first? How can I have a personal, lifelong, obedient relationship with Him?

REMAINING IN CHRIST

The secret of discipleship is lordship. When you truly acknowledge Christ as Lord in all areas of your life, He lives in you in the fullness of His Spirit. He provides what you need to be like Him and to do His will.

 Read in the margin *John 15:5*, your Scripture-memory verse for this week, and complete this sentence:

Without Jesus' living in you and your living in Him, you can do

_____.

"I am the vine; you are the branches. If a man remains in me and I in him, he will bear much fruit; apart from me you can do nothing" (John 15:5).

You may try to make it on your own. You may try your own remedies and the world's remedies. You may do good deeds to satisfy your ego or to please others. But ultimately, the victory is His. You can do nothing to bear fruit without Him.

Jesus said that three things will characterize your life when He lives in you and you live in Him. Read the Scriptures in the margin. Match those three things with the appropriate verses.

_____ **1.** *Luke 6:46*	**a.** obedience
_____ **2.** *John 15:8*	**b.** love
_____ **3.** *John 13:34-35*	**c.** fruit

"Why do you call me, 'Lord, Lord,' and do not do what I say?" (Luke 6:46).

"This is to my Father's glory, that you bear much fruit, showing yourselves to be my disciples" (John 15:8).

"A new command I give you: Love one another. As I have loved you, so you must love one another. By this all men will know that you are my disciples, if you love one another" (John 13:34-35).

When He lives in you and you live in Him, obedience, love, and fruit are apparent to persons around you. The correct answers are 1. a, 2. c, 3. b. Remember these three things by putting them in sequence: love produces obedience, and obedience produces fruit.

In the diagram in the margin write the words obedience, love, and fruit in the correct sequence.

LIFE IN CHRIST

How do you abide in the Vine, as your Scripture-memory verse emphasizes? How do you make Christ the center of your life? Devote part of each day to a quiet time so that you can spend time with God and can stay attached to the Vine. Shut out distractions and totally turn over that portion of your day to Him. If you don't already do so, begin having a daily quiet time to stay in touch with God.

The two things that will help you grow most as a Christian are a quiet time and Scripture memory. Part of discipleship is setting aside from 15 to 20 minutes every day to spend with Jesus Christ, who is at the center of your life.

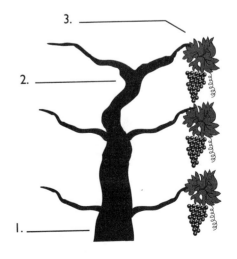

Daily Master Communication Guide

Luke 10:38-42

What God said to me:

What I said to God:

 Here are guidelines for having a daily quiet time. As you read, write decisions about your personal quiet time. Plan to explain to someone the importance of a quiet time.

How to Have a Quiet Time

1. Make a personal quiet time the top priority of your day.
   - Select a time to spend with God that fits your schedule. Usually, morning is best, but you may want or need to choose another time.

My quiet time is/will be _____ every day.

2. Prepare the night before.
   - If your quiet time is in the morning, set your alarm. If it's difficult for you to wake up, plan to exercise, bathe, dress, and eat before your quiet time.
   - Select a place where you can be alone. Have your Bible, notebook, and a pen or a pencil handy so that you won't waste time in the morning.

The place for my quiet time is/will be _____.

3. Develop a balanced plan of Bible reading and prayer.
   - Pray for guidance during your quiet time.
   - Follow a systematic plan to read your Bible. This course suggests passages of Scripture for you to read each day. Later, you may want to follow the plan provided in *DiscipleHelps: A Daily Quiet Time Guide and Journal*.
   - Make notes of what God says to you through His Word (use Daily Master Communication Guide).

Read *Luke 10:38-42*. **Write your responses in the Daily Master Communication Guide in the margin.**

- Pray in response to the Scriptures you have read.
- As you pray, use various components of prayer. For example, using the acronym ACTS—adoration, confession, thanksgiving, supplication—helps you remember the components.

Write the components of prayer: A _____
C _____
T _____
S _____

4. Be persistent until it's a habit.
- Strive for consistency rather than for length of time spent. Spend time with God every day rather than long devotional periods every other day.
- Expect interruptions. Satan tries to prevent you from spending time with God. Plan around interruptions rather than being frustrated by them.

Check the days this week you have a quiet time. ❑ **Monday** ❑ **Tuesday** ❑ **Wednesday** ❑ **Thursday** ❑ **Friday** ❑ **Saturday** ❑ **Sunday**

5. Focus on God rather than on the habit of having the quiet time. If you scheduled a meeting with the person you admire most, you wouldn't allow anything to stand in your way. Meeting God is even more important. He created you for fellowship with Him, and He saved you to bring about that fellowship.

LEARNING THE DISCIPLE'S CROSS

Now focus on the Disciple's Cross. Life in Christ is Christ living in you. *John 15:5* says: *"I am the vine; you are the branches. If a man remains in me and I in him, he will bear much fruit; apart from me you can do nothing."* What can you do without abiding in Christ? Nothing!

 Again draw a circle in the margin. Write Christ in the center, and under Christ write *John 15:5,* your memory verse for the week, so that you'll remember this basis of discipleship.

Christ said that He is the Vine and that we are the branches. The branches are part of the Vine. We are part of Christ. He wants to live His life through us.

Is this the kind of life you would like to have? ❑ Yes ❑ No Describe actions you need to take for Christ to live in you like that.

You may have answered something like this: I need to stop watching TV late at night so that I could have a quiet time at bedtime or could get up earlier and have a quiet time in the morning. Or I need to give up certain bad habits so that I would be a better example of Christ living in me. No matter how you answered, remember Christ's words in *John 15:5:* "Apart from me, you can do nothing." It doesn't say that you can do some things on your own. Ultimately, you can do nothing without Him.

Stop and pray, asking God to help you remove stumbling blocks from your life that keep you from staying connected to Him.

 Continue memorizing *John 15:5,* this week's memory verse. Say the verse aloud from one to three times from memory.

Learning your memory verse is an important part of *MasterLife* because memorizing Scripture is vital to mastering life in Christ. You can recall memorized verses when you need them to strengthen you and to fight temptation.

> Memorizing Scripture is vital to mastering life in Christ.

You also abide in Christ by praying. Find a prayer partner if you haven't already found one—someone who is not in your *MasterLife* group. Pray with your partner each week. You can meet to pray, or you can pray on the telephone. In the margin write the initials of someone you are considering to be your prayer partner. Tomorrow you'll write the name of the person you selected.

Pray by name for each member of your *MasterLife* group. Refer to your Discipleship Covenant to recall members' names.

DAY 4

Learning Obedience

After I had made my commitment to be a true disciple of Christ and made some real progress in the six disciplines of the disciple's cross, I met a cute girl that I wanted to impress. She seemed so fun loving that I thought she might not be interested in my new way of life. I told her of a lot of funny incidents in High school in which my behavior was not Christlike. We had a lot of laughs and good times, I thought. I also took her with me on some of the witnessing opportunities at the little rescue mission downtown.

I will never forget the day she broke the news, "Avery I like you, but I don't think we should see each other any more. I don't understand you. I like what I see you doing at the mission, but all the stories you tell about that happened in high school don't match. I don't know which person you are."

No persuasion on my part made any difference. She was determined to break up.

I was crushed. I had compromised who I really was to try to get her to like me. I was even more crushed when I realized how Christ must have felt. I went home and threw myself across the bed and cried out to God for forgiveness. He did forgive me for disobeying Him and going back on my commitment. I promised God "If you will have me as your disciple I will obey you and never let anyone else ever come between us. I know now that my life is Yours, and the only way I can be happy and fulfill Your purpose is to abide in Christ."

That was another key turning point in my life. I lost a girlfriend but gained a relationship to Christ as my friend that has never changed. It taught me that obedience as a disciple is the key to abiding in Christ.

When you have life in Christ, a lifelong, obedient relationship with Him is a natural result.

Check any item below that has caused you to disobey Christ's commands.
___ **Girl or boy friend**   ___ **Trying to be someone you weren't**
___ **Wanting to be liked**   ___ **Competing with someone**
___ **Trying to be funny**   ___ **Wanting to impress someone**
___ **Compromising your convictions**
___ **Trying to hold on to worldly things and still abide in Christ**

When you have life in Christ, having completely turned over your life to Him, a lifelong, obedient relationship with Him is a natural result. And when you obey Christ, you want to stay connected to Him and to follow His teachings. As a result of obeying His commands, you bear fruit.

The key to discipleship is obedience to Christ's _____.

Find the following verses and match the benefits of obeying Christ's commands.
___ 1. *John 15:10*   a. You show that you are His disciple.
___ 2. *John 14:21*   b. You are blessed.
___ 3. *John 13:34-35*   c. You remain in His love.
___ 4. *John 13:17*   d. The Father loves you and reveals Himself to you.

Obeying Christ's commands is the key to discipleship. When you obey these commands, you benefit because you remain in His love (1. c), the Father loves you and reveals Himself to you (2. d), you show that you are His disciple (3. a), and you are blessed (4. b). Christ doesn't want you to obey Him just to be good; He wants you to be obedient so you can be involved in His mission.

OBEYING CHRIST'S COMMANDS

OK, you think, that sounds good. I want to obey Christ's commands. I want to have those benefits I just read about. I want to be involved in His mission. But how do I take the first step? How do I start the process of obeying Him? To obey Christ's commands requires two things: knowing them and doing them. Do you know them? Are you doing what Christ commanded?

Read the following verses and write in your own words what Christ wants you to emphasize.

1. *Matthew 5:19-20:*

2. *Matthew 7:21,24-27:*

3. *Matthew 28:19-20:*

4. *James 1:22:*

The Bible is very clear about what area Jesus wants you to emphasize. You may have answered something like this: 1. Doing and teaching His commands. 2. Doing His will and practicing His teachings. 3. Observing any or all of His commands. 4. Doing the Word.

Describe one step you can take to know and do His commands so that you can be obedient.

You may have answered something like this: I need to set aside time each day to read the Bible so that I'll know what the Scriptures tell me to do. I need to develop a consistent quiet time so that I can hear God speak to me through His Word. I need to respond immediately when I read Christ's commands or feel His Spirit urging me to obey a command or a Scripture in response to a situation.

Continue memorizing *John 15:5*. Say this verse aloud to someone in your group. Become better acquainted with the group member to whom you recited your memory verse. In the process of getting to know this person, describe in your own words how obedience relates to discipleship.

Have you chosen a prayer partner? Write the name of the person you chose: _____

TAKING ACTION

Have you heard someone say, "Actions speak louder than words"? That statement also applies to your Christian life. You may know the right thing to do, but what

Daily Master Communication Guide

Matthew 26:47-56

What God said to me:

What I said to God:

good is knowledge without action? If you are grounded in God's Word but it makes no difference in your life, your knowledge is fruitless. To show that you love Christ, you also need to obey, keep, and do His commandments.

Stop and pray, asking God to help you begin the practice you listed that will help you become more obedient.
Check one or more of the following that you are ready and willing to do.

❑ **Give Christ first priority in your life**
❑ **Follow Christ by obeying His commands**
❑ **Abide in Christ so that He can produce His life and fruit in you**

Suppose you lived in a country that wanted to put you in jail for being a Christian. Would members of a court of law be able to prove that you are a Christian? Write below the evidence they see in your life, based on the three choices above?

One way you demonstrate that you are a Christian is to follow Christ's command in *Matthew 28:19-20*, the ultimate demonstration of fruit bearing: *"Go and make disciples of all nations, baptizing them in the name of the Father and of the Son and of the Holy Spirit, and teaching them to obey everything I have commanded you. And surely I am with you always, to the very end of the age."* If you follow His commands, you'll be aware of the world's needs and will pray daily for those needs.

When I was a teenager God impressed on me that I should pray for people in trouble. When I would hear a siren I would shoot up a brief prayer for whoever was in danger. Later, I learned that all kinds of things can be prayer reminders.

Look at a globe or map of the world and begin to pray for specific countries or people groups. As you listen to news broadcasts read newspapers, and newsmagazines, or watch TV send up a quick, silent prayer for people in trouble. As you read magazines like *The Commission, Sports Illustrated,* **or** *Seventeen* **pray for the people you are reading about. When you become aware of people who are in crisis and need the Lord, immediately pray for them as an ongoing conversation with Christ.**

Continue having your daily quiet time. For your Bible reading use *Matthew 26:47-56,* **a passage about an act of supreme obedience. After you have read this passage, complete the Daily Master Communication Guide in the margin.**

DAY 5

Challenges to Obedience

Several years ago I was in the United States on furlough from missionary work in Indonesia. During this time in the United States I visited many churches that seemed almost dead, showing no excitement or energy in worshiping or serving the Lord. Our denomination had just made a commitment to enlist 50,000 volunteers for short-term mission trips overseas. Having seen little evidence of Christ's lordship in these churches, I couldn't imagine sending people with no excitement or energy for the Lord.

God directed me to return to the United States and make disciples so that our denomination could reach its commitment to share the gospel with everyone in the world. Deeply committed to my work as a missionary, I struggled to understand why God would call a missionary back to the United States indefinitely. For the next eight months I struggled with God about this matter.

As I preached about Peter's being commanded to eat unclean animals on a large sheet (see *Acts 10)*, I began to see in that sheet the dead churches I had visited. I sensed God saying to me, "Rise and eat." I told God that I didn't want to get involved with already dead churches and that I wanted to return to Indonesia. I even reminded God that Peter had three men at the gate telling him what to do, and that I didn't have anyone!

Immediately three men asked me to do things that applied to my struggle: (1) I was asked to translate *MasterLife* into English to train a church staff; (2) I was asked by this publisher if I would adapt *MasterLife* for an English-speaking audience; (3) I was asked to help design a plan to train people to witness. I struggled for months, but finally, God spoke very clearly to me about this matter. Even though I didn't want to leave my work in Indonesia I knew that I must obey God if I was going to teach others to be His obedient disciples.

I knew that I must obey God if I was going to teach others to be His obedient disciples.

COMMITTED TO OBEY

Are you like me—not as obedient as you could be or should be? Do you make excuses for not being obedient, as I did? Read *Philippians 2:13* in the margin. Christ created in His disciples a desire and an ability to obey Him. He didn't want them to obey just to be good; He wanted to involve them in His work. Jesus used the following process to teach the disciples: (1) He commanded, and they obeyed; (2) they learned by doing what He commanded them to do; (3) Christ then discussed the meaning of the experience with them.

God is always at work in you to make you willing and able to obey his own purpose (Phil. 2:13, GNB).

Jesus called His disciples to leave what they were doing and to follow Him. Andrew, Peter, James, and John left their fishing businesses and followed Him (see *Matt. 4:18-22*). Matthew left his job as a tax collector (see *Matt. 9:9*). In the margin describe something that would be difficult for you to leave behind or do if God asked you to.

Jesus told Peter to catch a fish, take a coin from its mouth, and pay their taxes (*Matt. 17:27*). In the margin write what you would do if God asked you to do something that didn't make sense to you.

Jesus told His disciples to get a colt for Him and, if the owners asked

what they were doing, to say: *"The Lord needs it" (Mark 11:3)*. If Jesus told you to get a car parked at Main and First streets, what would you do, especially if you had to answer the owner's questions with the statement "The Lord needs it"? Write your answer in the margin.

When Jesus told Philip to feed the five thousand, Philip said it was impossible. Andrew offered a boy's lunch *(John 6:5-11)*. Which disciple would you be most like? ❑ Philip ❑ Andrew

Have you been disobedient because you believed that what God asked you to do was unreasonable or didn't make sense? ❑ Yes ❑ No

Like the disciples, we are to obey Jesus' commands. Jesus provided resources to help His disciples obey: He prayed for them, sent the Holy Spirit, and provided His written Word. You and I have the same resources available to us. If you obey His commands, you'll experience His love and will bear His fruit. You can have a lifelong, obedient relationship with Him.

To review this week's theme, complete the sentence in the margin.

If you had difficulty completing the sentence, review the illustration on page 17. As you have studied, you can let Christ lead you and help you so that your life is characterized by obedience, love, and fruit.

LEARNING THE DISCIPLE'S CROSS

Your primary task is to abide in Christ, the Vine. If you do this, He will be at the center of your life. Below I have drawn for you all of the elements of the Disciple's Cross but haven't placed Christ at the center of the circle. Fill in the circle and under it write *John 15:5* as a reminder of the Vine and the branches.

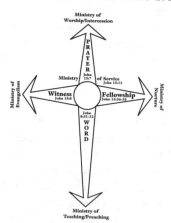

Today in your quiet time read *John 15*. As you read, look for ways this passage addresses your need to have Christ at the center of your life. Each week I'll ask you to read this passage and to look for ways God uses it to speak to that week's discipline. After you have read this passage, complete the Daily Master Communication Guide in the margin.

HAS THIS WEEK MADE A DIFFERENCE?

Review "My Walk with the Master This Week" on page 10. Mark the activities you've finished by drawing vertical lines in the diamonds beside them. Finish any incomplete activities.

Margin notes:

Like the disciples, we are to obey Jesus' commands.

If your life is characterized by _____, you will experience Christ's _____ and will bear _____.

Daily Master Communication Guide

John 15

What God said to me:

What I said to God:

The following inventory will help you evaluate your Christian life. It's for your private use, not for comparing yourself with anyone else. It's not a test, and no one is expected to make a perfect score. Your score reflects how you feel about your life of discipleship and what you do. Ask God to help you see where you are now and where He wants you to be in your relationship with Jesus Christ.

Evaluate your Christian life by filling in the circle that closely represents what you do.	Always	Usually	Sometimes	Seldom	Never

Spending Time with the Master
- I have a daily quiet time. ○ ○ ○ ○ ○
- I try to make Christ Lord of my life. ○ ○ ○ ○ ○
- I feel close to the Lord during the day. ○ ○ ○ ○ ○
- I try to discipline myself. ○ ○ ○ ○ ○
- I'm aware that the Lord disciplines me. ○ ○ ○ ○ ○

Living in the Word
- I read my Bible daily. ○ ○ ○ ○ ○
- I study my Bible each week. ○ ○ ○ ○ ○
- I memorize a Scripture verse weekly. ○ ○ ○ ○ ○
- I take notes at least once a week as I hear, read, or study the Bible in order to apply it to my life. ○ ○ ○ ○ ○

Praying in Faith
- I keep a prayer list and pray for the persons and concerns on the list. ○ ○ ○ ○ ○
- I've experienced a specific answer to prayer during the past month. ○ ○ ○ ○ ○
- Each day my prayers include thanksgiving, praise, confession, petition, and intercession. ○ ○ ○ ○ ○

Fellowshipping with Believers
- I seek to live in peace with my fellow Christians. ○ ○ ○ ○ ○
- I seek reconciliation with those who have a problem with me or with whom I have a problem. ○ ○ ○ ○ ○
- Others know I am a Christian by the way I love God's people. ○ ○ ○ ○ ○
- I live in harmony with other members of my family. ○ ○ ○ ○ ○

Witnessing to the World
- I regularly pray for lost persons by name. ○ ○ ○ ○ ○
- I share my testimony when I have an appropriate opportunity. ○ ○ ○ ○ ○
- I share the plan of salvation with those who are open to hear it. ○ ○ ○ ○ ○
- I witness for Christ weekly ○ ○ ○ ○ ○
- I follow up on and encourage persons I have won to Christ. ○ ○ ○ ○ ○

Ministering to Others
- I serve Christ by serving in my church. ○ ○ ○ ○ ○
- I give my tithe at my church. ○ ○ ○ ○ ○
- Each month I do kind deeds for persons less fortunate than I. ○ ○ ○ ○ ○
- I have goals for my life that I keep clearly in mind. ○ ○ ○ ○ ○

Subtotals ___ ___ ___ ___
x4 x3 x2 x1

Totals ___ ___ ___ ___

Score ___

Scoring: Each check in the "Always" column is 4 points; the "Usually" column, 3 points; the "Sometimes" column, 2 points; the "Seldom" column, 1 point; "Never" column, 0 points. Add the four totals together to get your overall score out of a possible 100.

Complete the following statements.

My score (does/does not) reflect my life of discipleship because

_____.

Other factors not mentioned in the inventory and my feelings about them are

_____.

My personal, overall evaluation of my discipleship is_____.

WEEK 2

Live in the Word

This Week's Goal

You will grow closer to Christ as you learn to live in the Word by having a daily quiet time and by memorizing Scripture.

My Walk with the Master This Week

You will complete the following activities to develop the six biblical disciplines. When you have completed each activity, draw a vertical line in the diamond beside it.

SPEND TIME WITH THE MASTER

◇ During your daily quiet time use the Daily Master Communication Guides in the margins of this week's material.

LIVE IN THE WORD

◇ Read your Bible every day. Write what God says to you and what you say to God on the Daily Communication Guide or in a personal notebook or journal.

◇ Memorize *John 8:31-32*

◇ Review *Luke 9:23* and *John 15:5*, which you have already memorized.

PRAY IN FAITH

◇ Pray for each member of your *MasterLife* group by name.

◇ Pray with your prayer partner once this week. If you don't have a prayer partner yet, find one this week.

FELLOWSHIP WITH BELIEVERS

◇ Get better acquainted with a member of your group. Visit or call that person. Tell the person that you are praying for him or her. Talk about any blessings or challenges you are having in MasterLife.

WITNESS TO THE WORLD

◇ List the names of at least five lost persons on your Prayer Covenant List. Begin praying regularly for them. Make any contacts the Spirit leads you to make.

MINISTER TO OTHERS

◇ Continue learning the Disciple's Cross. Learn the meaning of the bottom part of the cross to add to the information about the circle that you learned last week.

This Week's Scripture-Memory Verses

"If you hold to my teaching, you are really my disciples. Then you will know the truth, and the truth will set you free" (John 8:31-32).

DAY 1

A Close Relationship

I felt guilty when I was a teenager because I couldn't seem do a daily quiet time regularly. Then I read a tract that emphasized the importance of spending a short period with God every morning. It suggested a simple plan so I decided that no matter what, I would spend seven minutes with God every morning.

I learned that a quiet time is more than merely a habit. It's an appointment at the beginning of the day with Jesus Christ, who is at the center of my life. I suggest that you set aside a few minutes every morning with Jesus Christ, for He is also at the center of your life.

Your daily time with Christ is the first of six disciplines that are basic to a disciple's walk. Last week you studied denying yourself and putting Christ at the center of your life as part of becoming a disciple and developing a lifelong, obedient relationship with Him. This week you'll begin learning what it means for Christ to be at the center of your life.

A quiet time is more than merely a habit. It is an appointment with Jesus Christ.

LEARNING THE DISCIPLE'S CROSS

Last week you drew the center part of the Disciple's Cross for the role Christ is to have in your life. As you continue in *MasterLife*, you'll draw the cross around the center, one bar at a time, as you add to your life six disciplines that keep you abiding in Christ.

You can visualize the cross as representing the six disciplines a disciple needs to practice.

In the margin label each discipline on the Disciple's Cross. Refer to pages 6 or 202 if you need help.

By the end of your study you'll be able to explain the cross and to quote the Scriptures with it. Each bar of the cross represents one part of the Christian life. The bottom part represents the Word, and the upper part represents prayer. These form the vertical crossbar, which represents your relationship with God. The horizontal crossbar represents your relationships with others. In your life in Christ you have one Lord, represented by the circle with Christ as the center, and two relationships—with God and other persons.

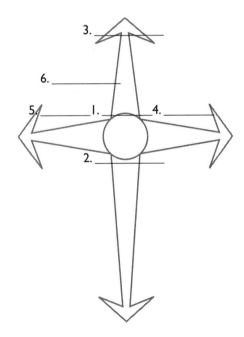

REMAINING IN THE WORD

The way to have Christ living in you is to have His Word in you. The first discipline is spending time with the Master by having a quiet time. The second and third disciplines, living in the Word and praying in faith, will support your quiet time. Jesus said in *John 8:31-32*: *"If you hold to my teaching, you are really my disciples. Then you will <u>know</u> the <u>truth</u>, and the truth will set you free."* The Word is food for you. You cannot grow unless you regularly spend time in the Word.

Reread *John 8:31-32*. Underline what the verses say about becoming Christ's disciple. Then begin memorizing *John 8:31-32* by saying the verses aloud from one to three times.

One way to experience Christ living in you more fully is to have His Word in you.

You likely underlined the phrase *"If you hold to my teaching."* Christ's teaching is found in the Word. The absence of a regular habit to read His Word keeps you from being the kind of follower Christ wants you to be. You may wonder: *What difference does it make if I remain in His Word? Won't I still have the same problems as anyone else? I'll still have sorrows in my life. Will it really matter if I live as a disciple of Christ?* As a Christian, you aren't free from problems. But remaining in His Word grows a relationship so you can successfully face your problems. The Scriptures point to Christ as the source of guidance and strength.

A DAILY APPOINTMENT

One way you can know Christ's teaching is through daily Bible reading, meditation, and prayer. No substitute exists for a quiet time. *Joshua 1:8* says of the Word, *"'Meditate on it day and night, so that you may be careful to do everything written in it.'"* Memorizing puts God's Word in your head. Meditating puts it in your heart. With God's Word in your heart you can face any circumstance.

Several years ago I was going to have surgery. In my quiet time I read *Psalm 116:1-9.* In *verse 3* I read:

> The cords of death entangled me,
> the anguish of the grave came upon me;
> I was overcome by trouble and sorrow.

I wrote in my prayer journal, "This operation is going to be more dangerous than I thought." I prepared for the worst and then put my trust in what God said in *verses 7-9:*

> Be at rest once more, O my soul, for the Lord has been good to you.
> For you, O Lord, have delivered my soul from death, my eyes from
> tears, my feet from stumbling, that I may walk before the Lord
> in the land of the living.

After the surgery the medical report showed one cancer cell. At first I was startled by the word *cancer,* but Scripture came to my mind and quieted my soul. Years have passed since that surgery, and I've had no other cancer cells. I thanked God for His warning about the cancer through His Word, which prepared me for the outcome of the surgery. Striving to live a life of obedience didn't make me immune to cancer, but my habit of a regular quiet time helped me get through a difficult time with strength and comfort.

Have you had an experience that led you to closer fellowship with Christ so that you could be more receptive to His direction? ❑ Yes ☑ No If so, in the margin describe your experience.

FELLOWSHIP WITH GOD

The first reason for a quiet time is that it helps you get to know God through fellowship with Him. This week you will study this and three more reasons. Read in the margin the four reasons for a quiet time.

It's natural to want to communicate with someone you love. Think about the way you feel when you go for a while without seeing or talking to someone you love. You can't wait to hear from them. When you are a child of God, you have a deep desire for fellowship with your Heavenly Father.

Reasons for a Quiet Time

____ 1. To know God through fellowship with Him

__✓__ 2. To receive direction and guidance for daily decisions

____ 3. To bring needs before God

____ 4. To bear spiritual fruit

Check the above reasons you would like to experience in your life.

In the Bible look up the verses and answer in your own words the following questions:

Why do you love God (see *1 John 4:19*)?

He has set me free from eternal damnation with everlasting life

How do you know that God loves you (see *1 John 4:9-10*)?

He died for us

You love God as a response to Him: He first loved you. You know that He loves you because He sent His Son to die for you. Failing to return God's love doesn't influence the way He feels about you. But your love for Him shrinks and grows stale if you don't have the food from daily fellowship with Him. A daily quiet time is important so you can enjoy a close relationship with God. Christ doesn't promise that you'll be free from death or that your struggles will be fewer if you fellowship with Him. But He promises that you'll have knowledge of Him, the power of the resurrection, and fellowship during times of suffering..

In the space below write the first reason for a daily quiet time.

1. *To walk closer with Christ*

When you love someone—and as a Christian, you are to love Christ above all else—you don't want to be separated from that person. You can't really know someone unless you spend time with him or her. To answer the question in the previous activity, you likely wrote something like "so that I can know Him through fellowship with Him" or "because I love Him."

Your habit of a daily quiet time strengthens your relationship with the Vine, without whom you can do nothing. Last week's memory verse, *John 15:5,* underscores your helplessness if you are not connected to Christ. He wants to change your character into Christlikeness as you stay connected to Him.

 Memorize *John 8:31-32* and review *Luke 9:23*. Say them aloud to a family member or a friend.

 Today read *Matthew 26:36-46*, a passage describing a time when Jesus sought to be alone for prayer. Complete the Daily Master Communication Guide in the margin.

Daily Master Communication Guide

Matthew 26:36-46

What God said to me:

What I said to God:

DAY 2

Guidance for Daily Decisions

As you begin living in the Word, the problem of time may come up. You may think: *Sure, it's good to read my Bible daily. I can try to establish that habit. But living in the Word sounds like something I do around the clock. Does anyone really have enough hours in the day to live in the Word all the time? I have school, family, and other responsibilities. I can't walk around with a Bible in my hand all day.*

Certainly, reading your Bible regularly is a primary way to live in the Word. You need that daily discipline. However, you can receive the Word in many ways besides reading it. These include listening to someone preach it, studying it, memorizing it, meditating on it, recalling it, and applying it. Making Christ Lord and having a personal, lifelong, obedient relationship with Him mean that you want to study and meditate on the Word regularly. Then you live what it says.

In the previous paragraph underline ways to receive the Word.

God's Word can be a part of your daily life in all kinds of situations, as you remember Scripture verses you have memorized. You'll also find yourself making countless decisions that require you to apply scriptural truths. Even when you can't have an open Bible in front of you, you can meditate on verses you've memorized. Hearing someone preach the Word teaches you what God plans for you. Developing daily habits of reading and studying the Scriptures helps you live in the Word. In the previous activity you likely underlined all of these ways.

Work on this week's Scripture-memory verses, *John 8:31-32*. Say the verses aloud several times. Be aware of times you apply these verses to your life this week.

LEARNING THE DISCIPLE'S CROSS
Draw the parts of the Disciple's Cross that you've studied. Draw a circle with Christ and *John 15:5* in the center and draw the lower crossbar with Word written on it. Write *John 8:31-32* on the lower crossbar. Say aloud what you've learned about the Disciple's Cross so far.

One way to get the Word into your mind and heart is through a daily quiet time. Today you'll study the second reason for a quiet time: to receive direction and guidance for daily decisions.

ASKING GOD TO SHOW YOU THE WAY

The second reason for a daily quiet time is it provides direction and guidance for your daily decisions. You learn God's will as you meditate on His Word and commune with His Spirit. *Psalm 143:8* can be your prayer: *Show me the way I should go, for to you I lift up my soul.*

In *Psalm 143:8* what did the psalmist ask God to do for him?

***First John 5:14* says, *This is the confidence we have in approaching God: that if we ask anything according to his will, he hears us.* What does this verse say about God's response if you pray according to His will?**

Like the psalmist, you can ask God to show you the way you should walk in your life in Christ. If you pray according to His will, you have the guarantee that He hears you. I know of no greater reason for taking time to strengthen your relationship with Him daily!

FINDING DIRECTION IN THE WORD

God has used His Word to reveal His direction for me over and over again. Once my wife and I were in South Africa leading *MasterLife* training for nine countries. Word arrived that because of a political boycott, no passengers from South Africa would be allowed to get off in Kenya, where we were to conduct training for nine countries. We couldn't find a solution. If we weren't allowed to enter Kenya, we would have to go on to Europe without leading the training.

The day before we were to leave, we decided to go to Zimbabwe, to get new passports, visas, and tickets in an attempt to travel to Kenya. On the morning we were to leave, I read in my quiet time *Psalm 118. Verses 5-8* say:

> *In my anguish I cried to the Lord, and he answered by setting me free.*
> *The Lord is with me; I will not be afraid.*
> *What can man do to me?*
> *The Lord is with me; he is my helper.*
> *I will look in triumph on my enemies.*
> *It is better to take refuge in the Lord than to trust in man.*

I felt that these verses were God's promise that we would be able to enter Kenya. *Verses 14-16* seemed to offer further affirmation:

> *The Lord is my strength and my song; he has become my salvation.*
> *Shouts of joy and victory resound in the tents of the righteous:*
> *"The Lord's right hand has done mighty things!*
>   *The Lord's right hand is lifted high;*
>   *the Lord's right hand has done mighty things!"*

A daily quiet time provides direction and guidance for your daily decisions.

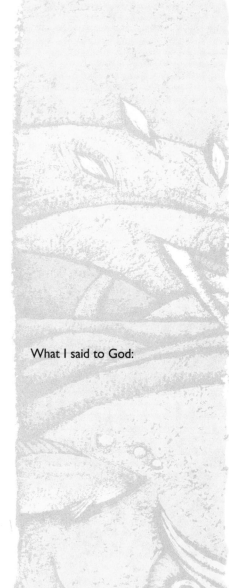

**Daily Master
Communication Guide**

Psalm 118

What God said to me:

What I said to God:

We arrived in Zimbabwe, with only one hour to obtain the new passports, visas, and tickets, but God did it! In Kenya, the officials turned back the three persons in front of us, but they examined our new passports and visas and let us walk through! Shouts of joy and victory came from us and from those who had prayed that we would be able to enter the country. God had performed a miracle, and I was thankful that I had sought answers from His Word. Without God's assurance, I wouldn't have been bold enough to start on the journey.

Has God ever helped you make a decision as you looked for answers from His Word? ☑Yes ☐No   If so, describe your experience.

To summarize what you've learned today, fill in the blanks below. Check your work by reviewing the list on page 31.

The first two reasons for a daily quiet time are:

1. For Direction

2. Closer Relationship

Read *Psalm 118* as your Bible passage today and see how God uses it to speak to you. After you've read this passage, complete the Daily Master Communication Guide in the margin.

Pray for each member of your *MasterLife* group. Refer to your Discipleship Covenant to recall their names.

DAY 3
Petitioning for Needs

By now you're realizing that remaining in Christ's Word, or holding to His teaching, is not a one-time action. Have you ever read your Bible, closed it, and had a self-satisfied feeling like "Whew! Now that's done"? This isn't a task that can be accomplished and then set aside indefinitely. Remaining in His Word, or holding to His teaching, means His Word is so much a part of your life that it's like the air you breathe. Your memory verses for the week are *John 8:31-32: "If you hold to my teaching, you are really my disciples. Then you will know the truth, and the truth will set you free."* Today you'll study what it means to hold to Christ's teaching.

BRINGING YOUR NEEDS TO GOD

If you hold to Christ's teaching, you won't wait to ask for His help as a last resort. He will be your first source of help. You'll seek the Scriptures first when you have needs. This is the third good reason to have a daily quiet time. Needs and problems in your life can make you realize your dependence on God. He wants to meet your needs. In a quiet time you can bring your needs before God.

Today you'll study the third reason for a quiet time: to bring needs before God. List in the margin the first two reasons for a quiet time.

Read the verses in the margin. Match the references in the left column with the prayer promises from the Bible in the right column.

C 1. *Philippians 4:4-7*   **a. God renews our strength as we wait on Him.**
B 2. *Psalm 34:17*   **b. In prayer we find grace in our need.**
D 3. *Hebrews 4:16*   **c. God delivers the righteous from trouble.**
A 4. *Isaiah 40:31*   **d. As we make our requests known to God, He gives us peace.**

These are wonderful promises about what happens when you pray! God provides grace, peace, strength, and deliverance from trouble. The correct answers are 1. d, 2. c, 3. b, and 4. a. Beautiful promises await you if you remain in the Word, as your memory verses, *John 8:31-32*, remind you.

 Take a few minutes to review your memory verses, *John 8:31-32*. Without looking back at page 26, write the verses in the margin to see how well you can recall them.

By this point in *MasterLife* you may be saying to yourself: *This memory work is tough. I've never been very good at memorizing things.* You may think that you are too busy or too young to begin memorizing Scripture. But Scripture memorization is a major part of remaining in the Word. Being able to recall verses as you need them is important in a Christian's daily walk.

My family always had what they called family devotions when I was growing up. We met after breakfast each morning for about 15 minutes. One of the things we

---

The first two reasons for a quiet time:
1. Direction

2. Relatioship

The third reason for a quiet time is to bring needs before God.

Rejoice in the Lord always. I will say it again: Rejoice! let your gentleness be evident to all. The Lord is near. Do not be anxious about anything, but in everything, by prayer and petition, with thanksgiving, present your requests to God. And the peace of God, which transcends all understanding, will guard your hearts and your minds in Christ Jesus (Phil. 4:4-7).

The righteous cry out, and the Lord hears them; he delivers them from all their troubles (Ps. 34:17).

Let us then approach the throne of grace with confidence, so that we may receive mercy and find grace to help us in our time of need (Heb. 4:16).

Those who hope in the Lord will renew their strength.
They will soar on wings like eagles; they will run and not grow weary, they will walk and not be faint (Isa. 40:31).

Being able to recall Scripture verses as you need them is important in a Christian's daily walk.

did was memorize and quote Scripture. I didn't realize that my parents were arming me to face temptations and to make right decisions for life. Once my father promised me a sum of money if I would memorize the Sermon on the Mount *(Matt. 5-7)*. I never did it. But later in my freshman year in college the professor said anyone who memorized the Sermon on the Mount and said it to the class would not have to take the final exam. I thought I could collect on both rewards and memorized it. I didn't have to take the final, but my dad said it was too late to collect on his offer! But I got much more out of the experience since Scripture memory has become a part of my life.

My wife and I helped our children memorize Scripture because along with the quiet time, Scripture memory made the greatest impact on my spiritual growth. Imagine my delight when my oldest son called one day and said that my grandson, Matt, age six, had something to say to me. He quoted *Isaiah 53:6!* Then his brother, Kyle, age three wanted to quote it—which he did but he gave a different reference since he didn't know numbers. They both eventually memorized a verse for every letter of the alphabet and before they became teenagers quoted *Colossians 3* in its entirety—big words and all! I have watched students memorize whole chapters, such as 1 Corinthians 13 on love, as well as whole books, such as Ephesians. If you memorize Scripture on a regular basis you will have God's compass inside you that can point you in the right direction every time.

Get to know someone in your *MasterLife* group better. Visit or call that person. Talk about any blessings or challenges you're having with Scripture memorization or with any other part of *MasterLife*. Pray together for their ability to memorize Scripture and for other needs they express. Together review the verses you have memorized in *MasterLife*.

TRACING ANSWERS TO PRAYER

Keep track with the way God meets your needs. We often forget to thank Him for the way He answers our prayers. Keep track of your requests and answers by keeping a Prayer-Covenant List. Many Christians use this system to remind them of what God has done in their lives. Here are some tips on how to use the list.

HOW TO USE THE PRAYER-COVENANT LIST

1. Use the list on page 205. Photocopy the list and make individual lists for different categories of prayer or for different days of the week. Make one list of requests for which you pray daily. Pray for other requests weekly or monthly.
2. List requests in specific terms so that you'll know when it's answered. For example, don't write, "Bless Aunt Sue." Instead, ask that she might be able to use her arm again. Date your request. If the Holy Spirit impresses on you a Bible verse related to that request, write it in the appropriate column. Be alert to verses that might apply to your request.
3. Leave two or three lines on which to write entries in the answer column. Your prayer may be answered in stages. Write the date when each prayer is answered.

✝ Begin keeping your **Prayer-Covenant List, using the one on page 205. Make copies of the list as needed. You may want to make a prayer notebook to use during *MasterLife*. At first you may not have enough prayer requests to fill all of the lines. Record only the requests that represent genuine concerns at the time.**

Your prayer list with dated answers may become the best evidence you have to convince yourself or someone else of God's concern and power. This was the case for a young construction worker named Dyke, a member of a *MasterLife* group I led at our church. Dyke consistently listed his boss on his Prayer-Covenant List as someone who needed salvation. Week after week he told of how he was witnessing to his boss, we prayed with him, but still no answer came.

Finally, Dyke found a way to take his boss to church and to lead him to the Lord. He excitedly told the group, "This is the best thing that has happened to me since I was saved!" What a joy to see this young man use his Prayer-Covenant List as a means to pray consistently for someone's salvation and to witness this result.

Approach God with your needs during your quiet time and keep track of how He meets those needs. A quiet time is an important habit to develop in your life-long, obedient, relationship with Him.

Review today's study by listing the first three reasons for having a quiet time.

1.

2.

3.

✝ **Pray with your prayer partner once this week. If you don't have a prayer partner yet, find one this week.**

✝ **Read *1 Samuel 1:9-20*, during your quiet time today. When you have read the passage, complete the Daily Master Communication Guide.**

Daily Master Communication Guide

1 Samuel 1:9-20

What God said to me:

What I said to God:

Abide and Obey

During a family devotional time I asked my children why they believed the disciples dropped their nets at Jesus' command and followed Him—no questions asked. My young son replied, "They were tired of mending those nets." I don't think that was the reason the disciples followed Jesus on command. They followed Jesus because they recognized Him as their Master. Discipleship is obedience to the lordship of Christ. To remain in the Word, or hold to His teaching, then, means to obey it. You can read the Word, meditate on it, pray about it, hear it preached and taught, and see it demonstrated, but if you don't obey the Word, you're wasting your time.

The disciples followed Jesus because they recognized Him as their Master.

Read the verse in the margin and answer the following questions.

What happens when you keep Christ's commands?

"If you obey my commands, you will remain in my love, just as I have obeyed my Father's commands and remain in his love" (John 15:10).

Whose example do you follow when you keep Christ's commands?

To abide in Christ means to _____obey_____ **Him.**

Obeying Christ's commands is the key to discipleship. When you obey them, you remain in a lifelong, obedient relationship with Him. You abide in His love. You obey because of the example of Christ. When you abide in Him, you obey Him.

You obey because of the example Christ set in obeying His Father's commands.

Connie, a schoolteacher, gets up at 5:30 each morning to have her quiet time before she gets ready to teach school. She says this practice helps her bear fruit throughout the day as she works with children and helps her prepare for her job. "Getting up at 5:30 for me is difficult because I'm not a morning person," Connie relates. "But I know that God has given me the strength and determination to get up early to spend that time with Him. I know when I get to heaven, I'll never say, 'I wish I had slept more.' I'll say, 'I'm so glad I got up and spent time with my Master!' "

When you have a daily quiet time, Christ's teaching is fresh on your mind. You don't have to wonder how Christ would have acted in a certain situation; those truths are hidden in your heart. And when you're obedient, you bear spiritual fruit—the fourth reason for a quiet time.

You don't have to wonder how Christ would have acted in a certain situation; those truths are hidden in your heart.

Write the first three reasons for a quiet time.

1.

2.

3.

BEARING FRUIT

In *John 15:4* Jesus said: *"Remain in me, and I will remain in you. No branch can bear fruit by itself; it must remain in the vine. Neither can you bear fruit unless you remain in me."*

What did Jesus say you must do to bear fruit?

God doesn't want you to work *for* Him. He wants to work *through* you. His work is accomplished only as you yield your will to Him daily through Bible study, prayer, and meditation. He will repeatedly show you how the Scripture points to Him. You can bear fruit only if you remain faithful to the Vine and remain in Him. That is what life in Christ is all about.

I hope that by now you are beginning to experience the benefits of having memorized verses to use instantly when you need them. When I give my testimony, I don't always have a Bible handy. I've found that the Holy Spirit helps me remember the verses that fit each situation. A woman who visited our church made a lot of excuses for not coming to Christ. Because I had memorized many verses, the Holy Spirit led me to choose the right verse for each excuse. To each excuse I didn't answer a word but asked her to read a verse I had memorized. After she read between 10 and 15 verses, she put her faith in Christ.

Describe a time when a memorized Scripture was helpful.

 Continue memorizing *John 8:31-32*. Say these verses aloud to someone in your family or to a friend.

Jesus was prepared to bear spiritual fruit because His relationship with the Father was always up to date. Even when He was tired, He led the Samaritan woman to Christ (see *John 4*). When He met the funeral procession for the widow's son, He had no time to get prepared. He immediately raised the young man from the dead (see *Luke 7:11-12*). When He was asleep during the storm and His disciples woke Him crying: "Lord, save us! We're going to drown!" He was ready to act (see *Luke 8:22-25*).

KEEPING YOUR RELATIONSHIP FRESH

Sometimes, when opportunities arise, you don't have time to prepare to meet them. But if your relationship has been established during your quiet time and has been kept fresh through prayer and remembering the Word through the day, you'll be ready. I'm often surprised by what God says to me in my quiet time and by the way it applies to my daily problems and opportunities. When I review what God revealed to me the day before, I often realize that He had prepared me for the situations that arose.

**Daily Master
Communication Guide**

Genesis 22:1-19

What God said to me:

What I said to God:

Check the opportunities you've had this week to bear spiritual fruit.

❑ **Comforting a friend**
❑ **Witnessing**
❑ **Giving advice**
❑ **Sharing a memory verse or an insight from your quiet time**
❑ **Praying with someone**
❑ **Helping a needy person**
❑ **Encouraging someone**
❑ **Choosing to not get even**
❑ **Controlling your emotions**
❑ **Loving the unlovely**

Review what you've learned this week. Without looking back, list the four reasons for having a quiet time. Draw a star beside the area in which you feel the greatest need for growth.

1.

2.

3.

4.

Develop your Prayer-Covenant List by including the names of lost persons. Add the names of lost persons to your list until you have at least five. Begin praying regularly for them. Make any contact the Spirit leads you to make.

Once when I was witnessing to an atheist, I showed him my prayer list. I pointed out the date I had asked for seemingly impossible things and the date God had answered those prayers. I said, "If there's not a God, a lot of coincidences happen when I pray." Praise the Lord that He answers our prayers in ways that move even the most resistant person!

In your quiet time today, use *Genesis 22:1-19*, which focuses on an Old Testament figure who was obedient. After you have read this passage, complete the Daily Master Communication Guide in the margin.

DAY 5

A Daily Discipline

Have you wondered, *Why was it necessary for Jesus to pray, since He was God's Son?* Jesus emptied Himself and became a human being (see *Phil. 2:6*). He placed Himself in the same relationship with God that we have: that of a learner (see *Luke 2:52; Heb. 5:7-9*). Jesus enjoyed a unique relationship with God. Although He was God's Son and was filled with God's Spirit, He still practiced regular, private worship. He modeled for us an obedient relationship with the Father.

The Scriptures in the margin show Jesus established patterns that enabled Him to maintain a special love relationship with God. He prayed in the early morning, during the night, and when He was alone. Since Jesus regularly fellowshipped with the Father, we should feel an even greater need. Read in the margin how you can have an effective quiet time.

A REGULAR TIME

A regular time is the first key to an effective quiet time. Having your quiet time in the morning begins the day with a recognition of your dependence on God and His all-sufficiency. It's an opportunity to yield your will to Him and consciously dedicate the day to His glory.

What time do you usually get up in the morning?_____
What adjustments would you need to make to get up 15 minutes earlier tomorrow morning?

I believe it's important to meet with God in the morning to seek His guidance and hear His word for the day. However, some Christians find that a quiet time at bedtime is better for them. The important factor is that the time be daily and regular so that it becomes a habit.

Do you have a time of day when you habitually pray? ❏ Yes ❏ No
If not, make a commitment to schedule a quiet time at _____
❏ a.m. ❏ p.m. each day.

A QUIET PLACE

A second requirement for an effective quiet time is a place where to be alone with God. *Matthew 6:6*, in the margin, describes how Jesus encouraged His followers to pray. Most people concentrate best when they have a place away from noise, distractions, and other people where they can focus on God.

Name the best place for you to have a quiet time: _____

A PROCEDURE TO FOLLOW

A third requirement for an effective quiet time is to follow a procedure. Unless

---

Very early in the morning, while it was still dark, Jesus got up, left the house and went off to a solitary place, where he prayed (Mark 1:35).

One of those days Jesus went out to a mountainside to pray, and spent the night praying to God (Luke 6:12).

After he had dismissed them, he went up on a mountainside by himself to pray. When evening came, he was there alone (Matt. 14:23).

After leaving them, he went up on a mountainside to pray (Mark 6:46).

Jesus modeled for us an obedient relationship with the Father.

How to Have an Effective Quiet Time
1. Schedule a regular time for it.
2. Find a place to be alone with God.
3. Follow a procedure.

"When you pray, go into your room, close the door and pray to your Father, who is unseen. Then your Father, who sees what is done in secret, will reward you" (Matt. 6:6).

you follow a pattern that keeps your mind focused on spiritual matters, you'll find that your mind tends to wander.

The following elements may be included in your quiet time. Check the ones you are currently using.
❑ **Fellowshipping with God in prayer** ❑ **Bible reading or study**
❑ **Praying for the day's schedule** ❑ **Praying your prayer list(s)**
❑ **Studying the day's *MasterLife* assignment**
❑ **Memorizing and/or reviewing memory verses**
❑ **Other:** _____

The following is my personal procedure. You may want to adapt it for yourself.
1. I kneel in prayer and renew my relationship with God after the night's rest. During this time I often use the ACTS model on page 18.
2. After fellowshipping with God, I read Scripture. I usually read a chapter a day as I read consecutively through a book of the Bible. During *MasterLife* I suggest that you read Scriptures related to the day's lesson. Later, you'll determine which book of the Bible to read and how much to read each day.
3. While I read or after I have finished reading, I summarize in my journal what God said to me and what I said to God.
4. I use my Prayer-Covenant List to pray for the requests listed. I add other subjects God leads me to pray about.

You may use my procedure or may develop another. You could try several different ways to organize your quiet time in the next several days to see which one is the best for you and which helps you best relate to God.

To recap what you've studied, explain in the margin the importance of the three requirements for a quiet time. Check your answers by reviewing what you've read. Write the procedure you'll use tomorrow.

LEARNING THE DISCIPLE'S CROSS
In this week's Scripture-memory verses, *John 8:31-32,* Jesus said that His disciples hold to His teaching.

Draw the portions of the Disciple's Cross you have studied so far. Draw the circle, the lower crossbar, and the words and verses that go in them. Explain mentally or aloud what you have learned about the Disciple's Cross this week.

Unless you follow a pattern that keeps your mind focused on spiritual matters, you'll find that your mind tends to wander.

A regular time:

A quiet place:

A procedure to follow:

First Peter 2:5 refers to believers as priests who may offer up *spiritual sacrifices, acceptable to God by Jesus Christ.* As priests, we have the privilege and responsibility to worship the Lord daily.

Evaluate the degree to which you do the following by filling in the circles in the appropriate columns.

	Always	Usually	Sometimes	Seldom	Never
Have a regular time	○	○	○	○	○
Have an established place to meet God	○	○	○	○	○
Have a procedure to follow	○	○	○	○	○

Enabling sinful people to fellowship with Him cost God His only Son. Yet God was willing to pay that price. Part of your life in Christ is daily communication with the Father. What is it costing you to have fellowship with Him?

Will you give God at least 15 minutes daily, starting tomorrow?
❑ **Yes** ❑ **No If this is your desire, tell Him so now in a prayer.**

Again read *John 15* in your quiet time today. Look for ways God uses this passage to speak to you about remaining in His Word, or holding to His teaching. After you've read this passage, complete the Daily Master Communication Guide in the margin.

HAS THIS WEEK MADE A DIFFERENCE?
Review "My Walk with the Master This Week" at the beginning of this week's material. Mark the activities you've finished by drawing vertical lines in the diamonds beside them. Finish any incomplete activities. Think about what you'll say during your group session about your work on these activities.

As you complete your study of "Live in the Word," think about the experiences you've had this week.
- Are you truly becoming a disciple, as *John 8:31-32* describes?
- Have you grown in your life this week as a result of what you learned?
- Are you abiding in Christ more this week than you were last week?
- Have you progressed in developing a personal, lifelong, obedient relationship with Him?

MasterLife encourages you to move forward in Christ. You wouldn't be participating in this study if you wanted only to stand still. I pray that God is working through your experiences to help you grow as a disciple.

**Daily Master
Communication Guide**

John 15

What God said to me:

What I said to God:

WEEK 3

Pray in Faith

This Week's Goal

You will grow in your relationship with Christ by learning to pray in faith.

My Walk with the Master This Week

You will complete the following activities to develop the six biblical disciplines. When you have completed each activity, draw a vertical line in the diamond beside it.

SPEND TIME WITH THE MASTER
◇ Have a quiet time every day, using the Daily Master Communication Guides in the margins of this week's material.

LIVE IN THE WORD
◇ Read your Bible every day. Write what God says to you and what you say to God.
◇ Memorize *John 15:7.*
◇ Review *Luke 9:23; John 15:5;* and *John 8:31-32.*

PRAY IN FAITH
◇ Pray for each member of your *MasterLife* group by name.
◇ Pray with your prayer partner in person or by telephone.
◇ Pray for the needs on your Prayer Covenant List.

FELLOWSHIP WITH BELIEVERS
◇ Share with someone your testimony of having a quiet time.

WITNESS TO THE WORLD
◇ Show God's love to a person who is not a Christian.

MINISTER TO OTHERS
◇ Continue learning the Disciple's Cross. Learn the meaning of the top part of the cross and memorize the Scripture that goes with it. Be ready to explain the top and bottom parts of the cross to someone in your group at the next session.

This Week's Scripture-Memory Verse

"If you remain in me and my words remain in you, ask whatever you wish, and it will be given you" (John 15:7).

DAY 1

Praying for What God Wants

When I was in college, God began to teach me to pray in faith. I read a sermon by an evangelist based on *John 15:7*, your memory verse for this week: *"If you remain in me and my words remain in you, ask whatever you wish, and it will be given you."* It impressed me so much that I said to God: "Lord, I'm trying my best to abide in You. I ought to be able to ask anything and have my prayer answered because You promised it." I then felt impressed to pray that someone would trust Christ as Savior as I witnessed on the street that night. I wrote in my diary, "I believe that someone will be saved tonight (*John 15:7*)."

I went out on the street and invited people to attend services at the rescue mission. When the sermon was over, I turned to the visitors and asked, "Are you Christians?" They said, "Yes." I couldn't understand that, because I had prayed that God would save someone. After the service I couldn't find anyone else to witness to. On the way home I questioned: "Lord, as far as I know, I'm abiding in You as *John 15:7* says. Why haven't You answered as You promised? Isn't Your Word true?"

When I got back to campus, I remembered that I had forgotten to bring home a friend's coat for which I was responsible. When I went back for the coat I witnessed to a young man standing on the street corner. After I explained how to be saved, he gave his life to Christ. I praised God for the man's salvation. But perhaps even more I rejoiced that His Word was true and that He did what He promised. Even before the man was baptized, he led someone else to Christ.

Eager with my new understanding of prayer and faith, I remembered that I would preach the next Sunday night at the church where my father was the pastor. I felt the Holy Spirit impressing me to ask that five persons be converted as I preached. At that time five persons had never made decisions when I preached unless they were decisions to leave! I said, "God, I believe your Word that You will save five persons." I asked my dad for prospect cards so that I could make visits, knowing that only if unsaved persons were at church could they be saved in the service. When the night arrived and I gave the invitation, five persons walked down the aisles to accept Christ, and another rededicated his life. I realized that God really wanted to do things when I prayed in accordance with His will.

The next week I asked God, "What about 10 persons this weekend?" But this time nothing happened. God wanted me to learn an important lesson about prayer. This time people weren't saved because I started telling God what I wanted rather than praying on the basis of what He revealed. I learned that prayer is to involve me in God's purpose rather than my involving Him in my plans.

Think of a time when you prayed for what you wanted rather than seeking God's will first. Describe this experience below.

God began to teach me to pray in faith.

I rejoiced that His Word was true and that He did what He promised.

We need to hear God's voice so that we'll know what to pray.

ASKING ACCORDING TO HIS WILL

God delights in answering prayer that is asked according to His will, but He refuses to answer prayer that isn't consistent with what He wants. We need to hear God's voice so that we'll know what to pray.

Not everyone is asked to make the sacrifices that some friends of mine were asked to make, although all need to deny self to follow Him. This couple, secure and prosperous, quit their jobs, sold their home, gave away most of their possessions, and went to Asia, where they began working for a humanitarian organization to share their faith. They took this drastic step joyfully because they wanted to follow God's will for their lives. They stayed close to the Vine and prayed in faith while making their decision. This gave them the courage and confidence for a major lifestyle change.

You may ask, *If I pray on the basis of what God wants rather than what I want, will I have to do what they did?* Who knows? The important question to ask is, *Am I willing to pray as they did?*

Do you read God's Word for direction and pray in faith when you need to make a major decision?
  ❑ **Yes, I always do this.**
  ❑ **I try to do this most of the time.**
  ❑ **I know I should, but I don't as often as I'd like.**
  ❑ **I usually consult God after I've made the decision.**

Read *John 15:7.* **Write in the margin what you think this verse says about consulting God first when making a decision. Give an example to explain your thoughts. Meditate on the verse. Ask God to show you what He wants and to give you faith to believe that He will do it. Write what you have asked according to His will.**

"If you remain in me and my words remain in you, ask whatever you wish, and it will be given you" (John 15:7).

LEARNING THE DISCIPLE'S CROSS

Fill in the blanks of the following sentences: The first discipline is _____ and keeping Him at the center of your life. The second discipline is _____.

You've been learning the disciplines around the Disciple's Cross. The first discipline is spending time with God and keeping Him at the center of your life. The second discipline is living in the Word. A third discipline is praying in faith. This week you'll learn the role of prayer in keeping Christ at the center of your life.

To preview what you'll learn this week about praying in faith, draw the portions of the Disciple's Cross you've studied in the space at the top of the next page. Draw a circle with *Christ* in the center and draw the lower crossbar with *Word* written on it. Add the verses that apply. Draw the upper crossbar with *prayer* written on it. Refer to the Disciple's Cross on page 205 if you need help with your drawing.

**Daily Master
Communication Guide**

Matthew 14:22-36

What God said to me:

The center of the cross represents one Lord, since He's the first priority in your life. The bars of the cross represent two relationships. Word on the bottom and prayer on the top, forming the vertical crossbar, represent your relationship with Christ. The horizontal crossbar represents your relationships with others.

 Read your Bible during your quiet time. Today read *Matthew 14:22-36*. After you've read this passage, complete the Daily Master Communication Guide.

What I said to God:

In the year that King Uzziah died, I saw the Lord seated on a throne, high and exalted, and the train of his robe filled the temple. Above him were seraphs, each with six wings: With two wings they covered their faces, with two they covered their feet, and with two they were flying. And they were calling to one another: "Holy, holy, holy is the Lord Almighty; the whole earth is full of his glory" (Isa. 6:1-3).

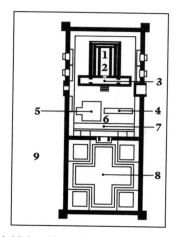

1. Holy of holies
2. Holy place
3. Porch
4. Slaughterhouse
5. Altar
6. Court of priests
7. Court of Israel
8. Court of women
9. Court of Gentiles

Since we have a great high priest who has gone through the heavens, Jesus the Son of God, let us hold firmly to the faith we profess. For we do not have a high priest who is unable to sympathize with our weaknesses, but we have one who has been tempted in every way, just as we are—yet was without sin. Let us then approach the throne of grace with confidence, so that we may receive mercy and find grace to help us in our time of need (Heb. 4:14-16).

Enter His Gates with Thanksgiving

As you studied day 1, you may have said to yourself: *I'd really like to learn to pray like that. But how do I begin? How do I know the right way to talk to the Father?* Maybe in the past you've prayed by reciting words you have memorized. Or maybe your prayers have merely been lists of requests rather than meaningful conversations with God. If you want to go deeper in your prayer life, you can learn to pray in faith as you develop your personal, lifelong, obedient relationship with Him.

ENTERING GOD'S PRESENCE

The Old Testament teaches that prayer is an act of actually coming into God's presence. If you think about prayer as a way to enter God's presence, you can understand why amazing things can happen when you pray.

Scripture can help you focus on entering God's presence. In *Isaiah 6:1-3*, in the margin, the prophet Isaiah depicted heaven as the temple. As Isaiah came into God's presence, he saw the train of God's robe filling the temple. Witnessing God's majesty, Isaiah experienced the holiness of His presence.

In *Isaiah 6:1-3* underline words or phrases that describe how Isaiah viewed God during this experience.

Isaiah obviously became aware of God's awesome holiness. You may have underlined the words *high, exalted, holy,* and *the whole earth is full of his glory.*

When you pray, you too can imagine entering the temple as you approach God and experience His awesome holiness. The drawing in the margin gives you a general idea of what the temple in Jerusalem looked like. The temple provided various levels of access, beginning with the gates and culminating with the holy of holies. Each level successively limited access to groups of people.

Only the high priest was permitted to enter the area that contained the holy of holies—the most sacred place and the innermost part of the temple. But Christ provided a way for all people to enter the holy of holies and to have an intimate relationship with God through prayer. His death on the cross broke through the limitations of earthly life, making it possible for you to enjoy direct access to God. Because Christ came to earth as a human being, His atoning death brought an end to the priests' role. He now represents you as your Great High Priest before God.

Read *Hebrews 4:14-16* in the margin.

APPROACHING GOD

The large, courtyard at the edge of the temple was open to everyone. As people entered through those beautiful temple gates, they gave thanks. The verses in the margin help you picture how the people approached the temple with thanksgiving. When you approach God, it's not proper to rush into His presence and bombard Him with your needs. First, thank Him for all He's done for you. Thanksgiving is the way to approach God.

T. W. Hunt, the author of *Disciple's Prayer Life*, described how he became aware of his need for an different attitude of thanksgiving. One morning as he brushed his teeth, T. W. asked himself, *What if tomorrow I had only the things for which I thanked God today?* He began to name things like his teeth, his eyes, the sense of touch, air, home, people—items he realized he sometimes took for granted. He changed his approach to prayer so that he began with thanksgiving to God.

What are things you take for granted for which you want to thank God? Write a prayer thanking God for some of these items.

Thank You, God, for—

Enter his gates with thanksgiving and his courts with praise; give thanks to him and praise his name (Ps. 100:4).

These things I remember as I pour out my soul: how I used to go with the multitude, leading the procession to the house of God, with shouts of joy and thanksgiving among the festive throng (Ps. 42:4).

In thanksgiving you express gratitude toward God, generally in response to His concrete acts. *Psalm 69:30-31*, shows the value God places on your prayers of thankfulness. He values prayers of thanksgiving more than acts of sacrifice.

What kinds of things do you thank God for? The Book of Psalms gives examples of areas in which you can give thanks.

I will praise God's name in song and glorify him with thanksgiving. This will please the Lord more than an ox, more than a bull with its horns and hoofs (Ps. 69:30-31).

• **Deliverance from trouble:**
The angel of the Lord encamps around those who fear him,
*   and he delivers them.*
Taste and see that the Lord is good;
*   blessed is the man who takes refuge in him (Ps. 34:7-8).*

• **God's faithfulness:**
The Lord is good and his love endures forever;
*   his faithfulness continues through all generations (Ps. 100:5).*

• **Forgiveness of sin:**
Sing to the Lord, you saints of his; praise his holy name.
For his anger lasts only a moment, but his favor lasts a lifetime (Ps. 30:4-5).

• **Creation:**
You make me glad by your deeds,
*   O Lord; I sing for joy at the works of your hands (Ps. 92:4).*

Does that list cause you to remember things for which you need to be thankful? Go back and draw a star beside one area in which you need to express gratitude. Then stop and pray, thanking God for what He brought to mind.

Daily Master Communication Guide

John 15

What God said to me:

What I said to God:

You can get so busy asking God for something that you forget to be thankful. What about earlier requests He answered? True, not everything you've asked for is granted. You may be waiting for an answer. Sometimes the answer you wanted wasn't part of His plan, and He gave you an answer that was better for you than the one you wanted. But He certainly answers many of your requests that are according to His will. How many of them have you thanked Him for? Your Prayer-Covenant List is a record of answered prayer. In the brief time you have kept a Prayer-Covenant List, what answers to prayer have you recorded?

Stop and review your Prayer-Covenant List or a list you kept previously. List two prayer requests below for which you've already seen answers. Then enter God's presence and thank Him for them.

1.

2.

Prayer is the discipline you're studying this week. A part of life in Christ is praying in faith. Jesus said in *John 15:7,* "*If you remain in me and my words remain in you, ask whatever you wish, and it will be given you.*"

Stop and review your memory verse, *John 15:7.* Say it to your prayer partner in person or by phone this week. Also say the verses you memorized previously.

Again read *John 15* as your Bible passage today. As you read the passage this time, look for ways God uses it to speak to you about praying in faith. After you've read this passage, complete the Daily Master Communication Guide.

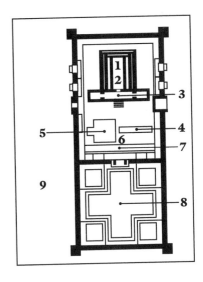

DAY 3

Enter His Courts with Praise

Learning to pray in faith involves focusing on who the Father is and what He means in your life. Jesus taught His disciples how to pray and how to know the Father through prayer. Focusing on Him will help you overcome distractions or demands and to acknowledge the One whose throne you are approaching. It will help you communicate with Him. Make a deliberate effort to set other thoughts aside as you concentrate on the Father.

Again, think about the way people approached the temple in Jerusalem in Bible times as you consider how to approach God's throne in prayer. As the people entered the courts of the temple, they came with praise, as *Psalm 100:4*, in the margin, indicates. Praise is based on adoration of God. Adoration is what you do in worship.

PROCLAIMING HIS WORTH

The word *praise* originates from a Latin word meaning value or price. Thus, to give praise to God is to proclaim His worth. How you do this—whether you are kneeling, standing, sitting, or reclining—doesn't matter. *John 11:41* implies that Jesus prayed with His eyes open. Regardless of how you praise Him and under what circumstances, praise is an important element of prayer. It's to be constant, as *Psalm 34:1*, in the margin, indicates. Praise raises your prayer life above yourself. Thanksgiving focuses on what God has done for you. Praise focuses on who God is.

Praise focuses on the person of God. Some of God's names that appear in the Bible reveal His character—ways He works in your life. You can praise God as you recognize the aspects of His character that are revealed in His names. To discover various aspects of God's character, study *Psalm 91*, which mentions several of His names.

 During your quiet time read *Psalm 91*. Then complete the Daily Master Communication Guide on page 50.

Here are the names of God that are used in *Psalm 91*:

El Elyon:

> He who dwells in the shelter of the Most High
> will rest in the shadow of the Almighty (Ps. 91:1).

The name *El Elyon* means "Most High," the strongest of all gods and the possessor of heaven and earth—the strongest of the strong. Do you believe that you win the daily battles of life in your own strength? The true victory originates with El Elyon. He is capable of arranging even the most tedious details of your life.

---

1. Holy of holies
2. Holy place
3. Porch
4. Slaughterhouse
5. Alter
6. Court of priests
7. Court of Israel
8. Court of women
9. Court of Gentiles

Enter his gates with thanksgiving and his courts with praise; give thanks to him and praise his name (Ps. 100:4).

I will extol the Lord at all times; his praise will always be on my lips (Ps. 34:1).

He did not waver through unbelief regarding the promise of God, but was strengthened in his faith and gave glory to God, being fully persuaded that God had power to do what he had promised (Rom. 4:20-21).

Daily Master Communication Guide

Psalm 91

What God said to me:

What I said to God:

Has God, El Elyon, worked out a circumstance in your life beyond anything you could have imagined? ❏ Yes ❏ No If so, describe this experience below. Stop and praise God as El Elyon, the Most High God.

El Shaddai:

> *He who dwells in the shelter of the Most High*
> *will rest in the shadow of the Almighty (Ps. 91:1).*

The name *El Shaddai* means "Almighty," the all-sufficient God. The name is first used in *Genesis 17:1*, when God appeared to Abraham and made great promises to Him. Even though Abraham was an old man, God promised to make of him a great nation and to give him a son. God keeps His promises. Read *Romans 4:20-21* in the margin.

Can you think of an occasion when God, El Shaddai, kept His promises to you? ❏ Yes ❏ No If so, describe it below and praise Him for being a promise-keeping God.

Yahweh:

> *I will say of the Lord, "He is my refuge and my fortress,*
> *my God, in whom I trust" (Ps. 91:2).*

The personal name of God—*Yahweh* or *Jehovah*, means "LORD," written in capital letters. (The word *Lord* in lowercase letters signifies "Adonai"—the master, the person with authority.) *Yahweh* signifies "the God who is with you all the time." God used this name to reveal Himself to Moses in *Exodus 3*. When God said to Moses, *"I AM WHO I AM,"* (see *Ex. 3:14*). He was probably saying, in effect, "I am always with you for I am present everywhere all the time." God is our contemporary.

Have you been aware of His, Yahweh, presence when you believed that He was asking you to do something difficult? ❏ Yes ❏ No If so, describe your experience below. Stop and pray, praising God for being Yahweh in your life.

Elohim:

The name *Elohim* means "My God, in whom I trust" *(Ps. 91:2)*. It first appears in *Genesis 1:1* in the creation story, referring to the strong, covenant-keeping God who is the Creator. Do you regularly approach God as the Creator and worship Him?

When have you been aware of Him, Elohim, as the One who gave you life and created everything around you? Describe your experience below. Then stop and worship God as the Creator.

Other names of God also help you focus on who He is and enable you to praise Him. Jehovah is another way to translate Yahweh. Consider these:
- *Jehovah Jireh*—the God who provides
- *Jehovah Shalom*—the God who brings peace
- *Jehovah Sabaoth*—the God who brings spiritual help
- *Jehovah Rapha*—the God who heals

You may want to use a Bible dictionary to examine some of the names of God. Understanding the characteristics of God helps you know how to praise Him. God's names are revealed in your experiences with Him. Let Him reveal Himself to you as you worship Him.

Understanding the characteristics of God helps you know how to praise Him.

REASONS TO PRAISE GOD

As you practice praying in faith, consider these other reasons God is worthy of praise. You can praise Him because—
- *He is the living God.* Matthew 16:16 states Simon Peter's answer when Jesus asked who He is: *"You are the Christ, the Son of the living God."*
- *He is holy.* As people entered the temple area, they were aware of God's holiness. Psalm 29:2 says, *Worship the Lord in the splendor of his holiness.*
- *He is spirit.* He is not material form but the highest form of existence. God's spirit form allows Him to be with people everywhere:

> *Where can I go from your Spirit?*
> *Where can I flee from your presence? (Ps. 139:7)*

- *He is love.* The primary purpose behind His revelation is love (see *John 3:16*).
- *He is Father.* He is the Father of our Lord Jesus Christ, whose death allows us to enter the Father's presence: *"No one comes to the Father except through me"* (John 14:6).
- *He is glory.* The word *glory* refers to His influence and importance in the universe. Hebrews 1:3 says, *The Son is the radiance of God's glory and the exact representation of his being, sustaining all things by his powerful word.*

Praise God because of who He IS, not just because of what He DOES. Praise is pure worship, and adoration, and an expression of your love for Him.

Praise God because of who He IS, not just because of what He DOES.

Stop and pray. Review the list of reasons God is worthy of your praise. Use each one to praise Him as you continue to develop the discipline of praying in faith.

I hope that by praying alone during your quiet time and praying with your prayer partner you've seen growth in your spiritual life. I hope that God has begun to reveal to you people who are not Christians for whom you need to pray. One way to begin building a witnessing relationship is to show God's love to someone who isn't a Christian. As you befriend that person, start sharing the gospel.

We became friends with a couple who lived across the street but they didn't respond positively to a gospel witness. One Christmas I took a poinsettia to them. Soon the woman came over and asked if I would pray for her. She had obviously been drinking. Later, I was able to lead her to receive Christ. The act of giving the plant paved the way for me to witness. I was thankful that God had allowed me the opportunity to share Christ with this woman.

 This week show God's love to a non-Christian by doing something kind for that person. Afterward, describe here what you did and the person's response.

 In the margin write this week's memory verse, *John 15:7*. Below the verse describe how you feel about beginning or developing the practice of praying in faith.

DAY 4

The Altar of Confession

After you've thanked God for what He has done and have praised Him for who He is, confess your sins to Him. In addition to glorifying and honoring God, you must also ask God to examine your heart.

THE NEED TO CONFESS SIN

When Isaiah saw God and witnessed His glory, Isaiah also saw the contrast between God's holiness and his own sinfulness.

Read *Isaiah 6:4-6* in the margin and complete the sentence:

When you approach God's throne and are in His presence, you become aware of your sins. It's appropriate to confess your sins, just as Isaiah did when he experienced God's glory.

Before the death of Christ, people sacrificed animal offerings to atone for their sins. Today no blood offering is required to atone for your sins. Christ offered Himself as a sacrifice so that your sins may be forgiven. Read *First John 1:8-10,* in the margin, that says when you confess your sins God is faithful to forgive you.

In confession God examines your heart and shows you what separates you from Him—the barriers that keep you from experiencing Him to the fullest. Full fellowship with God is blocked by unconfessed sin. *Psalm 139* illustrates the proper attitude about confession. Read *verses 23-24* in the margin. The psalmist asks God to make him aware of his unrighteousness so that he can grow. The Holy Spirit convicts us of things that offend God. You don't have to guess what might be sin in your life. If you open yourself to His leading, the Holy Spirit will show you things that offend God.

Reread *1 John 1:8-10.* According to this passage, why confess the sin in your life? Check the appropriate box(es) in the margin.

The Father wants you to confess sin so that He can do what He has promised to do: forgive you and cleanse you. You only fool yourself when you claim to be sinless. God knows the sin in your heart. Confessing sin makes you feel better, but that's not the purpose. The purpose is to restore your fellowship with God. All of the answers except the last one are reasons for confessing sin.

Psalm 66:18 reveals that God doesn't listen to your prayers if you continue to cling to your sins by refusing to acknowledge and confess them. Confessing your sin is a crucial next step in your fellowship with God.

✞ **In your quiet time read *Psalm 51,* David's confession. Complete the Daily Master Communication Guide (p. 54) before reading further.**

At the sound of their voices the doorposts and thresholds shook and the temple was filled with smoke. "Woe to me!" I cried. "I am ruined! For I am a man of unclean lips, and I live among a people of unclean lips, and my eyes have seen the King, the Lord Almighty" (Isa. 6:4-6).

When Isaiah experienced the Lord's glory, he _____ his sin.

If we claim to be without sin, we deceive ourselves and the truth is not in us. If we confess our sins, he is faithful and just and will forgive us our sins and purify us from all unrighteousness. If we claim we have not sinned, we make him out to be a liar and his word has no place in our lives (1 John 1:8-10).

❑ **The Father will forgive you and cleanse you.**
❑ **You deceive yourself and don't live in the truth if you claim to be above sin.**
❑ **The Father can show that He is faithful to His promise to forgive you when you confess sin.**
❑ **So that you will feel better.**

Search me, O God, and know my heart; test me and know my anxious thoughts. See if there is any offensive way in me, and lead me in the way everlasting (Ps. 139:23-24).

If I had cherished sin in my heart, the Lord would not have listened (Ps. 66:18).

**Daily Master
Communication Guide**

Psalm 51

What God said to me:

What I said to God:

❑ **deceitful/dishonest desires**
❑ **brawling/shouting insults**
❑ **falsehood/lying**
❑ **laziness**
❑ **anger**
❑ **slander/speaking unjustly
   about someone**
❑ **bitterness/holding a grudge**
❑ **unwholesome talk/harmful
   words**
❑ **rage/violent anger**
❑ **malice/hateful feelings**
❑ **stealing**

Your Prayer of Confession —

WHAT DO YOU NEED TO CONFESS?

As you study about confession and ask the Lord to search your heart, a good passage to read is *Ephesians 4:22-32*. In this passage Paul addressed all Christians, but his warnings apply in all relationships and to all behavior.

In your Bible read *Ephesians 4:22-32* and then ask yourself, *What do I need to confess?* As you open yourself to the Lord, ask Him to point out what is not right in your life and to help you confess it.

In the margin check anything of which the Lord convicted you. Now in the margin write a prayer of confession asking God to forgive you of the sins you checked.

Confession is an important part of keeping a right relationship with God. Maturity in discipleship is the degree to which you experience harmony, or wholeness, in relating to God and others. You experience this harmony when you regularly fellowship with Christ through daily prayer. That's why praying in faith is a major part of your relationship with Him.

LEARNING THE DISCIPLE'S CROSS

Draw below, or on a separate sheet of paper, the portions of the Disciple's Cross you've studied so far. Draw a circle with *Christ* in it, the lower crossbar with *Word* written on it, and the accompanying Scriptures. Then draw the upper crossbar with *Prayer* written on it. Under prayer write *John 15:7*. Explain the cross aloud as you draw these parts. Be prepared to explain it at your next group session.

Say the verse, *John 15:7*, aloud to a friend. Call a member of your MasterLife group for whom you are praying and practice saying the verse together. Remind the person of your prayers for them.

Every few days study your Prayer-Covenant List and praise God for answered prayers. Set aside time each week to examine your list. Every month review the requests to see what God has done. God answers so many prayers and He will show you how faithful He has been. Usually, not every request is answered the way you hoped, but He teaches you to walk in faith by answering many of them.

Spend time on your Prayer-Covenant List. Pray for the prayer needs on it. Then decide on a time during the next week when you will study what God is doing in your life. Write the day and time here:
Day_____Time_____.

DAY 5

In God's Presence

Now you find yourself in the presence of God—a holy place. The Father wants you to approach Him with your needs. He waits to grant what you ask that is in His will. He delights in doing so. Now that you've thanked Him, praised Him, and confessed your sins, you're ready to talk with Him about your and others' needs.

BRINGING YOUR NEEDS TO GOD

When you think about praying for needs, think of the place in the temple called the holy of holies, the temple's most sacred area. In Bible times only the high priest had access to this innermost area. Because of Jesus, however, you have access to God and can approach Him in all His holiness with the deepest needs of your heart. In that holy of holies everything is laid bare before Him *(Heb. 4:13)*.

 In your quiet time today read *Hebrews 4*, which states that Jesus Christ is the only high priest you need. After you have read this passage, complete the Daily Master Communication Guide.

Hebrews 4:14-16, in the margin on the next page, states that Jesus, as our Great High Priest, understands our needs.

How does *Hebrews 4:14-16* tell you that you are to approach God's throne of grace? With_____.

You can approach God's throne of grace with confidence because He is ready to grant you mercy and grace to help you in your time of need. He is pleased to hear your personal requests. How do you know that Jesus wants you to pray freely about your needs? Your memory verse for this week ensures it.

 As you think about the marvelous promise in *John 15:7*, say the verse aloud from memory. As you say it, think about a loving God who finds your requests pleasing to His ears.

PRAYING FOR YOURSELF

Today you'll study two types of requests: petition and intercession. Petition is asking for yourself. You know that God encourages people to pray for their personal concerns, because His Word is filled with answered requests. For example, *Luke 1:13* contains God's response to Zechariah's petition for a son. His request was answered with the birth of John the Baptist.

God's answers to your prayers help mold you into the person He wants you to become. He doesn't grant petitions that you pray for the wrong reason or that He knows would bring the wrong outcome in your life. Read *1 John 5:14-15* in the margin.

Nothing in all creation is hidden from God's sight. Everything is uncovered and laid bare before the eyes of him to whom we must give account (Heb. 4:13).

1. Holy of holies

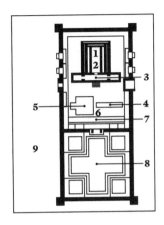

2. Holy place
3. Porch
4. Slaughterhouse
5. Altar
6. Court of priests
7. Court of Israel
8. Court of women
9. Court of Gentiles

Daily Master Communication Guide

Hebrews 4

What God said to me:

What I said to God:

Since we have a great high priest who has gone through the heavens, Jesus the Son of God, let us hold firmly to the faith we profess. For we do not have a high priest who is unable to sympathize with our weaknesses, but we have one who has been tempted in every way, just as we are—yet was without sin. Let us then approach the throne of grace with confidence, so that we may receive mercy and find grace to help us in our time of need (Heb. 4:14-16).

This is the confidence we have in approaching God: that if we ask anything according to his will, he hears us (1 John 5:14-15).

Confess your sins to each other and pray for each other so that you may be healed. The prayer of a righteous man is powerful and effective (Jas. 5:16).

"Holy Father, protect them by the power of your name—the name you gave me—so that they may be one as we are one. My prayer is not that you take them out of the world but that you protect them from the evil one. Sanctify them by the truth; your word is truth" (John 17:11,15,17).

Praying for others is called intercessory prayer.

God uses you as His vehicle to accomplish His will when you pray for others.

List your personal needs. Use the following categories to help your thinking, but don't limit your list to these or feel that you must write a request for each one. You may need to use extra paper to expand your list.

Christ-honoring relationships with others:

The ability to manage my time wisely:

Concerns at school:

My ministry at church:

Guidance for my future:

Physical and emotional health:

Ability to resist temptation:

Material needs:

Now stop and pray about your requests. Pray for God's will in the outcomes of the above situations and concerns.

PRAYING FOR OTHERS

The second type of request is intercession—prayer for others. The Bible instructs us to pray for one another, as *James 5:16*, in the margin, indicates. Jesus prayed for His disciples many times. One of the best examples is found in *John 17*, in which Jesus prayed for His disciples before He went to the cross. A portion of that prayer appears in the margin. You pray for others so that God can mold them into the persons He wants them to become. God uses you as His vehicle to accomplish His will when you pray for others.

How important to you is intercession for others? Check the answer that describes you.
❑ **I'm too busy taking care of my own needs to pray for others.**
❑ **I pray for others after I handle other areas of my life.**
❑ **I pray for others only when they have an extreme crisis.**
❑ **Praying for others is important to me because God can use my prayers to accomplish His will.**

Stop and pray. Ask God to help you pray for others more often.

As you've kept your Prayer-Covenant List for the past several weeks, you've prayed for others. By praying for others, God has used you to accomplish His will in the lives of others. Review some of your prayers of intercession.

List two persons on your Prayer-Covenant List and their needs. Describe ways God has answered your prayers for these individuals. Even if you've seen only small parts of an answer, list those below. Thank God for hearing your prayers. Ask Him to continue working His will in the lives of those individuals.

Name	Request	Answer

List in the margin the two types of prayers for needs you have studied.

 For several weeks you've practiced a daily quiet time. Share your testimony about having a daily quiet time with someone.

HAS THIS WEEK MADE A DIFFERENCE?
Review "My Walk with the Master This Week" (p. 42). Mark the finished activities by drawing vertical lines in the diamonds beside them. Finish any incomplete activities. Think about what you'll say during your group session about your work on these activities.

As you complete your study of "Pray in Faith," reflect on the experiences you have had this week.

• Have you been praying in faith this week?
• Is having a quiet time becoming a regular part of your life?
• Are you keeping a Prayer-Covenant List and making notes of answers to prayer?

Through this week's work I hope that you've become more aware of how praying in faith helps you develop the disciplines of a disciple and contributes to your lifelong, obedient relationship with Christ. Jesus' purpose in teaching His disciples how to pray was to teach them how to know the Father through prayer. Have you come to know more about Him this week? Where do you stand now in terms of your lifelong, obedient relationship with Him? Congratulations on taking these important steps. Learning to pray the way Christ wants you to isn't easy. It requires setting aside your self-centered way of life and looking for His will for you. Starting your prayers with thanksgiving, praise, and confession before making requests means that you have Someone besides yourself at the center of your life. Christ is the Master of your life.

Throughout *MasterLife* you'll continue to learn how to pray in faith. You'll see the fullness of all God wants to do in your life through prayer. Following Jesus means that you seek to know and do His will, not just coast through life. By now in *MasterLife* you've seen the sacrifices you need to make in order to walk with the Master and to live in Him. I affirm your willingness to make these sacrifices in order to grow as a disciple of Christ.

Praying for yourself:

Praying for others:

Starting your prayers with thanksgiving, praise, and confession before making requests means that you have Someone besides yourself at the center of your life. Christ is the Master of your life.

WEEK 4

Fellowship with Believers

This Week's Goal
You will experience growth in Christ through relationships with other believers.

My Walk with the Master This Week
You will complete the following activities to develop the six biblical disciplines. When you have completed each activity, draw a vertical line in the diamond beside it.

SPEND TIME WITH THE MASTER
◇ Have a daily quiet time. Check the box beside each day you have a quiet time this week:
❑ Sunday ❑ Monday ❑ Tuesday ❑ Wednesday ❑ Thursday ❑ Friday ❑ Saturday

LIVE IN THE WORD
◇ Read your Bible every day. Write what God says to you and what you say to God.
◇ Memorize *John 13:34-35.*
◇ Review *Luke 9:23; John 15:5; John 8:31-32;* and *John 15:7.*

PRAY IN FAITH
◇ Pray for your prayer partner.
◇ Pray about your priorities and your use of time.
◇ Add requests to your Prayer-Covenant List.

FELLOWSHIP WITH BELIEVERS
◇ Befriend someone in the church who is not a close friend and is not in your MasterLife group.

WITNESS TO THE WORLD
◇ Plan your time, using "How to Use MasterTime" and the MasterTime form. Read "Redeeming the Time" and underline portions that apply to you.

MINISTER TO OTHERS
◇ Continue learning the Disciple's Cross. Explain the meaning of the right crossbar to add to the information about the circle and the vertical crossbar that you learned in previous weeks. Learn the Scriptures that go with each part of the cross.

This Week's Scripture-Memory Verse
"A new command I give you: Love one another. As I have loved you, so you must love one another. By this all men will know that you are my disciples, if you love one another" (John 13:34-35).

DAY 1

The Mark of a Disciple

Bruce Schmidt was trying to buy some land in a Ugandan valley to begin missionary work among unreached people, and came face-to-face with a leader of the Karamojong, one of the most feared tribes in East Africa. "Why are you here, and what do you want?" the chief demanded.

Bruce replied that he was in the valley because of two great things: the Great Commission, which he explained, and the Great Commandment. "In the Great Commandment Jesus said that we are to love God first and to love our neighbor as ourselves. I want to be your neighbor."

To Bruce's surprise, the Karamojong leader voiced no objection. Instead, he appeared to be moved by Bruce's remarks. "Nobody wants to be our neighbor. We are the most hated tribe in Uganda. Neighboring tribes have had their cattle stolen, their women raped, and their men murdered. We can't believe you want to be our neighbor!" the man exclaimed.

By the time the meeting ended, God had melted hearts of stone. This feared Karamojong tribe gave Bruce and his coworkers 30 acres of land for their new mission work—all because of neighborly love that Bruce extended in Jesus Christ. Although most of us are not placed in a foreign land with hostile tribes as neighbors, we often face hostility as Christians in an evil world. Like Bruce, we are to love our neighbors.

As we love and fellowship with other believers, we gain strength from one another.

LOVING ONE ANOTHER

You can't be a balanced Christian if you neglect godly relationships with others. If you try to live apart from the fellowship of other believers—the church, which is Christ's body—you'll not experience fullness of life in Christ. The Lord put us in a body of believers because life outside the body is difficult. As we love and fellowship with one another, we gain strength from one another.

 Read this week's Scripture-memory verses, John 13:34-35, in the margin. What did Jesus say identifies His disciples?

"A new command I give you: Love one another. As I have loved you, so you must love one another. By this all men will know that you are my disciples, if you love one another" (John 13:34-35).

Now go back and read John 13:34-35 aloud from one to three times to begin memorizing these verses.

Jesus said your love for others shows the world that you are His disciple. Loving others and fellowshipping with them show that Christ is at the center of your life. Loving relationships are at the very heart of life in Christ. Jesus modeled fellowship with believers and wants us to demonstrate the love He modeled for us.

Love shows the world that you are His disciple.

Read the following case studies.

Amy loved the outdoors and enjoyed skiing. Although Amy was a

Christian, she didn't attend church, using an excuse many people do: "I can worship God better when I'm enjoying His creation." Members of the church youth group invited her to attend, but Amy chose to ski instead.

Joe had given his life to Christ several years ago but had never become involved in a church. Even though members of a church youth group in his neighborhood visited him, Joe wouldn't go. Since he was shy, Joe couldn't imagine himself talking to strangers.

Underline the excuses Amy and Joe used for not fellowshipping with believers. What kinds of activities do you choose to do instead of fellowship with believers? List them in the margin.

Exploring God's creation is a wonderful way to be aware of His blessings and glory, but it doesn't take the place of the fellowship Christ wants for you to have with other believers. Shyness is a painful matter for some people, but the Father can give you strength to overcome weaknesses so that you can be part of the body. When you have life in Christ and abide in Him, you follow His commands. *John 15:12* says, *"My command is this: Love each other as I have loved you."*

Why does *John 15:12* say that you are to love other persons?

Let us consider how we may spur one another on toward love and good deeds. Let us not give up meeting together, as some are in the habit of doing, but let us encourage one another—and all the more as you see the Day approaching (Heb. 10:24-25).

Love flows from God through Christ to us. Having modeled love for you, Christ commands you to exhibit His love to others. Not fellowshipping with others hurts your ability to show love to others and prevents their showing love to you. Your church represents the body of Christ, in which you can fellowship with other believers. *Hebrews 10:24-25,* in the margin, teaches that we are to meet together with other believers.

Isolation and individualism are not Christ's ways. Christ brings believers together as a family. Fellow Christians should express love for one another. Worshiping together is one way we gain strength and motivation from other disciples. *First Peter 4:10,* in the margin, says Christians as part of a body of believers, should use their gifts to serve others and receive instruction from God's Word. Christian's who don't attend church are disregarding God's Word and are living outside His will.

Each one should use whatever gift he has received to serve others, faithfully administering God's grace in its various forms (1 Pet. 4:10).

The love God has for His Son, Jesus, is the source of the love the Son has for His followers. It's also the model for the love you are to have for others. The depths of Jesus' love, which led Him to the cross, shouldn't surprise you, because it's modeled in the love the Father has for the Son. Read *John 15:9* in the margin.

"As the Father has loved me, so have I loved you. Now remain in my love" (John 15:9).

LEARNING THE DISCIPLE'S CROSS
The fourth discipline of a disciple's life, then, is fellowshipping with believers. While the vertical crossbar on the Disciple's Cross you've studied for the past two weeks emphasizes your relationship with Christ through the Word and prayer,

the horizontal crossbar you'll study this week and in week 5 stresses the importance of your relationship with others through fellowship and witness.

✝ **Draw the portions of the Disciple's Cross you have studied. Draw a circle with *Christ* in the center and draw the lower crossbar with *Word* written on it. Then draw the upper crossbar with *Prayer* written on it. Add the verses that apply. Now draw the right crossbar and write *Fellowship* on it. Under fellowship write *John 13:34-35.* Refer to the completed cross on page 204 if you need help.**

✝ **Read your Bible daily during your quiet time. Today read *1 Corinthians 12:12-31,* which explains the special relationship between you and other Christians. After you've read this passage, complete the Daily Master Communication Guide in the margin.**

Daily Master Communication Guide

1 Corinthians 12:12-31

What God said to me:

What I said to God:

The Gift of Accountability

God has often shown me the importance of working within the fellowship of believers in the body of Christ. When I was in college, my friends and I decided to conduct a huge youth revival in my friend's hometown. We secured the high-school auditorium, put up huge billboards, announced the event on the radio, and delivered posters to stores. But at the last minute high-school officials told us that church leaders in the community—members of our own denomination—had pressured the school not to let us use the facility. Because we didn't seek the local churches' involvement in advance, our plan was backfiring.

I prayed, "Lord, You can't let us down after we've done so much to prepare," but He taught us another lesson: that we could do nothing without Him. We did this task on our own for God rather than asking what He wanted. We had talked and prayed about the revival but had then gone ahead with our plans.

This experience was a crushing defeat but a lesson well learned. We left town, convinced that we wouldn't again try to do anything else without God's direct leadership and without working within the framework of the local church.

Have you ever had a disappointing experience in Christian service because you were working outside the fellowship of believers? ❏ Yes ❏ No If so, describe your experience.

I made several mistakes in my experience above. First, my friends and I didn't pray in faith for God's direction before we started. Second, we didn't ask God to search our hearts for selfish motives and desires for success of our plans. And finally, we didn't seek the local churches' support. We failed to live as part of the body of Christ.

 Say aloud your memory verses for the week. In the margin write what these verses say about the importance of fellowshipping with believers.

Did you answer something like this? I may obey Christ in a number of ways, but unless I demonstrate love for His people, I don't show that I'm His disciple.

GOD WORKS THROUGH OTHERS

God often reveals Himself through people that He places in your path. Life in Christ includes fellowshipping with your brothers and sisters in Christ. These people may speak a God-anointed word to you that helps you see a problem more clearly or make a right decision. Christian friends can help hold you accountable for times when you get off course. They can remind you of what the Word says. Friends can help you see your misplaced priorities. God works through others in the church to accomplish His will in your life.

God often reveals Himself through people that He places in your path.

Read these case studies and answer the questions that follow.

Anita and her former best friend hadn't spoken in months. Anita longed to make relations right between them. She invited her friend over for a special weekend to attempt to repair their relationship. Anita spent every spare moment of the weekend planning fun things to do and even bought her a present, hoping this would make her friend want to be her best friend again. She also asked her friends at church to pray for them.

How could Anita's friends at church show love for her?

Charles worked long hours at a job after school and on weekends to pay for his sports car and insurance. He was away from home so much that he seldom saw his family or friends. He wanted to participate in his school and church events, but Charles had to miss most of them. He managed to go to church about once a month.

How could fellowship with other believers help Charles?

In Anita's story, Christian friends could have prayed with her about her relationship with her best friend. Without giving her advice, they could have helped Anita see her choices. What had she done to make things right? Had Anita apologized to her friend for any wrong on her part? Had she discussed the situation with her youth leader or pastor? Christian friends could invite Anita to youth events at church to give her other friends in her life. They could lovingly model ways she could connect with the Vine as the source of help.

Christian friends could possibly help Charles with his job situation. They could help him network among church members to find a job with better pay, which would eliminate the need for such long hours. They could invite him to family activities planned by the church to provide opportunities for him to be with his family and friends in a church setting. The youth group could include him in their activities. They could lovingly help Charles see if he's off course in his priorities. They could help him connect with the Vine as the source of power.

AN INSTRUMENT OF CHRIST'S LOVE

True disciples that have a personal, lifelong, obedient relationship with Jesus show love for others by fellowshipping with them and by being Christ's instrument in their lives. Christ's love can flow through you to them. You can help them be all Christ wants them to be. The right crossbar of fellowship on the Disciple's Cross reminds you of the importance of your relationships with others.

**Daily Master
Communication Guide**

I Corinthians 12:31—13:13

What God said to me:

What I said to God:

Say aloud your Scripture-memory verses for this week, *John 13:34-35*. Now try to write them below from memory. Write them several times until you can easily write them from memory. Say them to your prayer partner in your prayer time this week.

Read *I Corinthians 12:31—13:13* during your quiet time. Let God speak to you through this passage about loving one another. After reading this passage, complete the Daily Master Communication Guide in the margin.

DAY 3

Help for Stuck Christians

Suppose you just walked onto an elevator. You watch the doors close. You push the button for the floor you want to go to a couple of times because you're in a hurry. Then you change your mind and push the button for another floor. The doors don't close fast enough so you push the close door button. But after standing there a few seconds you realize that you haven't moved--either up or down. You push the buttons again. You are stuck right where you were. You think you are doing all of the right things: pushing the open door button, pushing the alarm, pushing the floor indicator buttons, but the doors stay closed and the elevator doesn't move.

Then you spot the telephone and you call the emergency number on the phone. You shout to the operator, "I'm stuck, how do I get off the elevator?" The operator begins to tell you that she too had been stuck on that same elevator. She goes on to say that the elevator is stuck because so many buttons have been pushed that the circuits are confused about what to do. Her advice is to wait a few more minutes for the circuits to catch up with the commands. Then she directs you to the Master Control button. She also tells you before you get on the elevator the next time, to be prepared for the ride—to know how to use the master control: to not be in such a hurry and to remember when you step onto that elevator, you must allow it to work the way it's supposed to work.

Some Christians are spiritually stuck. They are busy and exhausted from doing good things. But just like the person stuck on the elevator, Christians need the fellowship, understanding, and advice of someone who has experienced the same situation. The operator was able to give direction to the person on the elevator. Christian friends who share their own experiences help encourage and restore other believers to a life of usefulness in God's kingdom. Fellowship with other Christians helps revive you in the midst of a spiritual crisis. Fellowship can also help you begin learning how to change your busy lifestyle to ensure a daily quiet time and a more personal relationship with Christ.

Just like the elevator, we can obey only so many commands at one time. If we overload our lives with commands without any direction we will experience a spiritual crisis. When we allow the Master to control our lives we won't be stuck in a spiritual crisis.

Has fellowship with a Christian friend ever helped you when you were experiencing a spiritual crisis? ❏ Yes ❏ No If yes, describe how they helped you experience a victorious life in Christ.

Daily Master Communication Guide

2 Timothy 1:1-14

What God said to me:

What I said to God:

 Read *2 Timothy 1:1-14,* which shows the special relationship between Paul and Timothy, during your quiet time today. After you have read this passage, complete the Daily Master Communication Guide in the margin.

A NETWORK OF SUPPORT

As you become an instrument of Christ you can encourage others. Your fellow church members become important to you. *First Corinthians 12:27* says, *You are the body of Christ, and each one of you is a part of it.* If one member of the body is stuck spiritually the entire body suffers, including you. The body cares for each member of the body so that together all of the members become more complete in Christ's love.

SHARING WHAT GOD IS DOING

Have you shared with other believers ways you are growing in Christ as you learn what being His disciple means?

In the space below write about your experience of praying in faith.

In the space below write about your experience of memorizing Scripture.

In the space below write about your experience of having a daily quiet time.

Read over what you have written above about your experiences of praying in faith, memorizing Scripture, and your daily quiet time. Share your experiences with another person. Sharing your experiences may lead that person to seek a closer relationship with the Lord.

 Work today on this week's Scripture-memory verses, *John 13:34-35,* by writing them several times in the space below. Tell someone how you have grown in Christ from the practice of memorizing Scripture.

Stop and pray, asking God to show you how He wants you to work within the body of Christ to encourage others.

DAY 4

What Christ Expects

Disciples are careful to develop Christ-honoring relationships with others. Relationships don't just happen. They require special care. Because all of us have sinful natures, we can become thoughtless in the way we treat others. Hatred, selfishness, jealousy, and backbiting have no place in the life of a follower of Christ. The Scriptures instruct us about how Christ expects us to treat others.

FRIENDSHIP: A HIGH PRIORITY
Read *John 15:9,12-13* in the margin, then answer the following.
• **Why are you to love other persons?**_____
• **At the heart of friendship is the willingness to_____ if necessary.**

"As the Father has loved me, so have I loved you. My command is this: Love each other as I have loved you. Greater love has no one than this, that he lay down his life for his friends" (John 15:9, 12-13).

You should love others because of the love that flows from God through Christ to you. Jesus valued friendship and fellowship so much that He said friends should be willing to give their lives for one another if necessary. Jesus made friendship a high priority! Jesus laid down His life for others, and later, some of His disciples did, too. Fellowshipping with believers and loving them with the kind of sacrificial love like Jesus demonstrated are important parts of life in Christ.

A friend loves at all times, and a brother is born for adversity (Prov. 17:17).

Study what the Bible says about the way friends are to act toward one another. Read the verses in the margin. Then match each reference in the left column with the correct statement in the right column.

____ 1. *Proverbs 17:17*   a. **Friends care enough to confront one another in love if necessary.**

____ 2. *Matthew 18:15*   b. **Friends don't gossip or make hurtful remarks about one another.**

____ 3. *James 4:11*   c. **Friends want the best for one another and therefore present the gospel to friends who don't know Christ.**

____ 4. *1 John 1:3*   d. **Friends love one another regardless of the situations they face.**

Review the statements in the right column that describe characteristics of friendship. Draw a star beside the trait or traits that represent the biggest challenges in your friendships. Stop and pray that God will change you in these areas through Christ's love.

"If your brother sins against you, go and show him his fault, just between the two of you. If he listens to you, you have won your brother over. But if he will not listen, take one or two others along, so that every matter may be established by the testimony of two or three witnesses" (Matt. 18:15).

Brothers, do not slander one another. Anyone who speaks against his brother or judges him speaks against the law and judges it (Jas. 4:11).

Was one of the statements you checked item a—caring enough to confront? This is a hard issue. You may think that confronting a friend is not Christlike because it seems to call for hostility. Actually, confronting a friend in love is a very caring act. Sometimes people tell others that they have a problem with a friend yet never go directly to that person. That type of indirect communication can hurt the relationship. It can also hurt the body of Christ. Disagreements between individuals in a youth group can increase, widening their circle to include others.

We proclaim to you what we have seen and heard, so that you also may have fellowship with us. And our fellowship is with the Father and with his Son, Jesus Christ (1 John 1:3).

**Daily Master
Communication Guide**

I Thessalonians 2:1-13

What God said to me:

What I said to God:

Eventually, small disputes can develop into major rifts that prevent the body of Christ from doing its work.

In those verses it's very clear about how Christians are to relate to and resolve difficulties with others. You can learn loving, diplomatic ways to communicate how you feel so that such communication strengthens and doesn't harm the relationship. The correct answers to the previous exercise are 1. d, 2. a, 3. b, 4. c.

THE COST OF NEGLECTING RELATIONSHIPS

Have you closed yourself off from persons who care about you? Do you shut out persons rather than get involved in their lives? Do you avoid persons rather than risk a relationship? Have you been hurt in past friendships so you withdraw rather than go through that again? Do you allow friendships to form at church?

In the previous paragraph underline statements or questions with which you can identify.

If you avoid fellowshipping with believers because you don't want to risk relationships, you miss opportunities to serve your family in Christ. When difficulties come your way, relationships with other believers can provide resources to meet your needs. The most serious result of neglecting fellowship with believers is that it inevitably creates distance between you and God.

Read *I Thessalonians 2:1-13* today during your quiet time. After you've read about Paul's love for and ministry with the Christians at Thessalonica, complete the Daily Master Communication Guide in the margin.

Paul's example with the Thessalonians can guide you in relating to your *MasterLife* group members. Likely by now, you're forming a special bond with your group members. Enduring friendships can form as a result of this fellowship. You may begin to see in these persons some of the traits of friendship you studied on page 67. Be thankful for the trust, support, and fellowship that's developing.

Take to heart *John 15:12-13,* the verses you have read several times this week, and lovingly lift your group members to the Father in prayer. Stop now and pray for each of your *MasterLife* group members by name. Ask God to bless each person through this study. Ask Him to help you be available as a friend to your fellow members.

USING YOUR TIME EFFECTIVELY

A lack of time is an excuse you may use when you assess why you don't take advantage of—or create—opportunities to fellowship with believers. Perhaps you've already had difficulty finding time to do your daily assignments. For the rest of today and in day 5 you'll learn ways to wisely use your time.

 As you read these suggestions to help you use your time more effectively, underline statements that seem relevant to you.

Redeeming the Time

• Time is a cherished possession.

Our world focuses on time, and the clock dictates the tempo of our lives.

Ask God's Purpose for Our Time

• Time is God's gift to us.

We have time when we live according to God's purposes. We are responsible to Him for every minute He gives us. If we listen to Him, our lives are more harmonious. When we treat time as a gift from God we spend our time in ways that are more consistent with His purposes, thus the events of our lives flow together smoothly allowing us the time to do the things that need to be done.

Ask God's Direction for the Day

• Time is an opportunity God gives us to discover and carry out His purposes.

If we believe that Christ is the Lord of our time, we can believe that He has a design for this day, as well as for our entire lives. Knowing and doing God's will involves knowing and doing God's will for this day.

Ask God for Right Priorities

• Time used wisely gives us opportunities for Christian ministry and witness.

Paul said that wisdom is related to time *(Eph. 5:15-16)*. *Making the most of every opportunity* means "buying up every chance." God's time is a priceless item. Using time wisely is being alert to opportunities for ministry and witness. Be prepared, expect opportunities to minister and witness, and take them!

Ask God's Help for a Daily Quiet Time

• A time for quiet mediation is good for our spiritual lives.

We rediscover how to take things easily, how to rest as God commanded, how to meditate and pray. In quietness we rediscover the inner peace the world needs. We make a clear distinction between what is really important and what is secondary. Do it in priority order, but leave yourself open for God to redirect you. We experience freedom when we obey God's purposes. Jesus was a truly free but purposeful person living an unhurried life. Jesus had plenty of time to speak to the woman He met at a well, to spend holidays with His disciples, to admire the lilies of the field, to wash His disciples' feet, to answer their questions patiently. Most important, He had time to spend a whole night in prayer before an important decision.

Be very careful, then, how you live—not as unwise but as wise, making the most of every opportunity, because the days are evil (Eph. 5:15-16).

The wise use of time means being alert to every opportunity for Christian ministry and witness.

Check the benefits you are receiving from your daily quiet time.

❑ **Learning how to take things easily**

❑ **Learning how to rest as God commanded**

❑ **Learning how to meditate and pray**

❑ **Rediscovering inner peace**

❑ **Learning to distinguish between what is really important and what is secondary**

Draw a star beside those areas you still need to improve on.

 Continue to memorize this week's Scripture-memory verses, *John 13:34-35*. Write them in the margin from one to three times. Review the verses you memorized earlier.

The Model of Friendship

Fellowship was the centerpiece of one of Jesus' last messages to His disciples as He was on the way to the cross. He wanted His followers equipped to carry on His work after He was no longer with them physically.

"You are my friends if you do what I command. I no longer call you servants, because a servant does not know his master's business. Instead, I have called you friends, for everything that I learned from my Father I have made known to you" (John 15:14-15).

Read *John 15:14-15* in the margin. Underline two things Jesus considered important to communicate to His disciples.

Jesus wanted the disciples to know that He considered them friends, not servants. Their relationship was that of friends who loved one another in fellowship. He taught them everything He learned from His Father. Jesus openly discussed His business with the disciples and reminded them that they would have all the knowledge they needed to do His work after He was gone.

Like the disciples, you have access to all the knowledge you need to do the Father's work. The disciples had the same marching orders from Jesus that you have. He set the model for fellowship, and you as His disciple can act on that model.

"You did not choose me, but I chose you and appointed you to go and bear fruit—fruit that will last. Then the Father will give you whatever you ask in my name. This is my command: Love each other" (John 15:16-17).

In *John 15:16-17*, in the margin, underline the three things Jesus wanted to happen in the lives of His disciples.

Jesus placed a high priority on fellowship with believers. He emphasized three reasons He chose the disciples: He appointed them to (1) bear fruit, (2) ask the Father in His name, and (3) love one another. Loving one another, is the emphasis of this week's study. Christian love is the identifying mark of all disciples. Those who obey His commands love one another.

A STRONG BODY

Encouragement from fellowship with believers also gives you strength to witness. *John 17:20-22*, in the margin, describes the complete unity that Christ wants in the body. A youth group united in Christ can be an effective witness for Him. Jesus wanted unity, not division, in the church so that others would believe in Him. To a lost world, members of a youth group or church who argue and fail to demonstrate love to one another look as if they have nothing to offer.

"My prayer is…that all of them may be one, Father, just as you are in me and I am in you. May they also be in us so that the world may believe that you have sent me. I have given them the glory that you gave me, that they may be one as we are one. May they be brought to complete unity to let the world know that you sent me and have loved them even as you have loved me" (John 17:20-22).

Believers need one another's encouragement when they witness to others. Fellow church members can pray for you, encourage you, help ground you in Scripture, and support your efforts as you prepare to share your faith.

Pray in faith for those on your Prayer-Covenant List. Pray that you will seek strength from the body of Christ for witnessing opportunities that the Father puts in your path.

 Review your Prayer-Covenant List. If today's study brought other persons or requests to mind, add them to the list.

Say aloud your Scripture-memory verses, *John 13:34-35,* to a caring friend. Thank them for their friendship.

 Read *John 15* in your quiet time today and complete the Daily Master Communication Guide. Look for teachings about the discipline a Christian needs to fellowship with believers.

MOVING BEYOND YOUR COMFORT ZONE

Perhaps fellowshipping with believers is easy for you as long as you are within your comfort zone. You likely have a comfortable circle of friends in your youth group, in your *MasterLife* group, or in another area of your church. But when Christ commands you to love others, He doesn't put restrictions on those you are to love. Sometimes you may need to reach outside your close circle of friends to extend fellowship.

 Find someone who isn't in your close circle of friends or in your *MasterLife* **group and begin to develop a relationship.**

You may be wondering how you'll find the extra time to befriend someone. Yesterday you read about redeeming the time to become a better steward of your time. Today you'll learn to use a MasterTime form to set your priorities. You'll find the description of How to Use MasterTime form below.

Although I like to do things spontaneously, I've learned that in order to get the priority things done, I must plan my schedule every day, using the MasterTime process. I never get everything I planned to do finished, but I know that I've done the priority things. If I don't prioritize my time, others will prioritize it for me. As you use MasterTime remember the following helps:

• Trust the Lord to direct you in all you do.

• Plan your daily work under the Master's leadership.

• When listing major goals think of working toward them as you complete your other tasks. For example, if one of your major goals is college, you can work toward that goal by doing your best when you spend time studying for the junior or high school classes that you have now.

• When listing your daily and weekly responsibilities remember to include items such as church, family, school, and job commitments—daily quiet time, homework, cleaning your room, etc.

• When listing your daily and weekly appointments include items such as doctor appointments, piano lessons, meetings, football games, band, etc.

• Rank tasks by priority, but also think of ways to save time such as ranking by category and then by doing similar tasks in order. Work toward long-term goals by your efforts on short-term goals and daily tasks.

• Spend time every morning planning your schedule. Having a plan helps you get started on the right tasks and keeps you focused on priorities. Check off the tasks on your MasterTime form as you complete them.

• Do the tasks in the order planned but be flexible according to God's direction. Interruptions and unplanned events are sometimes God's ways to get you to do His will. However, ask His leadership, because Satan can also stop

**Daily Master
Communication Guide**

John 15

What God said to me:

What I said to God:

you from doing God's will. Ask yourself:

___ Is this one of God's priorities I might not have thought about?

___ Is God trying to teach me something?

___ Does He want me to help someone I had not considered?

___ Does it contribute to one of my long-term goals? If so, is it a high enough priority to interrupt my list of priorities for today?

___ Is it important or just urgent?

___ Is this the best time to do it? Could I do it some other time?

___ Can it be delegated to someone else?

___ How much do someone else's responsibilities depend on my doing this task at this time?

• Stick to your plan as much as you can. If you do fail, don't waste time blaming yourself and feeling guilty. Ask forgiveness and submit to the Master's will.

• Don't worry about being unable to do everything you planned, since you did the most important things in priority under God's direction. Leave them to the Lord and add them to tomorrow's list with the priority each deserves that day.

• Leave the results to God.

Trust in the Lord with all your heart. Never rely on what you think you know. Remember the Lord in everything you do, and he will show you the right way (Prov. 3:5-6, GNB).

"Seek first his kingdom and his righteousness, and all these things will be given to you as well" (Matt. 6:33).

You may make your plans, but God directs your actions (Prov. 16:9, GNB).

Ask the Lord to bless your plans, and you will be successful in carrying them out (Prov. 16:3, GNB).

How to Use MasterTime

1. Read the Scripture verses in the margin (*Prov. 3:5-6; Matt. 6:33; Prov. 16:9; Prov. 16:3*). Think how these Scripture verses relate to the way you should plan.

2. Ask God to show you His purposes for you in His kingdom.

3. List major goals that you believe God has given you. Group them by year, month, week, and day.

4. List your daily and weekly responsibilities and the amount of time they will require.

5. List your daily and weekly appointments and the amount of time they will require.

6. Rank your goals, responsibilities, and appointments according to your priorities and time necessary.

7. Each morning plan your task schedule. Write these on your MasterTime form for that day.

8. Do the tasks in the order planned to save time and to receive immediate direction about the next task to do. Ask the Lord to direct your actions.

9. Discipline yourself to carry out your plans.

10. At the end of each day reevaluate and pray about any unfinished tasks on your MasterTime form.

Evaluate how often you accomplish the goals in "How to Use Master-Time." Circle the appropriate number 4 = always, 3 = usually, 2 = often, 1 = sometimes. Then pray about areas in which you need to improve.

I trust the Lord to direct me in all I do.

4   3   2   1

I plan my daily work under the Master's leadership.

4   3   2   1

I ask the Lord to bless my plans.

4   3   2   1

I depend on the Lord to direct my actions.

4   3   2   1

Now begin to plan your time, using "How to Use MasterTime" and the MasterTime worksheet and the MasterTime form on page 206. Use the MasterTime principles for at least the next six weeks. If you already use another system for time management, apply these same principles to that process.

Stop and pray, asking God to help you establish Christ-honoring priorities and to help you use your time wisely.

LEARNING THE DISCIPLE'S CROSS

You can use the Disciple's Cross to keep your time priorities balanced and to work toward the goals in "How to Use MasterTime." The cross shows two means of intake for a Christian: prayer and God's Word. It shows two means of output: fellowship and witness. If you manage your life so that you keep a proper balance between intake and output, spiritual and physical growth, mental and social stimulation, and time for your needs and those of others, you can keep ministering to others without depleting your spiritual resources.

> If you manage your life so that you keep a proper balance, you can keep ministering to others without depleting your spiritual resources.

To summarize what you've learned this week, draw the portions of the Disciple's Cross you have studied, with the verses that accompany each discipline. Be ready to explain the cross.

HAS THIS WEEK MADE A DIFFERENCE?

Review "My Walk with the Master This Week" at the beginning of this week's material. Mark the activities you've finished by drawing vertical lines in the diamonds beside them. Finish any incomplete activities. Think about what you will say during your group session about your work on these activities.

As you complete your study of "Fellowship with Believers," I hope that you'll ask Christ to examine areas in which you're not loving others as He commanded. Sometimes this kind of examination is uncomfortable. Your best intentions will not make you a disciple of Christ until you follow His command about fellowship and loving others.

WEEK 5

Witness to the World

This Week's Goal

You will bear witness of Christ and your relationship with Him.

My Walk with the Master This Week

You will complete the following activities to develop the six biblical disciplines. When you have completed each activity, draw a vertical line in the diamond beside it.

SPEND TIME WITH THE MASTER

◇ Have a daily quiet time. Check the box beside each day you have a quiet time this week:
☐ Sunday ☐ Monday ☐ Tuesday ☐ Wednesday ☐ Thursday ☐ Friday ☐ Saturday

LIVE IN THE WORD

◇ Read your Bible every day. Write what God says to you and what you say to God.
◇ Memorize *John 15:8.*
◇ Review *Luke 9:23; John 15:5; John 8:31-32; John 15:7;* and *John 13:34-35.*
◇ Study the reasons for memorizing Scripture in "How to Memorize Scripture."

PRAY IN FAITH

◇ Pray about your priorities and your use of time.
◇ Pray for the members of your *MasterLife* group.

FELLOWSHIP WITH BELIEVERS

◇ Share with your prayer partner some of your problems and pray about your and your partner's needs.

WITNESS TO THE WORLD

◇ Review "How to Use MasterTime." Use it to plan your days and week.
◇ Make a new friend who is not a Christian. Learn all you can about your new friend and be ready to tell your *MasterLife* group about him or her.

MINISTER TO OTHERS

◇ Continue learning the Disciple's Cross. Explain the meaning of the left crossbar to add to the information you have already learned.

This Week's Scripture-Memory Verse

"This is to my Father's glory, that you bear much fruit, showing yourselves to be my disciples" (John 15:8).

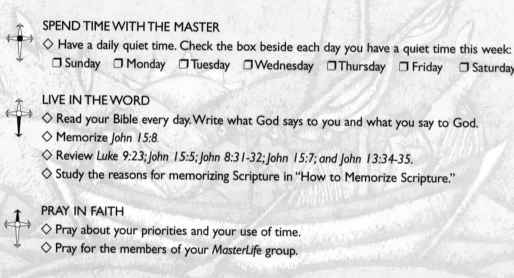

DAY 1

Bearing Fruit for Christ

After my initial commitment to be Christ's disciple, I felt a strong need to witness. Four nights a week I went to a rescue mission operated by college students. I tried to witness on the street, but no one came to Christ. I memorized Scriptures to counter the excuses people game me when they rejected my witness. Armed with about 50 Scriptures, I could answer almost any objection, but I hadn't discovered the real secret: the Holy Spirit is the One who empowers us to witness. He bears witness through us. When I allowed Him to fill me, the people I witnessed to began to trust Christ.

The Holy Spirit empowers us to witness.

A NATURAL DESIRE TO SHARE

Christ intends for His disciples to bear fruit. *John 15:8,* says the way to show that you're His disciple is to bear fruit. If you have an obedient relationship with Christ, you'll want to share with friends about that relationship. The branch that lives in the Vine bears fruit. If you practice the disciplines around the Disciple's Cross, you have a desire to share with non-Christians. If you fellowship with God's people as you live daily in the Word and pray in faith, you naturally share Christ with others. When God's love flows through the Son to you and others, you want to share Christ with others. The Holy Spirit empowers you to do so.

"This is to my Father's glory, that you bear much fruit, showing yourselves to be my disciples" (John 15:8).

✝ **What does *John 15:8* say you'll do to show that you are Christ's disciple?**

How does *John 15:8* say that you bring glory to God?

When God's love flows through the Son to you and others, you want to share the good news of Christ with those around you.

If you are Christ's disciple, you show it by bearing fruit for Him. This is a natural result of following Him. You don't do it in your own strength, as I first tried to do, but you allow the Holy Spirit to empower you. When you bear fruit for Him, you bring glory to God. The Lord uses you to teach others about Himself.

THE FRUIT OF A LIFE IN CHRIST

What does Christ mean when He talks about bearing fruit? *Galatians 5:22-23,* in the margin, describes the fruit of the Spirit—the traits of Christ that the Holy Spirit produces when you abide in Christ. How does bearing fruit relate to your life in Christ?

The fruit of the Spirit is love, joy, peace, patience, kindness, goodness, faithfulness, gentleness and self-control. Against such things there is no law (Gal. 5:22-23).

✝ **Read aloud *John 15:8,* this week's Scripture-memory verse, in the margin. What is the fruit you are expected to produce?**
❑ **The fruit of the Spirit, as listed in *Galatians 5:22-23***
❑ **Producing other Christians**

"This is to my Father's glory, that you bear much fruit, showing yourselves to be my disciples" (John 15:8).

Actually, both answers are correct. To better understand the purpose of fruit bearing, consider what occurs when a vine produces grapes. A vine doesn't produce fruit just so that a person can eat; it also enables the seed from that plant to be scattered. You're a Christian not merely to produce the sweet fruit of good deeds and good actions, but to cause others to want the life you are living. The fruit of the Spirit mentioned in *Galatians 5:22-23* naturally flows from your life if you abide in Christ. Your fruit bearing results in producing other Christians.

Check the qualities in the margin from *Galatians 5:22-23* that the world needs.

The result of your fruit bearing is to produce other Christians.

☑ love   ☑ patience
☑ faithfulness   ☑ joy
☑ kindness   ☑ gentleness
☑ peace   ☑ goodness
☑ self-control

When grapes get ripe you want to eat them. As you walk along eating them, you spit out the seeds. Without realizing it you are helping the vine reproduce more vines and fruit. Is love one of the things you checked that the world needs? One way you show Christ's character is to demonstrate love, for example, in loving your enemy. When others see you do that, they may ask: "How can you love like that? How can you love someone who mistreats you?" That's your opportunity to plant the seed. You can do that by praising the Vine. Say, "The truth is, I can't love like that, but Christ can love that person through me." Your life is a witness, but a verbal witness is also necessary to glorify God instead of yourself. Accepting credit for your good deeds would be wrong, because that's your chance to give credit to Christ. Only through Christ can you love your enemy. Demonstrating this fruit of the Spirit enables you to plant a seed that bears fruit.

What would happen if you demonstrated love without telling others why? *ppl would wonder who you are, question you.*

If you planted the seed without telling others why, they might think you're just different. A follower of Christ demonstrates and confesses Christ as the reason for his or her love. Each witnessing opportunity plants the seed of love and it bears fruit in your life. The Lord uses you to teach others about Himself.

You may have answered that the world needs peace. When others see peace in your life that is different from the world's chaos, they wonder what makes you different. But if you don't tell them that it's because of Christ's peace living in you, they won't understand the source. If a person comments on your calmness during difficulty, you can say, " An experience that I had with Christ helps me respond this way." This introduces Christ as your source of peace.

The world needs joy. You can be a joyful person and radiate that joy. Instead of being bitter or sad when facing difficulties, look on the positive side. When you look for the good in bad situations or refuse to give up in sickness, people take notice. Saying Christ is the source of your joy, produces the fruit Christ desires.

❏ patience   ❏ faithfulness
❏ goodness   ❏ kindness
❏ gentleness   ❏ self-control

We've looked at three fruit of the Spirit mentioned in *Galatians 5:22-23*—love, joy, and peace—and ways they could lead to a witness. Now choose one of the remaining fruit (in the margin) and describe in the margin how it could become the seed of a verbal witness.

THE FRUIT OF NEW BELIEVERS

As you've learned, bearing fruit can mean having the fruit of the Spirit in your life. Bearing fruit also includes the result: producing another follower of Christ. Jesus said in *Matthew 4:19*, *"Come, follow me, and I will make you fishers of men."* Fruit bearing is the normal, natural result of a life that has Christ at the center.

You might wonder: *How do I learn to witness, since all of my friends are Christians? I'm willing to be obedient and bear fruit, but how can I find someone with whom I can share the gospel?* One way is to reach beyond your circle of friends. You have persons all around you with whom you can become acquainted. Perhaps the following assignment will help.

 Make a new friend this week who isn't a Christian. Learn all you can about your new friend. Make notes and be ready to tell your *MasterLife* group about him or her.

LEARNING THE DISCIPLE'S CROSS

This week introduces you to the fourth bar of the Disciple's Cross, witness to the world. Just as the vertical crossbar represents the two ways a disciple relates to God—through the Word and prayer—the horizontal crossbar represents the two ways a disciple relates to others—through fellowship and witness. The cross illustrates a disciple's balanced life in Christ.

 Draw the portions of the Disciple's Cross you've already studied. Now draw the left crossbar and write the discipline *witness* on it. Refer to the completed cross on page 204 if you need help.

 In your quiet time today read *Galatians 5*, the chapter containing the verses you studied about the fruit of the Spirit. When you have read it, complete the Daily Master Communication Guide in the margin.

Daily Master Communication Guide

Galatians 5

What God said to me:

What I said to God:

"I am the true vine, and my Father is the gardener. He cuts off every branch in me that bears no fruit, while every branch that does bear fruit he prunes so that it will be even more fruitful. You are already clean because of the word I have spoken to you. Remain in me, and I will remain in you" (John 15:1-4).

Has Christ been your power source when you have witnessed? Describe an occasion when, as you witnessed, Christ was giving you the words to say and the strength to say them.

DAY 2

Relying on Christ

Read *John 15:1-4* in the margin. Then mark the statements that are true.

❑ **Fruit bearing is not a choice for a Christian.**
❑ **Some Christians are expected to bear fruit, while others are not.**
❑ **Christ cleanses you so that you can bear more fruit.**
❑ **Fruit bearing depends on remaining in Christ.**

Do you think that witnessing is only for persons with outgoing personalities? Or that you're excused from witnessing if you're not particularly talkative or don't have time? Do you think that witnessing is not your major strength? *John 15:1-4* says that persons who are in Christ bear fruit. It doesn't say that only a few believers are fruit bearers. All Christians are expected to bear fruit. You can't bear fruit apart from Him, as I learned when I tried to witness in my own strength. When Christ became my source of power and I shared from my lifelong, obedient relationship with Him, I became more effective in witnessing. In the previous exercise all of the statements are true except the second one.

Has Christ been your power source when you've witnessed? Describe in the margin an occasion when, as you witnessed, Christ was giving you the words to say and the strength to say them.

Have you ever made excuses for not witnessing? ❑ Yes ❑ No

 Try to say *John 15:8*, this week's Scripture-memory verse, several times from memory. Try to write it from memory. Write what it says about making excuses for not witnessing.

You may have answered like this: The verse indicates that Christ's disciples bear fruit. If I want to be His disciple, there's no real excuse for not witnessing.

How are you doing with the discipline of memorizing Scripture? By now you've likely memorized several verses you can use in different situations. I've found Scripture memorization helpful in times of temptation, trial, and testimony. When I'm tempted, I remember *1 Corinthians 10:13,* one of the earliest Scriptures I memorized. The Holy Spirit uses that verse to assure me that He will not allow me to be tempted more than I can bear but will offer an escape every time. Many times I have faced trials I couldn't understand. Each time the Holy Spirit reminded me of *James 1:2-3: Consider it pure joy, my brothers, whenever you face trials of many kinds, because you know that the testing of your faith develops perseverance. Perseverance must finish its work so that you may be mature and complete, not lacking anything.*

By now, the fifth week of your study, you've likely memorized five verses and are beginning to learn a sixth. Describe situations where these memorized verses have helped you. Be ready to share what you've written at your next group session.

Luke 9:23: Then he said to them all: "If anyone would come after me, he must deny himself and take up his cross daily and follow me

John 15:5: I am the vine; your are the branches. If a man remains in me and I in him, he will bear much fruit; apart from me you can do nothing

John 8:31-32:

John 15:7: If you remain in me and my words remain in you, ask whatever you wish, and it will be given

John 13:34-35:

Read *Acts 8:26-40,* about Philip's witness to the Ethiopian, during your quiet time today. Then complete the Daily Master Communication Guide in the margin.

Daily Master Communication Guide

Acts 8:26-40

What God said to me:

What I said to God:

Every Disciple's Orders

Witnessing is part of every disciple's marching orders.

Maybe you think that witnessing is something Jesus expects only of preachers, evangelists, or missionaries. You may think that Jesus doesn't expect ordinary Christians to bear fruit for Him in this way. But *John 15,* the passage you have been reading, makes clear that witnessing is part of every disciple's marching orders.

Read *John 15:16* in the margin and answer the questions below.

What did Jesus say His purpose was in choosing the disciples?

"You did not choose me, but I chose you and appointed you to go and bear fruit—fruit that will last. Then the Father will give you whatever you ask in my name" (John 15:16).

What did Jesus promise fruitful disciples they could do?

Fruit bearing wasn't optional for the disciples. It was expected of them as part of their relationships with Him. Jesus told the disciples that to bear fruit that would last was the reason He chose them. Along with this expectation Jesus promised that they could pray in His name and have their prayers answered. Obedient disciples seek to live to do the Father's will and to pray accordingly.

Daily Master Communication Guide

John 15

What God said to me:

What I said to God:

WITNESSING IS NOT OPTIONAL

In *John 15:27* Jesus once again told the disciples that witnessing is not optional; it is a discipline He expects. The verse says, *"You also must testify, for you have been with me from the beginning."*

Why did Jesus tell the disciples that they must testify?

Jesus commanded the disciples to testify about Him because they had been with Him from the beginning and knew firsthand of His saving truth.

Again read *John 15* in your quiet time today. Let God speak to you about the importance of bearing fruit and of testifying about Christ. After you have read this passage, complete the Daily Master Communication Guide.

Although you didn't physically live alongside Jesus, as the disciples did, you know firsthand of His saving truth, and you experience a growing relationship with Him. You can tell others what Christ has done in your life just as the disciples did. You can tell others about Him, based on your experience.

As you study about witnessing to others, you may find yourself thinking: *I want to do that! I know that Christ wants me to be His witness. But how will I know the words to say? How do I know I won't freeze up or embarrass myself?*

Read *John 15:4* in the margin and complete this sentence:

I'm unable to bear fruit unless I <u>remain in him</u>.

No branch can bear fruit by itself. The branch is part of the vine; it's not just attached to the vine. As the sap and the life-giving power that produces the fruit flow through the branch, they originate in the vine. The end of the branch that bears the fruit is the part you see, but the vine is always the life-giving source.

"Remain in me, and I will remain in you. No branch can bear fruit by itself; it must remain in the vine. Neither can you bear fruit unless you remain in me" (John 15:4).

THE PROMISE OF CHRIST'S POWER

When you were saved, you became part of the Vine. You can't bear fruit if you don't remain in the Vine, that is, stay in fellowship with Christ. If you stay in fellowship with Christ, you'll be empowered to witness. In my early attempts at witnessing I learned that I couldn't succeed just because I willed myself to succeed. Only when I allowed the Holy Spirit to control my thoughts, my words, and my actions could I witness effectively.

 Recall *John 15:5*, a previous memory verse. Write in the margin what it promises will happen if you remain in Christ?

If you stay in fellowship with Christ, you will be empowered to witness.

The verse doesn't say that perhaps you'll bear fruit or that only exceptional disciples will bear fruit. It says that if you remain in Christ, you'll bear fruit. This is a precious promise from God's Word to you about what happens to a person who abides in Christ and witnesses to others. He will enable you to bear fruit if you remain in Him and seek His will.

What are some ways you can remain in Christ so that you can bear fruit for Him?
❑ **Live in the Word by studying it and memorizing it.**
❑ **Pray that the Father will direct you to witness according to His will.**
❑ **Fellowship with other believers to hear instruction from God's Word and to draw encouragement from the body of Christ.**
❑ **Have a daily quiet time to hear God speak to you.**

Which discipline do you most need to work on? Draw a star beside it. Then ask God to help you with that discipline.

How did you evaluate yourself on having a daily quiet time with God? I've found that nothing takes the place of a personal quiet time with God every day. Like manna, it doesn't last long enough to provide for tomorrow. If I write in my Daily Master Communication Guide each day, God says more and more to me. Then when times are difficult, I can go back and read what God said to me in the previous days, weeks, or months. Many times this perspective gives me new insights about my relationship with God and restores my spirit.

Complete this statement: The time that works best for my daily quiet time is ___night (late)___.

If finding time for your daily, personal time with Christ is still a challenge for you, review what you learned in week 4 about ways to set priorities using MasterTime. Use MasterTime to plan your days and weeks.

Stop and pray, asking God to help you with your priorities and your use of time so that you'll be able to find a consistent time every day to remain connected to the Vine.

You can also abide in Christ by fellowshipping with other believers and by expressing your care and concern for them. For example, the time you spend with your prayer partner can be a time of fellowship.

Share with your prayer partner some of your problems. Pray about each other's needs. Before you finish your conversation, say *John 15:8,* this week's Scripture-memory verse, to your prayer partner.

As you studied in week 4, your fellowship with others naturally leads you to share Christ with them. The Lord will use you to teach others about Him. You'll have fellowship as you demonstrate your love for fellow believers, as you did with your prayer partner. You also need to relate to persons who don't know Christ, attempting to bring them to a saving knowledge of Him. Continue to cultivate the friendship with your new non-Christian friend.

LEARNING THE DISCIPLE'S CROSS

To reinforce what you're learning, draw the portions of the Disciple's Cross you've studied. Now draw the left crossbar and write *witness* on it. Write *John 15:8,* the Scripture reference that accompanies the left crossbar, under witness.

DAY 4

Compelled to Tell

When I was six years old, I accepted Christ as my Savior while my father was preaching a revival service in a local rescue mission. I recognized that I was a sinner and felt that if a trap door were under me, I would go straight to hell. Realizing that I needed to repent of my sins, I almost ran down the aisle. I felt that a burden had been lifted from me. With the enthusiasm of a new convert I told my neighbor, my barber, and even the president of the seminary where my dad had graduated that I had trusted Christ. I couldn't help telling what I'd seen and heard.

WHAT HAS CHRIST DONE FOR YOU?

The Bible says, *"We cannot help speaking about what we have seen and heard" (Acts 4:20)*. Has Christ ever been so real to you that you couldn't help but tell about what you saw and heard? Has He answered a prayer in such a way that you responded, "Only the Lord could have done that!" Have you experienced physical or emotional healing? Has He provided you special encouragement or help from a friend just when you needed it? You didn't live at the time of Christ to observe His miracles firsthand, but have you experienced modern-day miracles? If so, how can you keep from telling people you meet how awesome Christ is?

How ready are you to share about what Christ has done in your life? Evaluate yourself by circling the appropriate number of the statements in the margin: 1 = never, 2 = sometimes, 3 = often, 4 = usually, 5 = always. Then pray about areas in which you need to improve.

Don't feel embarrassed or awkward if you answered with a 1 or 2 on several or most of the statements in the exercise. Learning to share your faith boldly can be a building process. As a student I was concerned about my best friend. I invited him to go to church with me, but it was not a good experience for him. Later, when I was spending the night at his house he asked how to become a Christian. I stumbled and stuttered all around the subject, but I couldn't make it clear to him. He didn't receive Christ then or later when I learned to explain it better. For many years I carried the guilt that Jack might go to hell because I couldn't tell him how to be saved when he asked. On my first missionary furlough he told me that someone else had led him to Christ. I was relieved but I realized that I had cheated him out of several years of Christian living because I couldn't clearly explain how he could be saved. Could you explain how to be saved to your best friend who was lost? This is the time to learn how before you blow it like I did.

MAKE SURE OF YOUR RELATIONSHIP

As you think about witnessing to the world, first be sure of your own salvation so that you can bear fruit. Be sure that you are connected to the Vine so that you have Christ's love flowing through you in a lifelong, obedient relationship with

I couldn't help telling what I'd seen and heard!

I build relationships with non-Christian friends or acquaintances so that I can eventually have opportunities to witness to them. 1 2 3 4 5

I pray with persons or offer to pray for persons who have needs, and I remind them that God cares about them. 1 2 3 4 5

I visit or contact persons who visit my church and express concern for them. 1 2 3 4 5

I tell lost persons about Christ even though it means risking that they will reject me. 1 2 3 4 5

I don't hesitate to tell others when God answers my prayers. 1 2 3 4 5

Learning to share your faith boldly can be a building process.

I am not ashamed of the gospel, because it is the power of God for the salvation of everyone who believes: first for the Jew, then for the Gentile (Rom. 1:16).

God's kindness leads you toward repentance (Rom. 2:4).

All have sinned and fall short of the glory of God (Rom. 3:23).

God demonstrates his own love for us in this: While we were still sinners, Christ died for us (Rom. 5:8).

Him. The following gospel presentation is called the Roman Road.[1] You'll read eight passages from the Book of Romans explains the gospel message. Study the presentation to see how you measure up in your relationship with Christ. Start by memorizing the verses and marking them in sequence in your Bible so that you can also share the good news with others.

THE POWER OF GOD

Read *Romans 1:16* in the margin. Many people today live without hope. They have no resources to strengthen them and guide them through their struggles in life. According to *Romans 1:16,* the focus of the Christian faith is the gospel, which is the good news that God's power is available to help you in whatever problems you face. Through Jesus Christ a power great enough to bring salvation and deliverance is available to any person who believes.

God's _____ can make you secure.

THROUGH GOD'S POWER, PEOPLE CAN CHANGE

Read *Romans 2:4* in the margin. Through God's power, people can change. The biblical word for *change* is "repentance." This means allowing God to change the direction of your life.

God's power results in _____.

SIN MAKES CHANGE NECESSARY

Read *Romans 3:23* in the margin. Why do people need to change? From what does Jesus offer deliverance? According to the Bible, everybody has a problem. The problem can be described in many ways, but the most common biblical word is *sin.* One meaning of *sin* is to "fall short of the mark God has set." The Bible teaches that God's standard for us is Jesus Christ. If Jesus were standing in front of you in person, could you say that you are as good as He is? The failure to meet God's standard is sin, which means that all people have a sin problem. You may do much that is good, and you may not want to do anything bad, but none of us can measure up to God's standard of always doing right.

_____ makes change necessary.

How would you answer someone who claims that he has done nothing wrong?

GOD STILL LOVES US

Read *Romans 5:8* in the margin. God still loves you. Some people think that their failure to meet God's standard means that God is their enemy. Because they don't live up to His expectations, God must be against them. But the message of Jesus is that in spite of our sin, God still loves us. That's good news!

God's love for you isn't based on ignorance and an unawareness of sin. Nor is His love based on a toleration that overlooks your sin. Knowing your sin, God chose to love you, even though it meant His Son's death for you. In doing what was necessary to overcome your problem with sin, God demonstrated the depth and reality of His love for you (also see *John 3:16*).

God still _____ us.

THE WAGES OF SIN IS DEATH

Read *Romans 6:23* in the margin. Sin earns death, but God offers life. Sin wouldn't be a problem if it didn't have serious consequences. According to the Bible, the consequences of sin are too serious to overlook. Although God is not your enemy, He is your judge. As judge He can't ignore your failure to meet His standard of perfection. *Romans 6:23* it says that *the wages of sin is death*. Whenever you sin, you earn the wages of death. Since every person is guilty of sin, every person is subject to the consequences of eternal death and separation from God (see *John 3:36; Rev. 20:11-15*).

The wages of sin is death, but the gift of God is eternal life in Christ Jesus our Lord (Rom. 6:23).

GOD'S GIFT IS ETERNAL LIFE

An alternative exists. Through your works you earn death, but *the gift of God is eternal life in Christ Jesus our Lord (Rom. 6:23)*. Jesus died on the cross in your place (see *1 Pet. 3:18*). He took your guilt for sin upon Himself so that His death would fulfill the judgment of God against your sin (see *2 Cor. 5:21; Col. 2:13-14*). Your sin is judged in the death of Jesus on the cross as our substitute. By your works you earn death, but by His grace you can receive eternal life. God offers eternal life and the forgiveness of sin through Jesus Christ as His gift.

Sin earns _____, but God gives _____.

If you confess with your mouth, "Jesus is Lord," and believe in your heart that God raised him from the dead, you will be saved. For it is with your heart that you believe and are justified, and it is with your mouth that you confess and are saved. For, "Everyone who calls on the name of the Lord will be saved" (Rom. 10:9-10,13).

ACCEPT CHRIST AS SAVIOR AND LORD

Underline the words in *Romans 10:9-10,13*, in the margin, that indicate what you need to do to accept Christ as Savior and Lord.

Read *Romans 10:9-10,13* in the margin. The words *confess, believe,* and *call* summarize what someone must do to receive God's free gift and be saved.

The biblical word translated *confess* means "to say the same thing." *Lord* may be translated "ruler, boss, or sovereign authority." When we confess Jesus as Lord, we are saying the same thing about God that He says about Himself (see *Isa. 45:5-7,22-24; Phil. 2:10-11*). We recognize His rightful authority over us. In acknowledging Jesus as Lord, we admit our sin in failing to meet His standard of perfect obedience and righteousness.

Confessing Jesus as Lord means that we recognize His rightful _____ over us.

To confess Jesus as Lord also means to repent of our sins. In accepting His rightful authority over you, you turn away from life on your terms in order to obey and serve Him. This turning away from sin in order to follow Jesus is called repentance. More than feeling sorry, it is changing the direction of your life and living a God-oriented rather than a self-oriented life (see *Luke 3:7-14*).

Repentance means changing the _____ of your life and living a _____ life.

Believe means "to trust." When you *believe in your heart that God raised him from the dead (Rom. 10:9)*, you have confidence that the death and resurrection of Jesus are enough to secure your salvation. You trust in the work of Christ rather than in the work of your life for your salvation. When you look at a bridge, you might know that it would hold you up if you crossed it. The bridge never actually holds you up, however, until you get on it and cross. Similarly, you may know a lot about Jesus, but until you trust Him with your life, putting your life into His hands, you are not believing in Him. To believe in Jesus is to put your life, both physically and spiritually, into His hands.

To believe in Jesus is to put your life, both physically and spiritually, into His hands.

Believing means _____ Jesus with your life.

When you acknowledge that Jesus is the rightful Lord or boss of your life and when you are willing to believe in Him, trusting in His work alone for your salvation, you need only call on Him to be saved. In *Romans 10:13* Paul wrote, *"Everyone who calls on the name of the Lord will be saved."* Note how broad the invitation is. *Anyone* who is willing to call on the name of the Lord will be saved. No other qualifications are needed. If you are willing to call on Him, you can be saved.

Anyone who is willing to call on the name of the Lord will be saved.

To call on the name of the Lord is to ask Him for forgiveness of sin and for salvation. When you ask Him for salvation, you're acknowledging Him as your Lord and expressing your intention to live a life of obedience and service. Persons who call on Him will be saved.

Calling on the name of the Lord means asking Him for_____ of sin and for _____.

The three words that summarize what someone must do to be saved are: _____, _____, _____.

Lord Jesus, I need You. I want You to be my Savior and my Lord. I accept Your death on the cross as the payment for my sins, and I now entrust my life to Your care. Thank You for forgiving me and for giving me new life. Please help me grow as a Christian so that my life will bring glory and honor to You. Amen.
Signed_____
Date_____

You may have experienced some questions about where you stand in your commitment to Christ since you've started this study. As you've read about being totally committed to Christ, you may not be able to state firmly that you've taken that initial step of following Him that occurs when you receive Christ in salvation. *MasterLife* was designed for persons who have accepted Jesus as their Savior and Lord and who want to learn what it means to be His true followers. If you find that you can't say with 100-percent surety that you've made that commitment, you can accept Him now by inviting Him into your life. If you wish, use the sample prayer in the margin to express your commitment.

The Spirit himself testifies with our spirit that we are God's children. Now if we are children, then we are heirs—heirs of God and co-heirs with Christ, if indeed we share in his sufferings in order that we may also share in his glory. For I am convinced that neither death not life, neither angels nor demons, neither the present nor the future, nor any powers, neither height nor depth, nor anything else in all creation, will be able to separate us from the love of God that is in Christ Jesus our Lord (Rom. 8:16-17,38-39).

Receiving Christ does not guarantee that you will not struggle with issues like self-denial, cross bearing, and following Jesus. It does not mean that you will not be tempted to give your devotion to someone or something else. It doesn't mean that you won't shy away from the costs of discipleship. It means that He forgives you; that He has a lasting relationship with you that extends into eternity; and that

He will grant you strength, power, and wisdom as you seek to be His disciple. If you just now received Christ as your Savior and Lord, talk with your *MasterLife* leader, your youth leader, your pastor, or a trusted Christian friend about any new commitment you've made.

A CHILD OF GOD

Read *Romans 8:16-17,38-39* in the margin. When you are saved, God adopts you as His child, and His Holy Spirit assures you that you are part of His family. According to Roman law at the time of Paul's writing, someone's adopted son also became his heir. While Christ is God's heir by nature, Christians have become God's heirs by adoption. Therefore, you are a joint-heir with Christ.

Verses 38-39 tell us that we are eternally secure in God. Because Christ has defeated the principalities and powers of this earth, we need not fear human and superhuman enemies. Nothing can separate us from God's love in Christ Jesus. Believers have hope because they are a child of God and are secure in His love.

We now have _____.

LIFE FOR GOD.

Read *Romans 12:1-2* in the margin. Faith = life for God. When you become a Christian, you begin to live your life for God. You can expect your life to be different. God wants your life to change as you follow Jesus, even if it means sacrifice. The goal for believers is to look and live less like the unsaved people of the world and more like Jesus. That change happens because God brings it about. He will transform your life, making it more like the life of Jesus (see *Phil. 1:6; 2:13*). Jesus will make you look and live like one of His children as you follow Him.

Faith = life for _____.

YOU ARE HIS WITNESS

Whether you just received Christ or have been His disciple for many years, you are His witness. Plan your testimony in advance so that you can explain to a lost person how to receive eternal life. You may first want to go with your *MasterLife* leader when he or she uses it to witness to an unsaved person. Don't be afraid to share your salvation experience with non-Christians.

 In your quiet time today, read *Acts 16:11-15*. Then complete the Daily Master Communication Guide in the margin.

 Pray for your *MasterLife* group members by name. Ask God to bless each person with *MasterLife* and especially from the gospel presentation you've studied. Ask Him to help you be available as a friend to your fellow members.

Memorize *John 15:8*, this week's memory verse, which goes with the left crossbar of the Disciple's Cross. Write the verse several times in your journal or on a separate sheet of paper.

I urge you, brothers, in view of God's mercy, to offer your bodies as living sacrifices, holy and pleasing to God—this is your spiritual act of worship. Do not conform any longer to the pattern of this world, but be transformed by the renewing of your mind. Then you will be able to test and approve what God's will is—his good, pleasing and perfect will (Rom. 12:1-2).

Daily Master Communication Guide

Acts 16:11-15

What God said to me:

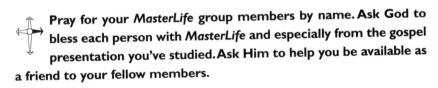

What I said to God:

"Remember the words I spoke to you: 'No servant is greater than his master.' If they persecuted me, they will persecute you also. If they obeyed my teaching, they will obey yours also. They will treat you this way because of my name, for they do not know the One who sent me" (John 15:20-21).

While he was still speaking a crowd came up, and the man who was called Judas, one of the Twelve, was leading them. He approached Jesus to kiss him, but Jesus asked him, "Judas, are you betraying the Son of Man with a kiss?" (Luke 22:47-48).

Jesus left there and went to his hometown, accompanied by his disciples. When the Sabbath came, he began to teach in the synagogue, and many who heard him were amazed. "Where did this man get these things?" they asked. "What's this wisdom that has been given him, that he even does miracles! isn't this the carpenter? Isn't this Mary's son and the brother of James, Joseph, Judas and Simon? Aren't his sisters here with us?" And they took offense at him (Mark 6:1-3).

He then began to teach them that the Son of Man must suffer many things and be rejected by the elders, chief priests and teachers of the law, and that he must be killed and after three days must rise again (Mark 8:31).

DAY 5

The Price of Bearing Fruit

Old Wang, Little Wang, and Cai Wen—rode 10 hours on a bus to tell the Zhou villagers about Jesus. As they witnessed, the Zhou people became an angry mob shouting to them, "You... know nothing... you wish to steal our gods...!" The mob beat them with sticks and farm implements. Little Wang, a Christian for only five months, died, paying the ultimate price for his faith. Old Wang and Cai Wen lived, but suffered from bruises and broken bones.

The following Sunday the church determined to send Old Wang and Cai Wen back to the Zhou village to evangelize again. Someone had to take the message of salvation to that village. The church grew silent when Liang, Little Wang's widow, requested to go with Old Wang and Cai Wen on their trip.

Their church and nearby churches prayed for Old Wang, Cai Wen, and Liang, and for the salvation of the Zhou villagers. When the threesome arrived in the Zhou village word quickly spread and a mob again formed. People yelled threats. Fear swept over Old Wang. Suddenly Liang stepped forward and said, "I'm the widow of the man you killed three weeks ago. My husband isn't dead, because God has given him eternal life. Now he is living in paradise with our God. My husband came here to tell you how you could have that same eternal life.... If you would like to hear more about this God, then meet us under the big tree this evening." The crowd grew quiet and left.

Most of the village gathered under the big tree to listen to Liang. Old Wang, and Cai Wen. Many of the villagers decided to follow God. Old Wang stayed behind to baptize them and to teach them how to serve God. When Old Wang returned home, three men from the new Zhou church also came. They expressed appreciation to the church and then one of the men said, "I'm the man who murdered Little Wang. The Lord has forgiven me and I ask for your forgiveness as well. I, and our entire church owe an eternal debt of gratitude to Little Wang and Liang for bringing us the message of life. We want to give this love offering and a pledge of a regular amount each month to help support Liang."

Witnessing to the world as you bear fruit for Christ has its price. As *John 15:20-21*, in the margin, reveals, when you have a relationship with Him, you'll be persecuted, just as He suffered. Everything you endure for Christ, He endured also. He knew rejection and suffering, and so will you.

In *John 15:20-21* what do Jesus' words "No servant is greater than his master" mean to you?

YOUR COMPANION IN SUFFERING

You are subject to the same rejection Jesus encountered. The same type of hard-hearted, closed-minded people who rejected the Master will also reject you. In contrast, the same type of people who were open to His teachings while He was on earth will be open to your words and actions today.

What did Christ suffer for you? Read the three verses in the margin of page 88. Then match the statements in the right column with the correct references on the left.

___ 1. *Luke 22:47-48* a. **Respected persons in authority rejected Him.**
___ 2. *Mark 6:1-3* b. **A friend betrayed Him.**
___ 3. *Mark 8:31* c. **People in His hometown took offense at Him.**

Go back and draw a star beside any type of persecution you have experienced. Have you had an experience in which you felt persecuted because you witnessed for Christ? ❏ Yes ❏ No If so, describe it below.

How does it make you feel to realize that Christ has already endured any type of heartache you have suffered?

Christ's suffering for you was so great that listing all of the trials He endured on earth would be impossible in this book. The Scriptures in the margin on page 88 represent only a few. Because of Christ-honoring stands you take, you may experience the rejection of friends, family, your community, and people you respect. I hope you described feeling strengthened and encouraged by considering the depths of His suffering and love for you. The correct answers to the previous matching exercise are 1. b, 2. c, 3.a.

LEARNING THE DISCIPLE'S CROSS

You know that the left crossbar of the Disciple's Cross represents bearing fruit by witnessing. The Disciple's Cross itself embodies fruit bearing. If you learn and practice the six disciplines, you will live an obedient life and thus will bear fruit.

 Draw the Disciple's Cross on a separate sheet of paper, writing *witness* on the left crossbar. Also include *John 15:8,* the Scripture that accompanies the left crossbar.

 Say aloud *John 15:8,* this week's memory verse. Sometime today recite it to a family member or a friend.

SCRIPTURE MEMORIZATION: A KEY TO BEARING FRUIT

Memorizing Scripture enables you to claim victory over Satan, to claim victory over sin, to win others to Christ, to meditate on the Word, and to direct your daily life. Most importantly, you memorize Scripture because God commands it.

 Try to memorize in your own words the six reasons listed in the following chart.

REASONS TO MEMORIZE SCRIPTURE
1. To claim victory over Satan.

 Read *Matthew 4:1-11,* the account of Christ's temptation in the wilderness, during your quiet time today. When you finish, complete the Daily Master Communication Guide.

Daily Master Communication Guide

Matthew 4:1-11

What God said to me:

What I said to God:

a. Jesus set the example. Read *Matthew 4:7,10.*

b. Satan misuses the Scriptures. Compare *Matthew 4:6* with *Psalm 91:11-12:*
He will command his angels concerning you
    to guard you in all your ways;
      they will lift you up in their hands,
      so that you will not strike your foot against a stone.

c. The Word is the sword of the Spirit:
How can a young man keep his way pure?
    By living according to your word.
I have hidden your word in my heart
    that I might not sin against you (Ps. 119:9,11).

2. To claim victory over sin. See *Psalm 119:9,11.*

3. To win others to Christ.

a. You will always be ready to give an answer about your faith: *Always be prepared to give an answer to everyone who asks you to give the reason for the hope that you have (1 Pet. 3:15).*

b. The Holy Spirit can bring to mind the word that is needed for any situation: *"When he, the Spirit of truth, comes, he will guide you into all truth. He will not speak on his own; he will speak only what he hears, and he will tell you what is yet to come" (John 16:13).*

c. Understanding the Word makes you bold in your witness: *After they prayed, the place where they were meeting was shaken. And they were all filled with the Holy Spirit and spoke the word of God boldly (Acts 4:31).*

4. To meditate on the Word.
His delight is in the law of the Lord,
    and on his law he meditates day and night.
He is like a tree planted by streams of water,
    which yields its fruit in season
    and whose leaf does not wither (Ps. 1:2-3).

5. To direct your daily life.
Your word is a lamp to my feet and a light for my path (Ps. 119:105).

6. Because God commands it.
These commandments that I give you today are to be upon your hearts (Deut. 6:6). Let the word of Christ dwell in you richly as you teach and admonish one another with all wisdom, and as you sing psalms, hymns, and spiritual songs with gratitude in your hearts to God (Col. 3:16).

Give an example in the margin of how memorizing Scripture has helped you in one of the above ways.

Read the following suggestions for memorizing Scripture. Check any suggestion you've tried. Draw a star beside any you pledge to try.

HOW TO MEMORIZE SCRIPTURE

1. Choose a verse that speaks to your need or, if the verse is assigned, discover how it meets a particular need in your life.

2. Understand the verse. Read the verse in relation to its context. Read the verse in various translations.

3. Record memory verses on a cassette tape. Leave a space after each verse so that you can practice quoting it after hearing it. Then record the verse a second time so that you can hear it again after you've quoted it.

4. Locate and underline the verse in your Bible so that you can see where it is on the page.

5. Write the verse, Scripture reference and topic on a card. The verse is related to a particular subject so that you can find it when a need arises.

6. Place the written verse where you can review it often such as on your locker, your mirror, the car dashboard, and on your school notebook or folders.

7. Commit the verse to memory. Divide it into natural, meaningful phrases and learn it word by word. If you learn it word-perfect in the beginning, it will be set in your memory, will be easier to review, will give you boldness when you are

tempted, and will convince the person with whom you are sharing that he or she can trust your word.

8. Review is the most important secret of Scripture memorization. Review a new verse at least once a day for six weeks. Review the verse weekly for the next six weeks and then monthly for the rest of your life.

9. Use these activities to set a verse in your mind: see it in pictorial form; sing it; pray it back to God; do it by making it a part of your life; and use it as often as possible.

10. Use the version of the Disciple's Cross in the margin to master the verse. Make the Scriptures a part of every facet of your life (see *John 8:31-32*).

11. Have someone check your memorization. Or write the verse from memory and then check it yourself, using your Bible.

12. Make Scripture memorization fun. Make a game of remembering verses with your family and friends. A game I have used is to say a reference to a *MasterLife* group member before the person can say it to me. For instance, if you cite *John 15:5*, the other person must quote it. If the other person says the reference first, you must quote it.

13. Set a goal for the number of verses you'll memorize each week. State your goal: _____ per week. Don't try to learn too many verses so fast that you don't have time for daily review, which is essential to memorizing Scripture.

 Since review helps you memorize, go back and work on this week's memory verse. Choose one of the suggestions you read and practice it to reinforce your memorization of *John 15:8*.

HAS THIS WEEK MADE A DIFFERENCE?
Review "My Walk with the Master This Week" at the beginning of this week's material. Mark the activities you've finished by drawing vertical lines in the diamonds beside them. Finish any incomplete activities.

Think about your study of "Witness to the World" this week.
• Are you developing new relationships with persons who don't know Christ?
• Do your relationships with non-Christian friends have a new meaning because of this week's study?
• Are you aware of new opportunities to witness?
• Have you committed to bear fruit in a new way?
I hope because of this week's study you'll commit to abide in Christ and to continue developing your lifelong, obedient relationship with Him. Making new commitments requires honesty. Look on these as opportunities to grow rather than judging your old ways of doing things.

[1] Adapted from Chuck Kelley, *Learning to Share My Faith* (Nashville: LifeWay Press, 1994), 27–34.

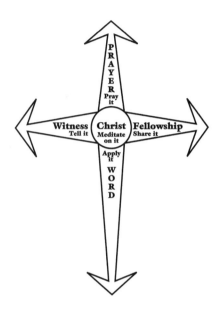

Review is the most important secret of Scripture memorization.

Making new commitments requires honesty, because you may realize that you need to make improvements in your life.

Minister to Others

...eek's Goal

...ll minister to others as you take up your cross and follow Jesus.

My Walk with the Master This Week

You will complete the following activities to develop the six biblical disciplines. When you have completed each activity, draw a vertical line in the diamond beside it.

SPEND TIME WITH THE MASTER

◇ Have a daily quiet time. Check the box beside each day you have a quiet time this week:
☑Sunday ☑Monday ☐Tuesday ☐Wednesday ☐Thursday ☐Friday ☐Saturday

LIVE IN THE WORD

◇ Read your Bible every day. Write what God says to you and what you say to God.
◇ Memorize *John 15:13*.
◇ Review *Luke 9:23; John 15:5; John 8:31-32; John 15:7; John 13:34-35; and John 15:8.*

PRAY IN FAITH

◇ Pray for your pastor, youth group, and church.
◇ Pray for the lost persons the group members talked about at the previous session.
◇ Ask God to lead you as you plan your time with Him, using the MasterTime form.

FELLOWSHIP WITH BELIEVERS

◇ Share with someone what the Lord has done for you since you started *MasterLife.*

WITNESS TO THE WORLD

◇ Use MasterTime to plan your days.
◇ Do a kind act for your new non-Christian friend this week. Learn all you can about your new friend. Be ready to tell your *MasterLife* group what happened.

MINISTER TO OTHERS

◇ Finish learning the Disciple's Cross. Share it with a member of your *MasterLife* group before the Growing Disciples Workshop. Say all of the verses that go with the Disciple's Cross.

This Week's Scripture-Memory Verse

"Greater love has no one than this, that he lay down his life for his friends" (John 15:13).

DAY 1

Take Up Your Cross

People rushed into the room where my friend, a Christian relief worker in Asia, was ministering. They pleaded, "Please come help…or he will die!" In the war-torn area of the country where he served, mine fields were plentiful. The people had found a shepherd injured by a mine. My friend knew he must quickly decide what to do. "I knew it was not wise to enter a mine field, but I felt that the Lord wanted me to help this person," he recalled. "As I crossed the field, I noticed that everyone following me was walking single file in my footsteps."

He carried the shepherd to the road, and stopped a truck. He begged the truck driver to carry the injured man to a hospital, but no one on the crowded vehicle would give up his place. To a worker who spoke English he said, "Tell the truck driver that I will pay twice what any rider paid if you will take this man to the hospital." The worker, in translating to the truck driver, commented, "This Christian is going to pay the man's way when we Muslims won't do anything." At that point the driver refused the money and made a place for the injured man.

In this Asian country where Christianity is not accepted, this modern-day Good Samaritan story spread all over the countryside with the message "This is what a Christian does. This is the kind of service a Christian does in Jesus' name."

WHAT A CHRISTIAN DOES
When Christ is at the center of your life, how do you serve others? What does being a disciple of Christ lead you to do? Although you may not serve as a relief worker in a war-torn country as my friend does, your opportunities for sacrificial service for others are endless.

In the margin describe a time when you served someone sacrificially.

What opportunities for service do you have that you're not taking advantage of? Write your answer in the margin. School & Golf

You probably identified someone in need or opportunities for sacrificial service in Jesus' name. I'm not talking about being a pastor or church minister. Every Christian is a minister if he or she follows Jesus and serves others as He did.

BEARING YOUR CROSS
To learn how a disciple ministers to others, review one of your memory verses, *Luke 9:23,* in which Jesus outlined the three basic commitments of a disciple.

 Complete *Luke 9:23* in the margin by filling in the blanks. Then say this verse from memory.

The three basic commitments a disciple makes are to deny self, take up his or her cross, and follow Christ. For Jesus, the cross meant that He gave Himself to

"If anyone would come after me, he must ___deny___ himself and take up his ___cross___ daily and ___follow___ me" (Luke 9:23).

"I tell you the truth, unless a kernel of wheat falls to the ground and dies, it remains only a single seed. But if it dies, it produces many seeds" (John 12:24).

❏ 1. **Death to the old way of life brings forth new life.**
❏ 2. **Dying to self means that you will probably live your life alone.**

"Anyone who does not carry his cross and follow me cannot be my disciple" (Luke 14:27).

_____

Being found in appearance as a man, he humbled himself and became obedient to death—even death on a cross! (Phil. 2:8).

redeem the world. For believers, cross bearing is voluntary, redemptive, sacrificial service for others. You enter His ministry by taking up your cross.

Read John 12:24 in the margin. Check the statement in the margin that best explains Jesus' comparison.

You must die to your old way of life before you can commit yourself to Christ. Self-denial emphasizes turning from commitment to self to commitment to Him. Taking up your cross means turning with Christ to the world in need. The correct answer is 1.

Read Luke 14:27 in the margin. What happens to a person who refuses to be a cross bearer? Write your answer in the margin under the verse.

If you refuse to be a cross bearer, you can't be Jesus' disciple. To follow Christ, you must bear your cross. In *Philippians 2:8,* in the margin, Paul explained why Jesus was willing to take up His cross. Jesus was obedient to God's will for His life even when it meant dying on a cross. We learn from Jesus' example that a Christian's cross has two characteristics: (1) it is a voluntary commitment, and (2) it is an act of obedience.

If you fail to take up your cross, which of the following sins have you committed? ❏ **disobedience** ❏ **disloyalty** ❏ **disbelief**

Disloyalty and disbelief may be involved, but you're disobedient to Christ if you fail to take up your cross, because cross bearing is a direct command of Christ. Obeying Jesus' commands is the primary motive for taking up your cross. *John 15:13,* states the value Jesus placed on sacrificial service to others.

 Memorize John 15:13. Read it aloud. What did Jesus say that a disciple would be willing to do to demonstrate love for others?

Jesus said that a disciple ministers to others, even if means hardship or death.

LEARNING THE DISCIPLE'S CROSS
The final addition to the cross indicates how you relate to the world if you're Christ's disciple. If Christ is at the center of your life, you grow as His disciple through the discipline of ministering to others. As you grow in Christ, you reach out to others through service.

 Draw the Disciple's Cross over the picture of the world in the margin to show how a disciple reaches out to the world in witness and ministry. Label each part of the cross.

 Read Luke 10:26-35 during your quiet time today. After you've read this passage, complete the Daily Master Communication Guide in the margin on page 95.

DAY 2

Ministry in Christ's Name

Daily Master Communication Guide

Luke 10:26-35

What God said to me:

What I said to God:

I hired a former lieutenant colonel in the Indonesian Army to manage the Indonesian Baptist Theological Seminary property and the employees who took care of it. He had been a Christian for only about six months and was very committed to the Lord. The problem was that he tried to manage the seminary property and employees as he would manage an army. I had to intervene often to keep war from breaking out between the employees and this supervisor.

Rather than fire him as soon urged me to do, I took on the difficulties required to disciple this man and to teach him to be an effective manager. Using the Scriptures, I taught him how to relate to his employees with patience, kindness, and self-control. This man effectively served at the seminary for more than 10 years.

Throughout your study of *MasterLife* you've learned six biblical disciplines of a follower of Christ. In these disciplines four resources can be identified that are available to every disciple: (1) the Word; (2) prayer; (3) fellowship; (4) witness.

A growing disciple uses these four resources to help others in Christ's name. Your service expresses itself in various ministries:

> 1. The Word leads to a ministry of teaching/preaching.
> 2. Prayer leads to a ministry of worship/intercession.
> 3. Fellowship leads to a ministry of nurture.
> 4. Witness leads to a ministry of evangelism.
> 5. Fellowship and witness lead to a ministry of service.

A MINISTRY OF TEACHING/PREACHING

Look at the first ministry which appears in the box above. You may think: That lets me out. I'm not called to be a pastor. How can I minister this way?

God definitely calls some people to be preachers or evangelists. If you live in the Word, you may learn that this role is His will for you. But you can be involved in the ministry of teaching or preaching even if you never preach a sermon in front of a congregation. Most people who stay in the Word long enough have the opportunity to share in a variety of ways what God has said to them.

In my story about the lieutenant colonel at the seminary, how did I use the resource of the Word in the ministry of teaching or preaching? Write your answer in the margin.

I used Scripture to teach this man how the Lord wanted him to relate to his employees. By sharing what the Word says about patience, kindness, and self-control as fruit of the Spirit, I helped him manage in a more Christ-honoring manner.

To understand how to use the resource of the Word in a ministry of teaching/preaching, you can look at ways teaching occurs in the Bible. Match the Scriptures in the margin with the following examples.

"God is exalted in his power. Who is a teacher like him?" (Job 36:22).

"Go and make disciples of all nations, baptizing them in the name of the Father and of the Son and of the Holy Spirit, and teaching them to obey everything I have commanded you" (Matt. 28:19).

Fathers, do not exasperate your children; instead, bring them up in the training and instruction of the Lord (Eph. 6:4).

The elders who direct the affairs of the church well are worthy of double honor, especially those whose work is preaching and teaching (1 Tim. 5:17).

____ 1. *Job 36:22*

____ 2. *Matthew 28:19*

____ 3. *Ephesians 6:4*

____ 4. *1 Timothy 5:17*

a. **God is a teaching God. Many prophets such as Samuel also functioned as teachers.**

b. **Parents are urged to tell their children about God's mighty acts and to instruct them in God's commandments.**

c. **In Jesus' ministry, teaching was His primary identity. In the Great Commission Jesus commanded His followers to make disciples and to instruct them in His teachings.**

d. **Whenever new churches were founded, Christian teachers were present.**

Today teaching is part of sharing your faith. To witness to the world, believers must first understand the gospel and then teach others. A person can be involved in a teaching ministry whether from the pulpit, in a classroom, in a small-group study, or one-to-one. The correct answers are 1. a, 2. c, 3. b, 4. d.

In the margin, name ways you might be able to use the resource of the Word in a ministry of teaching or preaching.

Don't be concerned if ideas for ministry don't immediately occur to you. The goal is to open your thinking to new possibilities for you as a follower of Christ.

Memorizing Scripture is one way to use the resource of the Word. When you hide God's Word in your heart, you have it at instant recall when you want to share about Christ or to give scriptural guidance or encouragement.

 By now you've likely memorized six verses and are working on a seventh one. On a sheet of paper, see how accurately you can write each of the six by memory.

If you had difficulty writing any of the six verses, review "How to Memorize Scripture" in week 5. Try to quote them perfectly by the next group meeting.

 Continue your work on this week's Scripture-memory verse, John 15:13. Say it aloud a few times. Ask a family member or friend if you can practice saying it aloud to him or her.

A MINISTRY OF WORSHIP/INTERCESSION

The more you get involved in prayer, the more you worship. Prayer is ministering before the Lord (see *1 Chron. 23:13*). It's bowing before God and worshiping Him through praise, adoration, and devotion. Prayer enables you to develop a closer relationship with the Father. Intercession is a way you can minister to others by bringing their needs before God.

The ministry of worship can be individual worship during your quiet time and fellowship with the body of Christ, gathered as His church. Worship as a church family has occurred since the time of the first Christians. Read the verses from Acts in the margin.

They devoted themselves to the apostles' teaching and to the fellowship, to the breaking of bread and to prayer. Every day they continued to meet together in the temple courts. They broke bread in their homes and ate together with glad and sincere hearts (Acts 2:42,46).

You may think: *I'm not a minister or a church-staff member. How can I perform a ministry of worship?* The focus of true worship is on God and your personal relationship with Him. If you never lead others in worship, you can serve the LORD through worship. Worship is the primary way you glorify the Lord and is God's primary reason for creating and redeeming you (see *1 Pet. 2:9*). The early church didn't limit leadership in worship to professional ministers. Everyone has a responsibility for worship by leading, participating, or ministering to the persons closest to us. Read *Deuteronomy 6:6-9* in the margin. Underline any you have experienced as a minister or recipient.

As you've learned, intercession is a disciple's ministry to bring church and world needs to God. Intercession changes lives and churches. Staying alert to persons' needs and concerns allows you to intercede for them as you pray.

In the space below write how you think God wants you to use the resource of prayer in a ministry of worship and intercession.

You can start by interceding for missionaries. Pray for them as they witness to the world and as they lead others to witness. Become a prayer partner with them. Let them know that you are praying for them and that they can depend on your prayers. You may want to add the names of your pastor and other church-staff members to your Prayer-Covenant List and to pray for their specific needs. Think about what God could do through missionaries, your pastor and your church-staff members if you and others regularly prayed for them! Pray for the one-third of the world's population who have never heard about Christ.

Stop now and pray for your pastor and church-staff members by name. Pray for the other members of your church who serve in the areas of teaching, prayer, outreach, benevolence, missions, music, and others. Ask God to bless each person as he or she ministers to others. Ask Him to help you think of ways you can support and demonstrate love for your church leaders.

Read *John 17:6-19* during your quiet time today. Let God speak to you through this passage about Jesus' intercession for His disciples. After you have read this passage, complete the Daily Master Communication Guide.

These commandments that I give you today are to be upon your hearts. Impress them on your children. Talk about them when you sit at home and when you walk along the road, when you lie down and when you get up. Tie them as symbols on your hands and bind them on your foreheads. Write them on the doorframes of your houses and on your gates (Deut. 6:6-9).

Daily Master Communication Guide

John 17:6-19

What God said to me:

What I said to God:

When they had finished eating, Jesus said to Simon Peter, "Simon son of John, do you truly love me more than these?"

"Yes, Lord," he said, "you know that I love you."

Jesus said, "Feed my lambs." Again Jesus said, "Simon son of John, do you truly love me?"

He answered, "Yes, Lord, you know that I love you."

Jesus said, "Take care of my sheep." The third time he said to him, "Simon son of John, do you love me?" Peter was hurt because Jesus asked him the third time, "Do you love me"

He said, "Lord, you know all things; you know that I love you."

Jesus said, "Feed my sheep" (John 21:15-17).

___❑ counseling new Christians at the time of decision;

___❑ helping spiritual infants understand what it means to have life in Christ;

___❑ leading a small group of disciples to know what following Christ means;

___❑ serving on your church youth council;

___❑ training leaders;

___❑ teaching persons how to witness;

___❑ counseling persons about their interpersonal needs.

Discipling is leading others to develop personal, lifelong, obedient relationships with Christ in which He transforms their character into Christlikeness, changes their values to His values, and involves them in His mission.

DAY 3

More Ways to Minister

A MINISTRY OF NURTURE

To carry out the Great Commission, you need to lead others into lifelong, obedient relationships with Jesus Christ. Through fellowship you help them grow in their relationships with Him until He transforms them into His likeness and involves them in His mission. Every disciple is to help other believers to grow.

In the Bible this happens over and over, as when Jesus saw Simon's potential and helped him grow into the rock called Peter (see *John 21:15-17* in the margin). Barnabas encouraged John Mark, who later wrote one of the Gospels. Christ will show you Himself as you fellowship with other believers.

In all situations nurture can involve role modeling, as Christ did with those He trained as His disciples. Others need examples of the Christian life that point them to Christ. In the margin is a list of ministries of nurture.

In the margin, check the ways you already serve and draw a star beside the one(s) God might want you to do in a ministry of nurture.

Remember the definition of *discipleship* you learned earlier? Read in the margin the definition of *discipling,* or *making disciples.* Has someone seen you reaching out to nurture others as you've fellowshipped with believers? Has your family witnessed you having a quiet time? I hope that your lifestyle has changed since you began your study of *MasterLife* so that new ways of thinking and behaving are obvious. They may have asked or wanted to ask you how you have changed.

 Tell a friend how you've benefited from your study of *MasterLife*.

A MINISTRY OF EVANGELISM

The well-known evangelist D. L. Moody had a personal commitment to witness to someone every day. Even if he had already gone to bed when he remembered that he hadn't witnessed that day, he would get up and tell someone about Christ.[1] The final resource you have for living the Christian life is the resource of witness. Many believers don't think of witness as a resource. However, nothing encourages Christians more than sharing Christ, especially when they see someone accept Christ. From the resource of witness grows a ministry of evangelism. Many types of evangelism exist but all start with personal witness.

Evangelism is proclaiming the good news of salvation in Christ. The Holy Spirit uses our evangelism to convert the lost. It's the way the Lord uses us to teach others about Himself. Evangelism is telling others about Christ, calling them to repentance, and giving God the glory for what occurs.

Read the Great Commission, *Matthew 28:19,* in the margin on the next page. What does Christ say about your responsibility for evangelism? Write your answer in the margin of the next page.

The Great Commission calls you to use the resource of witness. Through the Great Commission, Christ gave you the responsibility to share with others your knowledge of His love. You may think: *How do I do this? I'm not a D. L. Moody. I'm not a Billy Graham. I don't have the abilities of a TV evangelist or someone who draws crowds to tell about Christ.* Remember that D. L. Moody used the resource of witness to deal with one person at a time long before he became a preaching evangelist. Personal witness is a significant way to express the ministry of evangelism.

 Write your memory verse, *John 15:13,* in the margin. Describe under the verse what you think a person who is willing to give his or her life for a friend would do about witnessing.

You may have said that a person who would give everything for a friend would make sure that friend has the gift of eternal life. The ministry of evangelism can be expressed in many ways. Some of these ways are listed in the margin.

In the list in the margin, check the ways you've already served and draw a star beside the one(s) you think God might want you to do.

Maybe you don't know exactly how God wants you to minister in this area. The purpose of these exercises is to encourage you to begin thinking of ways you can use the valuable resources that are yours as a disciple of Christ.

LEARNING THE DISCIPLE'S CROSS

Draw the Disciple's Cross over the picture of the world. Then add pointed arrows to the ends of the crossbars. At the ends of the pointed arrows write the ministry areas that go with each part of the cross: ministry of teaching/preaching below the cross, ministry of worship/intercession above the cross, ministry of nurture to the right of the cross, and ministry of evangelism to the left of the cross.

 Read *1 Timothy 6:11-21* in your quiet time today. After you've read this passage, complete the Daily Master Communication Guide in the margin on page 100.

All evangelism starts with personal witness.

"Go and make disciples of all nations, baptizing them in the name of the Father and of the Son and of the Holy Spirit, and teaching them to obey everything I have commanded you" (Matt. 28:19).

___❑ Lifestyle—living a Christian life that attracts a lost person's attention and provides an opportunity for witness

___❑ Small-group evangelism—participating in small groups of persons with similar interests to share the gospel of Christ

___❑ Church evangelism—visiting homes, taking a religious survey, or using other actions to ensure that every person in your church's range of influence hears the good news

___❑ Mass evangelism—helping your church gather people for a community-wide proclamation of the gospel in a church building or a stadium

___❑ Missions ministry—entering other cultures to tell others about Jesus as a career, short-term, bivocational missionary, volunteer, or through giving and praying for missions causes

___❑ Other: _____

The Demands of Christ

Jesus didn't always paint a rosy picture for the disciples as He talked about what was ahead for them. During His last days on earth Jesus outlined what they could expect if they followed Him. Any suffering the disciples would encounter for taking up His cross would be sorrow He had already experienced. In the verse in the margin He told them that the world would hate them because they were associated with Him and because they would witness in His name. You may want to skip over verses like *John 15:18* because they indicate that life in Christ will be difficult. Read what an Argentine pastor says about this subject:

> The gospel which we have in the Bible is the gospel of the Kingdom of God. It presents Jesus as King, as Lord, as the maximum authority. Jesus is at the very center. The gospel of the Kingdom is a Christ-centered gospel.
>
> But in recent centuries we have been hearing another gospel—a man-centered, human gospel. It is the gospel of the big offer. The gospel of the hot sale. The gospel of the irresistible special deal. ... We have told people, "If you accept Jesus, you will have joy, you will have peace, health, prosperity. ... If you give Jesus ten dollars, you will get twenty dollars back." ... We are always appealing to man's interests. Jesus is the Savior, the Healer, and the King coming for me. Me is the center of our gospel.
>
> We take all the verses we like, all the verses that offer something or promise something—John 3:16, John 5:24, and so forth—and we make a systematic theology from these verses, while we forget the other verses that present the demands of Jesus Christ. ... Who said we were allowed to present only one side of Jesus? ... He is our Savior and our Healer, true. But we cannot cut Jesus Christ into pieces and take only the piece we like best.[2]

We can't accept the part of Jesus' message that we like and reject what we don't like. We must accept it all.

In the margin list commands Christ gave for disciples that you've ignored.

EXPECT TO BE REJECTED

The reality is, when you meet the demands of Christ as you minister to others, you may experience rejection. For example, did you feel rejection or a lack of openness to you as you began reaching out to your new non-Christian friend? Sometimes you may feel subtle rejection at first. Or you may initially sense that your friend isn't open to learning about Christ.

One of my neighbors who wasn't a Christian played on the church softball team I played on. I shared my faith with him as we became better acquainted, but I never felt that he was ready to respond. I felt somewhat rejected when I con-

---

Daily Master Communication Guide

I Timothy 6:11-21

What God said to me:

What I said to God:

"If the world hates you, keep in mind that it hated me first" (John 15:18).

tinually sensed that he wasn't open to my witness.

One day I sensed God leading me to talk to my neighbor. That night my wife and I visited him and led him to Christ. Befriending him and regularly expressing concern for him eventually provided a witnessing opportunity. I was glad I hadn't become discouraged when at first I felt rejected.

 Do something kind for the non-Christian friend you made last week. Get to know them better this week.

THE PROMISE OF HIS PRESENCE

After warning His disciples about the possibility of rejection, however, Jesus painted another picture designed to compel them to spread the good news despite what they encountered. Read the verses in the margin.

Jesus assured the disciples that they would have the Holy Spirit to assist them as they testified about Christ. He wouldn't leave them without help or resources. The Holy Spirit would guide them as they moved out to serve others.

Two thousand years later, Jesus makes the same promise to you and gives you the same commands. He warns that the world will hate you, but He gives you the Holy Spirit to empower you and to make you bold.

 Pray for lost persons the group members mentioned at the previous session. Continue praying that your fellow *MasterLife* group members will live Christlike lives that model Christ to others.

A MINISTRY OF SERVICE

Could a ministry of service be the ministry to which Christ calls you? Your witness and your fellowship involve Christian service to other persons. *John 15:13* says, *"Greater love has no one than this, that he lay down his life for his friends."* You are to be involved in a ministry of service as Christ was.

LEARNING THE DISCIPLE'S CROSS

Draw the Disciple's Cross as you learned to do in day 3, with the cross over the world and with the pointed arrows on the crossbars. Label the ministry areas. Then write *ministry of service, John 15:13* above the horizontal crossbar. As you label it with the disciplines, ministries, and Scriptures that accompany it, explain it aloud. Be sure to say aloud all of the memory verses you recorded on it.

"When the Counselor comes, whom I will send to you from the Father, the Spirit of truth who goes out from the Father, he will testify about me. And you also must testify, for you have been with me from the beginning" (John 15:26-27).

1 Lord as the first priority of your life
- The center of the cross emphasizes spending time with the Master.

2 relationships
- The vertical crossbar represents your relationship with God.
- The horizontal crossbar represents your relationship with others.

3 commitments
- Deny yourself
- Take up your cross
- Follow Christ

4 resources to center your life in Christ
- The Word
- Prayer
- Fellowship
- Witness

5 ministries that grow from the four resources
- Teaching/preaching
- Worship/intercession
- Nurture
- Evangelism
- Service

6 disciplines of a disciple
- Spend time with the Master
- Live in the Word
- Pray in faith
- Fellowship with believers
- Witness to the world
- Minister to others

Are your daily quiet times making a difference in your life? Are you interceding for others? Are you gaining strength? Has your quiet time raised your entire walk with the Lord to a different level? If so, draw a star in the blank here: _____.

A Growing Disciples Workshop will conclude this study. At this workshop you'll review what you've learned so far and will be prepared for the rest of this *MasterLife* study. Before the workshop share the Disciple's Cross with a member of your group.

WHAT IT MEANS TO BE A DISCIPLE
Read in the margin an easy way to remember what you've studied so far in *MasterLife*. Summarizing what it means to be a disciple is as simple as 1-2-3-4-5-6.

To reinforce this 1-2-3-4-5-6 plan for discipleship, fill in the blanks that follow. If you don't have enough space, use a separate sheet of paper.

A disciple of Christ has—
1 _____.
2 relationships: _____.
3 commitments: _____
_____.
4 resources: _____
_____.
5 ministries: _____
_____
_____.
6 disciplines: _____
_____
_____
_____.

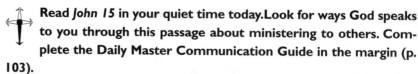 **Read *John 15* in your quiet time today. Look for ways God speaks to you through this passage about ministering to others. Complete the Daily Master Communication Guide in the margin (p. 103).**

Everything you've done in your study of *MasterLife*, including memorizing seven Scriptures and learning the Disciple's Cross, has required quite a time commitment. I pray that you have found this commitment worthwhile. I hope that the MasterTime form is becoming a regular part of your life.

Stop and pray, asking God to lead you as you plan your time, using the MasterTime form. Be ready to share with your group how your planning has benefited from using MasterTime.

HAS THIS WEEK MADE A DIFFERENCE?
Review "My Walk with the Master This Week." Mark the activities you've finished and finish the ones you've not completed. Then look back through this book. Finish any activities from previous weeks that you haven't completed. Consider what you'll report during the Growing Disciples Workshop about what these activities have meant to you.

A Disciple Indeed

**Daily Master
Communication Guide**

John 15

What God said to me:

What I said to God:

Communists took control of Ethiopia, and banned worship in churches and ordered that no more than five persons could meet without a permit. An Ethiopian Christian told me "Seven other men and I decided that we must do something to carry on the work."

They asked missionary veterinarian Jerry Bedsole, to disciple them secretly at his house, using *MasterLife*. Jerry was allowed to stay in Ethiopia because he took care of the animals at the palace. Later, each of those men discipled four persons. "We couldn't meet at the same place or time each week; we couldn't take Bibles to a meeting; and we prayed with our eyes open, using conversational prayer, so that we wouldn't be discovered," the man said.

Because the Ethiopian Christians feared that the Communists would soon destroy their Bibles, they planned for each person to memorize a part of the Bible so that they could reproduce it. "I'm memorizing one of the Gospels," he told me. They also knew that they could be put in jail. "Some of us already have been, but the government doesn't know what to do with us once we are behind bars. We witness and win the other prisoners, so they soon kick us out," he said. Eventually, these men began underground discipleship groups in 170 places around the country.

Several years later, after the Communists were overthrown, the churches of Ethiopia requested one hundred thousand sets of *MasterLife* to train Ethiopians to be disciples.

When the door seems to be closed, God can make a way for us to serve Him. Often, we must adjust our lives to follow Him in obedience.

What if you didn't have a church in which to worship? What would you do if you couldn't sing praises to God? What if a government took away your Bible to prohibit your witness? Describe in the margin how you would stay connected to the Vine.

I hope that as you've studied *MasterLife, Student Edition,* your relationship with Christ has become so important to you that you would bear your cross in any way possible to obey Christ.

LEARNING THE DISCIPLE'S CROSS

The Disciple's Cross has been the basis for sermons, conversations, and witnessing opportunities by persons who learned it and mastered its concepts. I hope that for you, however, the cross represents something even greater. It represents your relationship with Christ as His disciple. I hope that the Disciple's Cross is at the very core of your being—that it is a way of life for you. I hope that spending time with the Master, praying in faith, living in the Word, fellowshipping with believers, witnessing to the world, and ministering to others are becoming disciplines you use every day to live in Christ.

- you know six biblical disciplines of a disciple;
- you experience a closer relationship with Christ as you practice the disciplines each day;
- you use the Disciple's Cross as the standard to remind yourself and other Christians of the commitments required for being Christ's disciple;
- you use the six disciplines to follow the Holy Spirit's direction as you confront problems;
- you help other disciples live in Christ and bear fruit for His glory.

If a man cleanses himself from the latter, he will be an instrument for noble purposes, made holy, useful tot he Master and prepared to do any good work (2 Tim. 2:21).

In the margin are five ways to know if the Disciple's Cross is a part of your life. Review the list of ways that knowing the Disciple's Cross can help you as a disciple. Check the ways you are already benefiting from knowing the Disciple's Cross. Then draw a star beside ways you hope to continue growing in your use of the Disciple's Cross.

Your goal in discipleship is expressed in *2 Timothy 2:21*, in the margin. Grow in all of the disciplines to master life and be prepared for the Master's use. If you develop all of these disciplines, your life will be balanced and fruitful.

You learned the six disciplines by using a diagram of a cross. One way to reinforce the fact that you've learned these disciplines is to illustrate them in another form. Think about another item—a car, a tree, a mountain, a building, an ice-cream cone, or another object—you can draw to illustrate the elements of the Disciple's Cross. Perhaps you feel that you don't have artistic ability. Don't worry about how the final product looks; the most important point is to include all of the concepts.

In the margin draw the item you have chosen to illustrate the six disciplines. Include the memory verse references that go with them. If you need more room, use a blank sheet of paper. When you finish, insert the sheet of paper in your book at this place. Be prepared to explain your illustration at the Growing Disciples Workshop.

WHERE ARE YOU IN YOUR RELATIONSHIP WITH CHRIST?
How equipped are you to be Christ's disciple? The Growing Disciples Workshop that follows this study will help you determine the answer. Before you attend the workshop, complete the Discipleship Inventory on pages 207-212 to evaluate your growth in discipleship. The inventory, based on the characteristics of a disciple, can help you determine where you are in your growth as a disciple. Even though the inventory will help you look at yourself in terms of behavior and attitudes, the most important questions you can ask yourself are: *Where am I in my relationship with Christ? How far am I from the lifelong, obedient relationship with Him that I desire? If He desires to transform my values into Kingdom values, have I arrived?*

When you attend the Growing Disciples Workshop, you'll learn how to interpret your answers. At this point you may decide that you need to do additional work in certain areas of your relationship with Christ.

[1] R. A. Torrey, *Why God Used D. L. Moody* (Chicago: Moody Press, 1923), 42.
[2] Juan Carlos Ortiz, *Disciple* (Carol Stream, Ill.: Creation House, 1975), 12–16.

WEEK 7

Do God's Will

This Week's Goal
You will be able to understand and do God's will as the Holy Spirit works in you.

My Walk with the Master This Week
You will complete the following activities to develop the six biblical disciplines. When you have completed each activity, draw a vertical line in the diamond beside it.

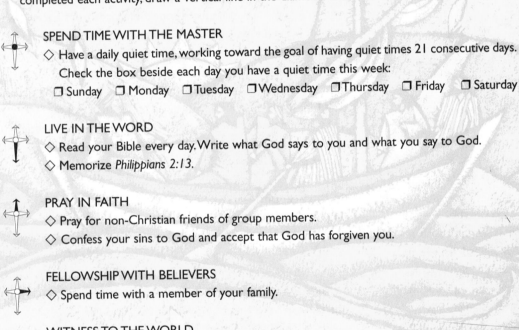

SPEND TIME WITH THE MASTER
◇ Have a daily quiet time, working toward the goal of having quiet times 21 consecutive days.
  Check the box beside each day you have a quiet time this week:
  ❑ Sunday ❑ Monday ❑ Tuesday ❑ Wednesday ❑ Thursday ❑ Friday ❑ Saturday

LIVE IN THE WORD
◇ Read your Bible every day. Write what God says to you and what you say to God.
◇ Memorize *Philippians 2:13*.

PRAY IN FAITH
◇ Pray for non-Christian friends of group members.
◇ Confess your sins to God and accept that God has forgiven you.

FELLOWSHIP WITH BELIEVERS
◇ Spend time with a member of your family.

WITNESS TO THE WORLD
◇ Think of five persons to whom you need to witness and write their names on the Prayer-Covenant List. Or make friends with five persons to whom you can witness in the future.

MINISTER TO OTHERS
◇ Learn the Unified Personality and Natural Person parts of the Disciple's Personality.

This Week's Scripture-Memory Verse
It is God who works in you to will and to act according to his good purpose (Phil. 2:13).

DAY 1

Who's in Charge?

My 16-year-old sister, Norma, asked me about God's will. I told her that God has a purpose for every person. To make my point, I used several illustrations: "Do you know how many sections are in an orange? An orange usually has 10 sections. A watermelon usually has an even number of stripes. Grains like wheat, barley, and rye have an even number of grains on a stalk. In a fully developed ear of corn an even number of rows are on each ear, an even number of grains are in each row, and an even number of silks are in the tassel." I asked her, "Do you think it's just an accident that so many things God has made have such symmetry?"

She asked, "Does that mean I have to do whatever God wants me to do?"

I answered: "No, although God has a perfect will for your life that He wants you to follow, He doesn't force you to. He leads you to do His will, but He gives you the freedom to make your own choice." I explained: "It's as if God has a blueprint for your life. Although He may want to build a beautiful mansion from your life, you can still choose to build a shack. But God's intent is that you build according to His will. Make sure that Christ is the foundation of your life. Let the Holy Spirit be the Builder. He can build far better than you can."

I watched to see how God worked in her life. Later she became a pastor's wife, and today she and her husband serve God as missionaries in Argentina. She made Christ the foundation and let the Holy Spirit guide her and build her life.

In the account you read, what was the key to this young woman's finding God's will in her life?

The key to finding God's will was making Christ the foundation and allowing the Holy Spirit to guide her instead of acting on her own will. When she allowed the Holy Spirit to lead her, He directed her to the center of God's will.

You may wonder: *How do I do that? How do I know that I'm living in the center of His will instead of acting on my own desires?* Jesus chose you and called you to do His will. Because you've chosen to deny yourself, take up your cross, and follow Him, He is now your Savior and Master.

YOU CAN CHOOSE

God has given you the ability to choose. This ability is called your will. The Bible refers to *will* as "a desire, intent, or purpose to do something."

Read the verses in the margin, which refer to a person's will. Indicate whether you agree with each statement:
1. A person's will can be used for good or evil. ❑ Yes ❑ No
2. God is always in control of a person's will. ❑ Yes ❑ No
3. A person can always do what he or she wills to do. ❑ Yes ❑ No

This day I call heaven and earth as witnesses against you that I have set before you life and death, blessings and curses. Now choose life, so that you and your children may live and that you may love the Lord your God, listen to his voice, and hold fast to him. For the Lord is your life, and he will give you many years in the land he swore to give to your fathers, Abraham, Isaac and Jacob (Deut. 20:19-20).

I know that nothing good lives in me, that is, in my sinful nature. For I have the desire to do what is good, but I cannot carry it out (Rom. 7:18).

Be very careful, then how you live—not as unwise but as wise, making the most of every opportunity, because the days are evil. Therefore do not be foolish, but understand what the Lord's will is (Eph. 5:15-17).

You may think that you're in control of your will, but your sinful nature may prevent you doing good. God wants you to do right, but He leaves that ultimate choice to you. In making your choice, you can choose good or evil. God wants you to choose His way, and His heart breaks when you don't. This week's Scripture-memory verse reminds you: *It is God who works in you to will and to act according to his good purpose (Phil. 2:13).* The correct answers are 1. yes, 2. no, 3. no.

God doesn't omit anyone in accomplishing His will. Every person is included in the scope of God's will. *Second Peter 3:9 says, The Lord is not slow in keeping his promise, as some understand slowness. He is patient with you, not wanting anyone to perish, but everyone to come to repentance.* When a person becomes a Christian, the Holy Spirit begins revealing to that person God's will. If you have life in the Spirit, you'll experience this type of activity in your life.

Describe ways the Holy Spirit began revealing God's will in your life after you became a Christian.

Your answer may be similar to one of these statements: After I became a Christian, the Lord revealed that He wanted me to stop using bad language. Or, He showed me that He wanted me to go to church regularly. He pointed out that He wanted me to have Christian friends.

The first four Scriptures in the margin mention God's will. Read them and mark the following statements T (true) or F (false).

_____ 1. Jesus claimed a special relationship with those who follow God's will.

_____ 2. Jesus said that His purpose was to do God's will.

_____ 3. Finding God's will is impossible.

_____ 4. You can discover God's will.

Jesus said that those who do His will have a special relationship with Him. For Jesus, doing God's will was like food—a constant part of His obedient life and purpose. You can find God's will when you are willing to be transformed and to have a renewed mind. All of the statements are true except 3.

CHARACTERISTICS OF GOD'S WILL

God's will and the human will are vastly different. They differ in capacity and purpose. Your capacity to carry out your own will is limited. Even good purposes can be ill motivated and corrupted. For example, you could desire to win persons to the Lord so that others think you are a great Christian. You could also waver in your desire to reach persons for Christ. When the task becomes difficult, you could decide that it is not worth the effort.

Unlike your frail, human capacity, however, God's capacity to carry out His will is unlimited. His purpose is always holy, upright, and constant. He doesn't change His mind on a whim or when the way is difficult. He always wants His will to be done, and He sends His Holy Spirit to help accomplish it.

"Whoever does the will of my Father in heaven is my brother and sister and mother (Matt. 12:50).

"My food," said Jesus, "is to do the will of him who sent me and to finish his work" (John 4:34).

Do not conform any longer to the pattern of this world, but be transformed by the renewing of your mind. Then you will be able to test and approve what God's will is—his good, pleasing and perfect will (Rom. 12:2).

For this reason, since the day we heard about you, we have not stopped praying for you and asking God to fill you with the knowledge of his will through all spiritual wisdom and understanding (Col. 1:9).

**Daily Master
Communication Guide**

Luke 2:41-52

What God said to me:

What I said to God:

He predestined us to be adopted as his sons through Jesus Christ, in accordance with his pleasure and will—to the praise of his glorious grace, which he has freely given us in the One he loves.

In order that we, who were the first to hope in Christ, might be for the praise of his glory. And you also were included in Christ when you heard the word of truth, the gospel of your salvation. Having believed, you were marked in him with a seal, the promised Holy Spirit, who is a deposit guaranteeing our inheritance until the redemption of those who are God's possession—to the praise of his glory (Eph. 1:5-6,12-14).

❏ **1. To make me happy**
❏ **2. To win the lost**
❏ **3. To bring glory to God**

1. *"Father, if you are willing, take this cup from me; yet not my will, but yours be done" (Luke 22:42).*

2. *"By myself I can do nothing; I judge only as I hear, and my judgment is just, for I seek not to please myself but him who sent me" (John 6:38).*

3. *"I have come down from heaven not to do my will but to do the will of him who sent me" (John 6:38).*

4. *"I have brought you glory on earth by completing the work you gave me to do" (John 17:4).*

 This week's Scripture-memory verse describes the way God works in you to help you find His will. To begin your memory work, read aloud *Philippians 2:13* a few times. Check this box when you have done so: ❏

FULFILLING GOD'S PURPOSE

When you think about finding God's will, you may wonder where to begin. You may feel that you can't think God's thoughts or learn what He has in store for you. God wants to teach you how He reveals His will and how you can do His will. Doing God's will begins when you have a vision of God and His purpose for your life and are open to letting the Holy Spirit teach you.

Read *Ephesians 1:5-6,12-14* in the margin. Below the verses, check what these verses emphasize as God's primary purpose for your life.

Your purpose for living is to bring glory to God so that His name will be praised. The correct answer is 3. Jesus' purpose for living was to bring glory to God so that His name would be praised. Jesus lived to do God's will. The Scriptures in the margin express how Jesus felt about doing God's will.

Read the Scriptures in the margin. Then match each Scripture reference with its summary statement.

_____	**1. *Luke 22:42***	**a. Jesus glorified God while He was on earth.**
_____	**2. *John 5:30***	**b. Jesus did not seek His own will.**
_____	**3. *John 6:38***	**c. Jesus prayed for God's will, not His.**
_____	**4. *John 17:4***	**d. Jesus came from heaven to do God's will.**

Jesus sought God's will and didn't seek to do His own will. Jesus experienced rejection and death because they were part of His Father's perfect will, not because He wanted them. The correct answers are 1. c, 2. b, 3. d, 4. a.

Jesus' commitment to God's purpose made His ministry on this earth effective. Your development in every part of your Christian life and ministry depends on your commitment to God's purpose.

Can you honestly state that the purpose of your life is to glorify God? ❏ **Yes** ❏ **No If you answered no, what takes priority over glorifying God?**

What changes would you need to make for your life purpose to be glorifying God?

You can find God's will by regularly feeding on His Word and by spending time with Him in prayer. I hope that having a daily quiet time and living in the Word is a regular part of your life now.

Read *Luke 2:41-52*, an early example of Jesus' doing His Father's will, during your quiet time today. Then complete the Daily Master Communication Guide on page 107.

DAY 2

About Your Personality

As you studied doing God's will in day 1, did you wonder why you often try to carry out your own will instead of first seeking God's will? Do you ever wonder why you have thoughts, feelings, and behaviors that don't honor Christ? Today you'll begin learning the Disciple's Personality, a simple illustration that is a major part of our study of life in the Spirit. The drawing will illustrate biblical teachings about your personality. It will show you how to make Christ the Master of your life and how to master life as you strive to do God's will instead of your own.

LEARNING THE DISCIPLE'S PERSONALITY

God created you as a physical and spiritual being. The physical part came from the earth. The spiritual part originated in God's Spirit. The illustration you will draw over the next few days will help you understand how you are made.

✝ **The first part of the Disciple's Personality is called "A Unified Personality." Read that section on page 212. Begin by drawing a circle below, leaving openings at the top and the bottom of the circle. Write *God* above the circle. Refer to the Disciple's Personality presentation (pp. 212-19) if you need help.**

The Bible describes you as a unity, a whole. That's why you drew one circle to represent your total personality. When you learned the Disciple's Cross, you drew a circle representing your life, with Christ at the center. In the Disciple's Personality presentation the circle also represents you. As you develop your understanding of your personality and behavior, you'll add to your drawing. When you understand each element of your personality and how it functions, you will discover how to integrate your personality under the lordship of Christ. The Dis-

Do you ever wonder why you have thoughts, feelings, and behaviors that don't honor Christ?

ciple's Personality also encourages you to continue practicing the six disciplines you've learned so far in *MasterLife*. By the end of this study you'll be able to draw the complete Disciple's Personality.

GROWING IN CHRISTLIKENESS

The Bible emphasizes building Christlike character, which is a part of the following definition of discipleship.

> Discipleship is developing a personal, lifelong, obedient relationship with Jesus Christ in which **He transforms your character into Christlikeness; changes your values into Kingdom values;** and involves you in His mission in the home, the church, and the world.

As you complete this study, you'll work on aspects of your character that Christ desires to mold into His likeness. When you read this definition, you may have asked yourself: *What exactly is Christlikeness? How will I know whether my character is Christlike?*

We know that in all things God works for the good of those who love him, who have been called according to his purpose. For those God foreknew he also predestined to be conformed to the likeness of his Son, that he might be the firstborn among many brothers (Rom. 8:28-29).

Read the verses in the margin. What is God's will for you?

God's purpose and will for you are that you become like Jesus. Transforming your character into Christlikeness means that the Holy Spirit helps you become more like Christ in every character trait.

In day 1 you read that Jesus did God's will. He came from heaven to do God's will. Doing God's will was a constant part of Jesus' obedient life and purpose. He glorified God while He was on earth. He prayed for God's will, not His own, to be done.

Do you desire to do what Jesus did? Check the statements that apply to you.
- [ ] **I want to be like Jesus and to do God's will, but I'm afraid that it may require me to give up something.**
- [ ] **I want to be like Jesus and to do God's will, but I'm afraid that I don't have the ability to do as He directs me.**
- [ ] **Being like Jesus is impossible for me. I can never do God's will if this is required of me.**
- [ ] **Yes, I want to do God's will, as Jesus did. Lord, please show me how.**

In this study you'll learn more about how to be like Jesus, how to develop Christlike character, and how developing His character traits helps you do His will.

Say aloud this week's Scripture-memory verse, *Philippians 2:13.* Write what God says to you through this verse about doing God's will and about building Christlike character.

You may have answered something like this: I need to allow the Holy Spirit to to remove harmful character traits in me and build new ones that honor Christ.

How are you doing in your practice of having a daily quiet time? Your goal is to have quiet times 21 straight days to establish it as part of your daily life. I hope that having a quiet time is a meaningful experience for you.

Read *John 5:16-30* during your quiet time today. See what God reveals to you through this passage about another time Jesus mentioned pleasing the Father. Then complete the Daily Master Communication Guide in the margin.

Daily Master Communication Guide

John 5:16-30

What God said to me:

What I said to God:

DAY 3

Committing Your Personality

Doing God's will depends on committing your whole personality to God. Even when you commit yourself to God, you soon discover that doing His will is not easy. Many factors influence you.

Connie and her husband, Mark, a church-staff member, were searching to know God's will. "Mark felt that God was leading him to another church," Connie said. "He received a few offers but turned them down, saying he didn't feel that these offers were part of God's will. Unfortunately, I didn't have as much faith. I felt that Mark was crazy for turning down those churches."

Connie then read *Ephesians 3:20-21*, which says that God is able to do immeasurably more than all we ask or imagine. "I realized that I was wrong to limit God's will and to mistrust my husband's faith. Then God called us to the church where we now serve. I never expected God's call to be to a church so loving, so God-centered, so caring—yet God knew all along!" Connie said that her lack of faith could have caused them to miss truly knowing and doing God's will and the Holy Spirit's leading.

GOD PROVIDES THE WAY
Read *1 John 2:15-17* below.

Do not love the world or anything in the world. If anyone loves the world, the love of the Father is not in him. For everything in the world—the cravings of sinful man, the lust of his eyes and the boasting of what he has and does—comes not from the Father but from the world. The world and its desires pass away, but the man who does the will of God lives forever (1 John 2:15-17).

Check the factor(s) that most hinder you from doing God's will.
❑ **sinful nature**   ❑ **environment**   ❑ **heredity**

Although you may have checked more than one answer, the verses from *1 John* clearly indicate that your sinful nature keeps you from doing God's will. Other factors may be a part of it. You may live in a sinful environment. You may come from a family that doesn't honor Christ. But you have a choice about whether to do God's will. Your sinful nature is the primary culprit that causes you to refuse to listen to the Holy Spirit and decline to do God's will.

How do you commit your whole personality to God? Does that mean losing your identity? Does that mean becoming passive and simply letting life roll over you? Does that mean never again struggling with what God wants you to do? Even Jesus struggled when He was tempted. But even though you struggle, God provides a way to accomplish His will in you when you commit your entire personality to Him.

 Read the Scriptures in the margin. Describe how God enables

you to commit each part of your personality to His will. The first reference is this week's **Scripture-memory verse**. See if you can recite it from memory.

Will *(Phil. 2:13):*

Mind *(Rom. 12:2):*

Body *(Rom. 12:1):*

Emotions *(Gal. 5:19-24):*

Life *(Gal. 2:20):*

Here are some ways you could have answered: *Will:* God works in me to provide the will and the ability to do His good pleasure. *Mind:* God renews my mind so that I can prove that His will is good, pleasing, and complete. *Body:* God tells me to present my body as a living sacrifice to Him as my reasonable service; Jesus encourages me to pray because my body is weak (see *Matt. 26:41*). *Emotions:* The Holy Spirit produces the fruit of the Spirit in me to replace evil emotions and actions. *Life:* Christ lives in me when I am crucified with Him, and He provides the power to do His will.

Here is a summary of what you have learned about God's will:

> The process of doing God's will is accomplished through—
> • a vision of God's purpose for your life;
> • a commitment of your whole personality to God;
> • actions based on God's provision for doing His will.

LEARNING THE DISCIPLE'S PERSONALITY

The Bible depicts you as a body and a soul. Read the sections "Body" and "Soul" (pp. 212-213) in the Disciple's Personality presentation.

✝ Draw a circle with *God* above it and *body* beneath it. Write the five senses—*sight, sound, smell, taste,* and *touch*—on each side of the circle. Now write *soul* on the inner top rim of the circle and *mind, will,* and *emotions* in the exact center of the circle. Use a separate sheet of paper if you need more room. Refer to the Disciple's Personality presentation (pp. 212-219) if you need help. By the end of this study you'll be able to draw the complete Disciple's Personality and to explain it in your own words.

It is God who works in you to will and to act according to his good purpose (Phil. 2:13).

Do not conform any longer to the pattern of this world, but be transformed by the renewing of your mind. Then you will be able to test and approve what God's will is—his good, pleasing and perfect will (Rom. 12:2).

Offer your bodies as living sacrifices, holy and pleasing to God—this is your spiritual act of worship (Rom. 12:1).

The acts of the sinful nature are obvious: sexual immorality, impurity and debauchery; idolatry and witchcraft; hatred, discord, jealousy, fits of rage, selfish ambition, dissensions, factions and envy; drunkenness, orgies, and the like. I warn you, as I did before, that those who live like this will not inherit the kingdom of God. But the fruit of the Spirit is love, joy, peace, patience, kindness, goodness, faithfulness, gentleness and self-control. Against such things there is no law. Those who belong to Christ Jesus have crucified the sinful nature with its passions and desires (Gal. 5:19-24).

I have been crucified with Christ and I no longer live, but Christ lives in me. The life I live in the body, I live by faith in the Son of God, who loved me and gave himself for me (Gal. 2:20).

Live by the Spirit, and you will not gratify the desires of the sinful nature. For the sinful nature desires what is contrary to the Spirit, and the Spirit what is contrary to the sinful nature. They are in conflict with each other, so that you do not do what you want. But if you are led by the Spirit, you are not under law.

The acts of the sinful nature are obvious: sexual immorality, impurity and debauchery; idolatry and witchcraft; hatred, discord, jealousy, fits of rage, selfish ambition, dissensions, factions and envy; drunkenness, orgies, and the like. I warn you, as I did before, that those who live like this will not inherit the kingdom of God. But the fruit of the Spirit is love, joy, peace, patience, kindness, goodness, faithfulness, gentleness and self-control. Against such things there is no law. Those who belong to Christ Jesus have crucified the sinful nature with its passions and desires. Since we live by the Spirit, let us keep in step with the Spirit (Gal. 5:16-25).

Daily Master Communication Guide

Exodus 4:1-17

What God said to me:

What I said to God:

What happens when you shift from the image of self to the image of Christ? What happens when you set aside the desires of the natural person and increasingly become more Christlike? In day 2 you learned that God expects you to be like Jesus, becoming more Christlike day by day. Today you'll learn more about what that means.

IN THE CARPENTER'S SHOP
When you think about setting aside old traits and becoming more Christlike, picture tearing down an old house and building a new one. What will you tear down and replace to become more Christlike? Ask the Holy Spirit to show you as you read *Galatians 5:16-25* in the margin.

Galatians 5:16-25 is one of three similar Bible passages that illustrate what it means to leave the old life behind, or tear it down, and to take up, or build, the new life. You will study the other two passages in days 4 and 5 this week.

Below are statements from the passage you just read from *Galatians 5*. Write O beside the statements that apply to the old person in Christ and N beside those that describe a new person in Christ.

_____ 1. *Keep in step with the Spirit.*
_____ 2. *Gratify the desires of the sinful nature.*
_____ 3. *[Desire] what is contrary to the Spirit.*
_____ 4. *[Crucify] the sinful nature.*
_____ 5. *Live by the Spirit.*
_____ 6. *[Be] led by the Spirit.*
_____ 7. *[Have] the fruit of the Spirit.*

As you know Christ more intimately, your life will change. You want to do God's will, to be like Christ, and to have Christ's character. The answers are 1. N, 2. O, 3. O, 4. N, 5. N, 6. N, 7. N.

✝ **Stop and pray for the salvation of the non-Christian friends group members mentioned during group session 1.**

In this study you're using your Daily Master Communication Guide to record what God says to you and what you say to God. You may want to begin keeping a journal so that you'll have more room to write. I suggest that you use *Disciple-Helps: A Daily Quiet Time Guide and Journal.*[1]

✝ **Read *Exodus 4:1-17* during your quiet time today. See how God speaks to you through this passage about Moses' struggle with doing God's will. Complete the Daily Master Communication Guide.**

DAY 4

Supplying Your Need

Do you feel helpless when you think about doing God's will? Do you believe that you need to be a scholar with vast Bible knowledge? Do you feel that only a pastor, an evangelist, or someone who studies the Bible and prays around the clock can know God's will under the Holy Spirit's leading.

The Scriptures say that God provides you exactly what you need to achieve His will. Both *Philippians 4:19* and *Romans 8:28*, in the margin, illustrate how well He equips you to know His will.

Read the verses in the margin. Describe what God has promised to do.

Philippians 4:19:

Romans 8:28:

My God will meet all your needs according to his glorious riches in Christ Jesus (Phil. 4:19).

We know that in all things God works for the good of those who love him, who have been called according to his purpose (Rom. 8:28).

These verses assure us that we don't have to be extra smart or brainy to know God's will. He will supply your needs and will work all things together for good.

Describe a time when God supplied your needs so that you could know His will.

You might read these verses and think, *If all of my needs are supplied, I can make it without God.* But doing God's will on your own is impossible. Only God has the ability to do exactly what He intends. Doing God's will involves a process in which God uses the provisions He has given you to accomplish His work. The two verses in the margin describe this process.

Being confident of this, that he who began a good work in you will carry it on to completion until the day of Christ Jesus (Phil. 1:6).

 In the margin write from memory this week's Scripture-memory verse, *Philippians 2:13*. Describe in your own words how God accomplishes His will in you.

The one who calls you is faithful and he will do it (1 Thess. 5:24).

You may have answered something like this: God works in me to will and to do what pleases Him. He also gives me the ability to do His will.

Reread *Philippians 1:6* in the margin. What good work do you think Christ has begun in you?

Write how you see He is being faithful to complete this good work in you?

Who among men knows the thoughts of a man except the man's spirit within him? In the same way no one knows the thoughts of God except the Spirit of God (1 Cor. 2:11).

The Spirit himself testifies with our spirit that we are God's children (Rom. 8:16).

Daily Master Communication Guide

Job 42

What God said to me:

What I said to God:

Is one of the good works Christ has begun in you a new willingness to witness to the world? Perhaps you've begun to see new opportunities to witness that you never thought about before. Have you started building relationships with persons that you can witness to? Christ promises that He will be faithful to complete work He has begun in you. He has given you the task of witnessing, and He will strengthen you for it.

Think of five persons who need you to witness to them. Write their names on your Prayer-Covenant List (p. 205). If you can't think of five unsaved persons, begin making friends with others so that you can witness to them in the future.

Do you want to do God's will, but internal conflicts and barriers arise? That's why it's important to continue learning to place your personality under the lordship of Christ. As you study the Disciple's Personality today, you'll learn (1) how the Bible pictures you as spirit and will; (2) understand how His will can truly be done in you as you live in the Holy Spirit.

LEARNING THE DISCIPLE'S PERSONALITY

Read the section "Spirit" (p. 213) in the Disciple's Personality presentation. Read the two verses in the margin to learn how the Bible pictures you as spirit.

Draw a circle in the space below, leaving openings at the top and bottom. Write God above it and body beneath it. Write the five senses—sight, sound, smell, taste, and touch—on each side of the circle. Write soul inside the top rim of the circle and mind, will, and emotions in the exact center. Write spirit vertically down the center of the circle, stopping at the word will. Refer to the Disciple's Personality presentation (pp. 212-19) for help. By the end of this study you'll be able to draw the complete Disciple's Personality and to explain it in your own words.

IN THE CARPENTER'S SHOP

As you become more like Christ, with the Holy Spirit's help you'll continue to put aside, or tear down, traits of the old person and to substitute traits of the new person. The verses from *Colossians 3*, in the margin, illustrate what leaving the old life behind and taking up the new one mean.

Read in the margin *Colossians 3*. Underline statements that describe the tendencies of the old life before Christ. Circle statements describing the tendencies of the new life after Christ.

I hope that this exercise continued to emphasize what must happen for you to become like Christ. For the old life, you may have underlined such phrases as *rid yourselves of all such things*, *Put to death, therefore, whatever belongs to your earthly nature*, and *you have taken off your old self with its practices*. For the new life, you may have circled *set your hearts on things above*, *Set your minds on things above*, *clothe yourselves with compassion, kindness, humility, gentleness and patience*, and *over all these virtues put on love, which binds them all together in perfect unity*.

Read *Job 42* during your quiet time today, describing the way God supplied the needs of someone who did His will. Then complete the Daily Master Communication Guide in the margin on page 116.

Sometimes people ask me: "Do I need to be alone when I have my quiet time? Can I have a quiet time with my friend or family?" Certainly, having family devotions and praying and studying the Bible with a friend are excellent ways to spend time with the Master. (You'll learn more about conversational prayer during this study.) But these can't take the place of individual time you spend with Christ. Make sure that your day includes a personal quiet time.

Ask God to help you continue to find the right time and setting each day to devote to a quiet time with Him.

Since, then, you have been raised with Christ, set your hearts on things above, where Christ is seated at the right hand of God. Set your minds on things above, not on earthly things. For you died, and your life is now hidden with Christ in God. When Christ, who is your life, appears, then you also will appear with him in glory.

Put to death, therefore, whatever belongs to your earthly nature: sexual immorality, impurity, list, evil desires and greed, which is idolatry. Because of these, the wrath of God is coming. You used to walk in these ways, in the life you once lived. But now you must rid yourselves of all such things as these: anger, rage, malice, slander, and filthy language from your lips. Do not lie to each other, since you have taken off your old self with its practices and have put on the new self, which is being renewed in knowledge in the image of its Creator. Here there is no Greek or Jew, circumcised or uncircumcised, barbarian, Scythian, slave or free, but Christ is all, and is in all.

Therefore, as God's chosen people, holy and dearly loved, clothe yourselves with compassion, kindness, humility, gentleness and patience. Bear with each other and forgive whatever grievances you may have against one another. Forgive was the Lord forgave you. And over all these virtues put on love, which binds them all together in perfect unity (Col. 3:1-14).

By faith Moses, when he had grown up, refused to be known as the son of Pharaoh's daughter. He chose to be mistreated along with the people of God rather than to enjoy the pleasures of sin for a short time. He regarded disgrace for the sake of Christ as of greater value than the treasures of Egypt, because he was looking ahead to his reward. By faith he left Egypt, not fearing the king's anger; he persevered because he saw him who is invisible (Heb. 11:24-27).

[Jesus] withdrew about a stone's throw beyond them, knelt down and prayed, "Father, if you are willing, take this cup from me; yet not my will, but yours be done" (Luke 22:41-42).

If anyone else thinks he has reasons to put confidence in the flesh, I [Paul] have more: circumcised on the eighth day, of the people of Israel, of the tribe of Benjamin, a Hebrew of Hebrews; in regard to the law, a Pharisee; as for zeal, persecuting the church; as for legalistic righteousness, faultless.

But whatever was to my profit I now consider loss for the sake of Christ. What is more, I consider everything a loss compared to the surpassing greatness of knowing Christ Jesus my Lord, for whose sake I have lost all things. I consider them rubbish, that I may gain Christ (Phil. 3:4-8).

DAY 5

Shutting the Door of the Flesh

You may think that you are the only person who struggles with knowing God's will. Perhaps you think that people in Bible times automatically knew exactly what God wanted them to do and never considered their own preferences. You may think that their lives were easy because they chose God's way.

Your daily Bible passages this week have focused on Bible figures and their struggles to do God's will. In today's study you'll examine three more. Read about Moses, Jesus, and Paul in the Scriptures in the margin.

Moses, Jesus, and Paul willingly suffered in order to follow God's will. Each displayed these three components of doing God's will:

> Doing God's will is accomplished through—
> ❏ a vision of God's purpose for your life;
> ❏ a commitment of your entire personality to God;
> ❏ actions based on God's provision for doing His will.

In the previous box check the component you believe is the most difficult for you in your effort to do God's will.

CONFORMED TO HIS LIKENESS

Read *Romans 8:29: Those God foreknew he also predestined to be conformed to the likeness of his Son, that he might be the firstborn among many brothers.* This verse says that if God's will is accomplished in your life, you'll be conformed to the likeness of Christ, God's Son. You will act like Him, will think like Him, and will have the kind of relationships with God and others that Christ did. You'll have Him at the center of your life, and you'll yield to the Holy Spirit's leading in your life.

 Say aloud this week's Scripture-memory verse, *Philippians 2:13*, to someone in your family or to a close friend. Tell that person how this verse has made you more aware of doing God's will.

Apply this verse to your life by writing your personal response to each of the following statements.

The vision I have of God's purpose for my life is—

If I said, "I commit my whole personality to God," that means that I—

Because I know that God will provide for me when I do His will, I will take the following action(s):

What hinders you from keeping these commitments? A look at the Natural Person, another part of the Disciple's Personality, provides an answer.

LEARNING THE DISCIPLE'S PERSONALITY

Read the section "The Flesh" (p. 213) in the Disciple's Personality presentation.

The Bible uses the word *flesh* in two ways.

Read the two verses in the margin and describe the two ways these verses refer to flesh.

Romans 6:12:

Galatians 5:16-18:

The general meaning of *flesh* is body, referring to the physical body (see *Rom. 6:12*). The other meaning is symbolic, referring to the lower nature (see *Gal. 5:16-18*). The *King James Version* uses *flesh* to mean "sinful nature." It refers to the human capacity to sin and to follow Satan instead of God.

Draw the portions of the Disciple's Personality you learned this week. Close the door of the spirit by completing the circle at the top. Leave the door of the flesh open at the bottom of the circle. Now draw an *I* in the center of the circle that surrounds the words *spirit* and *will*. Write *flesh* vertically under *will*. Draw a line through *spirit*. Write *Satan* outside the circle beneath *body*. Then write *1 Corinthians 2:14* above God and label your drawing *The Natural Person*. Refer to the Disciple's Personality presentation (pp. 212–19) if you need help. By the end of this study you'll be able to draw the entire Disciple's Personality and to explain it in your own words.

Do not let sin reign in your mortal body so that you obey its evil desires (Rom. 6:12).

Live by the spirit, and you will not gratify the desires of the sinful nature. For the sinful nature desires what is contrary to the Spirit, and the Spirit what is contrary to the sinful nature. They are in conflict with each other, so that you do not do what you want. But if you are led by the Spirit, you are not under law (Gal. 5:16-18).

I tell you this, and insist on it in the Lord, that you must no longer live as the Gentiles do, in the futility of their thinking. They are darkened in their understanding and separated from the life of God because of the ignorance that is in them due to the hardening of their hearts. Having lost all sensitivity, they have given themselves over to sensuality so as to indulge in every kind of impurity, with a continual lust for more.

You, however, did not come to know Christ that way. Surely you heard of him and were taught in him in accordance with the truth that is in Jesus. You were taught, with regard to your former way of life, to put off your old self, which is being corrupted by its deceitful desires; to be made new in the attitude of your minds; and to put on the new self, created to be like God in true righteousness and holiness.

Do not grieve the Holy Spirit of God, with whom you were sealed for the day of redemption. Get rid of all bitterness, rage and anger, brawling and slander, along with every form of malice. Be kind and compassionate to one another, forgiving each other, just as in Christ God forgave you.

Be imitators of God, therefore, as dearly loved children and live a life of love, just as Christ loved us and gave himself up for us as a fragrant offering and sacrifice to God (Eph. 4:17-24, 30-5:2).

Now read the section "The Condition of the Natural Person Today" (p. 214) in the Disciple's Personality presentation. These teachings help you understand why even a natural person's best intentions sometimes fail when he or she wants to do right but can't seem to. During the coming weeks, learning the Disciple's Personality will help you compare the way you live to God's plan for you.

How have you kept the door of the flesh open in your life? On a separate sheet of paper write the things you do that displease God. Confess your sins to God. Read *1 John 1:9: If we confess our sins, he is faithful and just and will forgive us our sins and purify us from all unrighteousness.* Accept that God has forgiven you. Tear up or burn the list to signify that your sins are forgiven.

Pray that as God works through the Holy Spirit, He will help you keep the commitments you wrote on page 118 and will shut the door of the flesh, which would prevent your carrying them out.

IN THE CARPENTER'S SHOP

Read in the margin the verses from Ephesians to continue learning how to build Christlike character. In the left column write statements that refer to actions of the old person. In the right column write statements that describe what a new person does after coming to know Christ.

Old Person   **New Person**

For actions of the old person, you may have listed *no longer live as the Gentiles do, put off your old self,* or *do not grieve the Holy Spirit.* For steps that the new person would take, you may have listed *be made new in the attitude of your minds; and to put on the new self, be like God in true righteousness and holiness,* or *live a life of love.* As you learn to live like Jesus, you'll learn that the ways of the world present a stark contrast to the Christian lifestyle.

Putting on the new person may involve new attitudes toward your family members.

 Spend time with a family member, maybe one with whom you haven't talked in a long time. Write or call the person if he or she doesn't live near you.

DAY 1

Making the Wrong Decisions

Your mind is much like a tape recorder or a video recorder. You record events and thoughts and continue to listen to them even when other options are open to you. These tapes from the past often lead you repeatedly to make the same wrong choices.

Read in the margin the verses of how Paul described his situation. Like me, you sometimes feel as Paul did—that you're trapped with a sinful nature that doesn't want to do God's will. Even though you want to do what is right, your mind thinks about doing wrong. I believe that the devil plays the tapes of wrong actions. As a result, you keep making wrong decisions.

In *Romans 7:25* Paul provided an answer to his dilemma: *Thanks be to God— through Jesus Christ our Lord!* He added in *Romans 8:1-2, There is now no condemnation for those who are in Christ Jesus, because through Christ Jesus the law of the Spirit of life set me free from the law of sin and death.*

The Holy Spirit takes God's Word and the words spoken by Christ, makes them real, and applies them to your life.

Read *John 14:16-20* in the margin and answer the following questions.

Why did Jesus say that He was sending the Holy Spirit?

So he will live in us. So we can be with him

How did Jesus say that the disciples would recognize the Holy Spirit?

?

Jesus told the disciples that He was sending the Holy Spirit to provide the same kind of help, comfort, and teaching He had provided them while on earth. He said that they would know the Holy Spirit because He would live within them. The Holy Spirit doesn't just walk with you but actually lives in your heart and life.

John 14:26, in the margin, also depicts the Holy Spirit as a counselor, or personal teacher. In this week's study you'll discover how to let the Holy Spirit renew your mind. When you've completed this week's study, you should be able to—

• describe the difference between the natural mind and the renewed mind;
• explain what it means to have the mind of Christ in you;
• describe the process of renewal of the mind;
• identify at least three ways to be more spiritually minded.

FOLLOWING THE NATURAL MIND

When I talk about the natural mind, I'm referring to lost people whose thinking process is limited to human reason and resources (see *1 Cor. 2:14* in the margin). Human history shows that the natural mind becomes progressively self-destructive if left to its own desires.

I do not understand what I do. For what I want to do I do not do, but what I hate I do. I know that nothing good lives in me, that is, in my sinful nature. For I have the desire to do what is good, but I cannot carry it out. For what I do is not the good I want to do; no, the evil I do not want to do—this I keep on doing. Now if I do what I do not want to do, it is no longer I who do it, but it is sin living in me that does it (Rom. 7:15,18-20).

"I will ask the Father, and he will give you another Counselor to be with you forever—the Spirit of truth. The world cannot accept him, because it neither sees him nor knows him. But you know him, for he lives with you and will be in you. I will not leave you as orphans; I will come to you. Before long, the world will not see me anymore, but you will see me. Because I live, you also will live. On that day you will realize that I am in my Father, and you are in me, and I am in you" (John 14:16-20).

"The Counselor, the Holy Spirit, who the Father will send in my name, will teach you all things and will remind you of everything I have said to you" (John 14:26).

The man without the Spirit does not accept the things that come from the Spirit of God, for they are foolishness to him, and he cannot understand them, because they are spiritually discerned (1 Cor. 2:14).

I tell you this, and insist on it in the Lord, that you must no longer live as the Gentiles do, in the futility of their thinking. They are darkened in their understanding and separated from the life of God because of the ignorance that is in them due to the hardening of their hearts (Eph. 4:17-18).

Since they did not think it worthwhile to retain the knowledge of God, he gave them over to a depraved mind, to do what ought not to be done. They have become filled with every kind of wickedness, evil, greed and depravity. They are full of envy, murder, strife, deceit and malice. They are gossips, slanderers, God-haters, insolent, arrogant and boastful; they invent ways of doing evil; they disobey their parents; they are senseless, faithless, heartless, ruthless (Rom. 1:28-31).

The god of this age has blinded the minds of unbelievers, so that they cannot see the light of the gospel of the glory of Christ, who is the image of God (2 Cor. 4:4).

Since they did not think it worthwhile to retain the knowledge of God, he gave them over to a depraved mind, to do what ought not to be done (Rom. 1:28).

...constant friction between men of corrupt mind, who have been robbed of the truth and who think that godliness is a means to financial gain (1 Tim. 6:5).

Do not let anyone who delights in false humility and the worship of angels disqualify you for the prize. Such a person goes into great detail about what he has seen, and his unspiritual mind puffs him up with idle notions (Col. 2:18).

Read *Ephesians 4:17-18* in the margin. What do these verses say about people who live according to their natural minds? Fill in the blanks.

Their thinking is ___darkened___.

They walk in the ___darkness___ **of their understanding.**

They are separated from God because of ___their thinking___.

They are ignorant because of their ___hearts___.

People who follow their natural minds and live as these natural minds direct walk in darkness and have futile thinking. Ignorance, which results because their hearts are hardened, separates them from God. They live hopeless lives.

The natural mind inevitably becomes enslaved to other masters. Read *Romans 1:28-31* in the margin. This verse shows how the natural mind enslaves a personality by reducing it primarily to the world of the senses and evil.

To what masters are you enslaved? Meditate on the words in *Romans 1:28-31* in the margin. Can you identify with some of these masters? If you can, underline the types of wrongdoing with which you struggle.

Read the Scriptures in the margin. Then draw a line between each word in the left column that describes the natural mind and the Scripture reference in the right column in which the word is found.

depraved	*2 Corinthians 4:4*
unspiritual	*Romans 1:28*
blinded	*1 Timothy 6:5*
corrupt	*Colossians 2:18*

These Scriptures clearly teach what happens to a person whose mind is not focused as the Spirit directs. The words used to describe such an existence are horrifying. The correct answers are: *depraved, Romans 1:28; unspiritual, Colossians 2:18; blinded, 2 Corinthians 4:4; corrupt, 1 Timothy 6:5.*

THE RENEWED MIND
The Holy Spirit uses God's Word to renew a person's mind. The natural mind and the renewed mind have the same basic functions: thinking, judging, reasoning, and evaluating. The difference is who controls these processes.

 Reread this week's Scripture-memory verses, *Romans 12:1-2.* Begin to memorize them as you reflect on what they say about the renewed mind.

The renewed mind is obedient to Christ. The natural mind thinks from a humanistic, sin-corrupted viewpoint. The renewed mind frees the personality by enlarging it to encompass the world of the Spirit in addition to the senses.

Write *N* beside the statements that describe the natural mind and *R* beside the ones that describe the renewed mind.

___N___ 1. **Becomes progressively self-destructive**

___N___ 2. **Is limited to purely human reason and resources**

___R___ 3. **Thinks from Christ's viewpoint as the Holy Spirit directs**

___R___ 4. **Frees the personality by including the Spirit**

___N___ 5. **Thinks from the viewpoint of the flesh**

The natural mind leads to a path of self-destruction. It doesn't rely on the mind of Christ but is limited to the resources of the human mind. The viewpoint of the flesh directs its thoughts. The renewed mind thinks from Christ's viewpoint as guided by the Holy Spirit. The correct answers are 1. N, 2. N, 3. R, 4. R, 5. N.

When the Holy Spirit rules your mind, you obey Christ. You think, *What would Christ have me do in this situation?* You try to understand what the Holy Spirit, who lives in you as your personal teacher, is leading you to do. In contrast, fleshly, worldly thoughts rule the worldly, sinful mind.

✛ **Read *Romans 8:1-14* in your Bible and mark the following statements *T* (true) or *F* (false).**

___F___ 1. **The worldly mind concentrates on spiritual things.**

___T___ 2. **To set your mind on things of the flesh brings death.**

___T___ 3. **The worldly mind doesn't submit to the Holy Spirit's control.**

___F___ 4. **A worldly mind sometimes pleases God.**

___F___ 5. **No hope exists for changing a worldly mind.**

The worldly mind is in the control of Satan, not of the Holy Spirit. Setting your mind on things of the flesh without turning to Christ brings death. Yet persons who set aside worldly ways and turn over their lives and thoughts to Christ can know forgiveness and joy. You can have a spiritual mind even if a worldly mind has ruled you in the past. The correct answers are 1. F, 2. T, 3. T, 4. F, 5. F.

✛ **Again read *Romans 8:1-14,* which contrasts the worldly mind and the spiritual mind, during your quiet time today. Then complete the Daily Master Communication Guide in the margin.**

✛ **This week spend time with a close Christian friend. Talk about the things that are most important. Satan would like nothing better than to gain control of your relationships. Spending time together can help keep you from a path of self-destruction in your personal life.**

Daily Master Communication Guide

Romans 8:1-14

What God said to me:

What I said to God:

As for you, you were dead in your transgressions and sins, in which you used to live when you followed the ways of this world and of the ruler of the kingdom of the air, the spirit who is now at work in those who are disobedient. All of us also lived among them at one time, gratifying the cravings of our sinful nature and following its desires and thoughts. Like the rest, we were by nature objects of wrath (Eph. 2:1-3).

Because of his great love for us, God, who is rich in mercy, made us alive with Christ even when we were dead in transgressions—it is by grace you have been saved. And God raised us up with Christ and seated us with him in the heavenly realms in Christ Jesus, in order that in the coming ages he might show the incomparable riches of his grace, expressed in his kindness to us in Christ Jesus. For it is by grace you have been saved, through faith—and this not from yourselves, it is the gift of God—not by works, so that no one can boast. For we are God's workmanship, created in Christ Jesus to do good works, which God prepared in advance for us to do (Eph. 2:4-10).

For this very reason, make every effort to add to your faith goodness; and to goodness, knowledge; and to knowledge, self-control; and to self-control, perseverance; and to perseverance, godliness; and to godliness, brotherly kindness; and to brotherly kindness, love. For if you possess these qualities in increasing measure, they will keep you from being ineffective and unproductive in your knowledge of our Lord Jesus Christ. But if anyone does not have them, he is nearsighted and blind, and has forgotten that he has been cleansed from his past sins (2 Pet. 1:5-9).

Ruled by the Flesh

When you studied about the natural person, you learned that this person doesn't know Christ. He or she lives a natural, sinful life without Christ.

Read *Ephesians 2:1-3* in the margin and underline the phrases that describe your former way of life. Now read *Ephesians 2:4-10* in the margin and underline what God did for you.

Before you knew Christ, you were dead in your transgressions and sins. When you repented of your sins and your sinful way of life and asked Christ to be your Savior and Lord, God made you alive with Christ. By His grace He saved you and raised you up with Christ. You are now God's workmanship, created in Christ Jesus to do good works.

However, many persons who have received Christ and have the Holy Spirit living in their hearts still don't live as God intended. That's why Paul told the Ephesians in *Ephesians 4:17-24* that they didn't learn their sinful, worldly ways from Christ and that they should move away from that way of living.

A WORLDLY CHRISTIAN

If a Christian lives like the unbelieving world, this person is a worldly Christian. The King James Version calls this person carnal, which means fleshly. It refers to a person who is controlled by human nature more than by the Spirit of God. Paul contrasts spiritual people—those who are under the control of the Holy Spirit—with those who are carnal—those who are under the control of the flesh. *First Corinthians 3:1* describes worldly Christians: *Brothers, I could not address you as spiritual but as worldly—mere infants in Christ.*

Second Peter 1:3 makes clear that God has provided you His power: *His divine power has given us everything we need for life and godliness through our knowledge of him who called us by his own glory and goodness.* He has given you the rich promise of eternal life. He has given you the resources you need for life and righteous living. However, a few verses later, in *2 Peter 1:5,* you are told to add certain things to your faith that God has provided for you.

In *2 Peter 1:5-9,* in the margin, underline the things you are told to add to your faith.

Did you underline goodness, knowledge, self-control, perseverance, godliness, brotherly kindness, and love? If you continue to manifest the traits of a worldly person, you—

- are ineffective and unproductive. A worldly person is sluggish and doesn't grow in faith. A worldly person doesn't have a productive life for Christ.
- are nearsighted and blind. This person is blind to the Holy Spirit's truth and listens to Satan's lies.

• have forgotten that you've been cleansed. This person isn't sensitive to sin and doesn't appreciate God and Christ for his or her forgiveness.

Reread the results if persons don't grow and add to their faith. Check any results you see in your life.

MASTERING THE MIND

God never intends for a Christian to be worldly. Yet some Christians are. Probably because they haven't been guided in how to grow, they are still guided more by fleshly desires than by spiritual desires. Christ secures your salvation, but you are responsible for following Him and living in Him.

The Holy Spirit wants to be to your mind what a rudder is to a ship. A rudder keeps the ship on course. In *2 Corinthians 10:3-5,* in the margin, Paul described a two-step plan for mastering the human mind. Paul described an offensive-defensive game plan that worked for his life, as it will for yours. In the defensive game plan you are to defeat worldly ideas that obstruct the knowledge of God. In the offensive game plan you are to keep Christ in control.

Underline the defensive plan and circle the offensive plan in the Scripture in the margin.

 This week's Scripture-memory verses address renewing your mind. Write them from memory in the margin. Then below it describe one way you need to renew your mind.

LEARNING THE DISCIPLE'S PERSONALITY

Read the section "The Worldly Christian" (p. 215) in the Disciple's Personality presentation. Begin drawing the Worldly Christian. Leave open the doors of the spirit and the flesh. Draw a big *I* in the circle. Above the circle write *The Worldly Christian.* Trace over the letter *s* in spirit with a capital *S.* Refer to the Disciple's Personality presentation (pp. 212–19) if you need help. By the end of this study you'll be able to draw the complete Disciple's Personality and to explain it in your own words.

Though we live in the world, we do not wage war as the world does. The weapons we fight with are not the weapons of the world. On the contrary, they have divine power to demolish strongholds. We demolish arguments and every pretension that sets itself up against the knowledge of God, and we take captive every thought to make it obedient to Christ (2 Cor. 10:3-5).

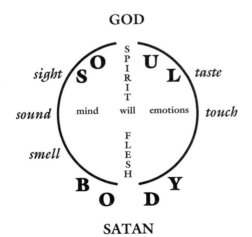

The World's Way

The acts of the sinful nature are obvious: sexual immorality, impurity and debauchery…(Gal. 5:19-21).

Put to death, therefore, whatever belongs to your earthly nature: sexual immorality, impurity, lust, evil desires and greed, which is idolatry…(Col 3:5-7).

Among you there must not be even a hint of sexual immorality, or of any kind of impurity, or of greed, because these are improper for God's holy people. Nor should there be obscenity, foolish talk or coarse joking…(Eph. 5:3-5).

The Spirit's Way

The fruit of the Spirit is love, joy, peace, patience, kindness, goodness, faithfulness, gentleness and self-control. Against such things there is no law (Gal. 5:22-23).

Since, then, you have been raised with Christ, set your hearts on things above, where Christ is seated at the right hand of God. Set your minds on things above, not on earthly things. For you died, and your life is now hidden with Christ in God (Col. 3:1-3).

Be imitators of God, therefore, as dearly loved children and live a life of love, just as Christ loved us and gave himself up for us as a fragrant offering and sacrifice to God (Eph. 5:1-2).

IN THE CARPENTER'S SHOP

Read the Scriptures in the margin that relate to immorality or impure thinking. From the verses under "The World's Way" identify a specific behavior you want to get rid of. From the verses under "The Spirit's Way" identify an action you'll take to replace it. Each day this week you will record your progress in working on this trait. If you feel that this matter is too personal to write about here, you may write about it elsewhere, but please address this critical change.

Here is an example.

Behavior I want to work on: sexually impure thoughts or actions
An action I will take to put off the old self: stop reading and looking at sexually explicit material
An action I will take to let the Holy Spirit make me more like Christ: memorize Scripture to have a pure heart and mind

Now you try it.
Behavior I want to work on:

An action I will take to put off the old self:

An action I will take to let the Holy Spirit make me more like Christ:

THE DESIRE TO CHANGE

A word about putting off old behaviors: *you can't always change these practices overnight.* Don't be discouraged if you don't see instant results. But by asking the Lord to renew your mind and by committing this process to Him, you'll eventually see the changes you want. If you need a quick reference on how to renew your mind, see the chart on page 135. Feel free to copy it to keep in a convenient place.

 Find a way to do something kind for a member of your family who does not know Christ. Be ready to share your experience at your next group session.

 Read *Ephesians 2:1-10*, a passage explaining how we are made alive in Christ, in your quiet time today. Then complete the Daily Master Communication Guide in the margin on page 129.

DAY 3

Replacing Your Thoughts

THE MIND OF CHRIST

As a Christian, you have the goal of thinking and acting from the mind of Christ. In *Philippians 2:5* Paul said, *Let this mind be in you, which was also in Christ Jesus* (KJV). He also referred to the mind of Christ in *I Corinthians 2:16:"Who has known the mind of the Lord that he may instruct him?"* But we have the mind of Christ.

In *I Corinthians 2:16* what did Paul claim that Christians have?

Paul said that Christians have the mind of Christ. Can you sincerely say that you desire to think Christ's thoughts? ❑ **Yes** ❑ **No**

Hopefully, you were able to answer yes to that question. You may sincerely desire to be Christlike and to think Christ's thoughts. But how do you do that? Renewing your mind is accomplished by filling your mind with Christ's thoughts.

Check the phrases that explain what having the mind of Christ means.
☑ **1. Making thoughts obedient to Christ**
☑ **2. Exercising the ability to think spiritually**
❑ **3. Having a high IQ**
☑ **4. Seeing things from Christ's viewpoint**
❑ **5. Meditating to empty your mind**

If you think Christ's thoughts, you try to see things as Christ would, and you let Him be the master of your mind. You make your thoughts obedient to Christ. Having a high IQ and emptying your mind by meditation have nothing to do with having the mind of Christ. Every Christian has the mind of Christ, but he or she doesn't always choose to engage it. The correct answers are 1, 2, and 4.

Fill in the blanks in the margin with one of the following words to describe a way Christ can be the master of your mind.

renewing   thought   mind   knowledge

You can make Christ the master of your mind by removing all obstacles to your knowledge of God, by making every thought obedient to Christ, by possessing the mind of Christ, and by renewing your mind.

 What do this week's memory verses say about renewing your mind? Say them aloud a few times. Review your memorization of *Philippians 2:13*.

THE RENEWAL PROCESS

To renew your mind, fill it with Scriptures to replace bad thoughts with good

---

Daily Master Communication Guide

Ephesians 2:1-10

What God said to me:

What I said to God:

- **By removing all obstacles to your** ___mind___ **of God**

- **By making every** _thought_ **obedient to Christ**

- **By possessing the** _Knowledge_ **of Christ**

- **By** _renewing_ **your mind**

Set your minds on things above, not on earthly things (Col. 3:2).

Those who live according to the sinful nature have their minds set on what that nature desires; but those who live in accordance with the Spirit have their minds set on what the Spirit desires. The mind of sinful man is death, but the mind controlled by the Spirit is life and peace (Rom. 8:5-6).

"When he, the Spirit of truth, comes, he will guide you into all truth. He will not speak on his own; he will speak only what he hears, and he will tell you what is yet to come" (John 16:13).

His delight is in the law of the Lord, and on his law he meditates day and night (Ps. 1:2).

Finally, brothers, whatever is true, whatever is noble, whatever is right, whatever is pure, whatever is lovely, whatever is admirable—if anything is excellent or praiseworthy—think about such things (Phil. 4:8).

thoughts. The more you live in the Word, the more your mind will be renewed.

The Scriptures in the margin give you further instruction on how Christ renews your mind. Read the verses and match the references in the left column with the summary statements in the right column.

____ **1. *Colossians 3:2***   **a. Think on praiseworthy things.**
____ **2. *Romans 8:5-6***   **b. Give attention to things of the Spirit.**
____ **3. *John 16:13***   **c. Let the Holy Spirit guide you into truth.**
____ **4. *Psalm 1:2***   **d. Set your heart's desire on heavenly things.**
____ **5. *Philippians 4:8***   **e. Meditate on God's Word.**

Don't let your mind linger on evil thoughts; instead, think about wholesome things, such as God's Word. Remember the computer saying: "Garbage in, garbage out." When you realize that you're having worldly thoughts, think of them as red, flashing emergency lights that warn you to turn your thoughts to spiritual things. The correct answers are 1. d, 2. b, 3. c, 4. e, 5. a.

Here are simple, practical steps for activating the mind of Christ when you are tempted to act in harmful ways.

ACTIVATING THE MIND OF CHRIST

1. Remember that Christ was tempted in every way you are tempted yet overcame the temptation (see *Heb. 4:15*).
2. Pray for grace in time of need (see *Heb. 4:16*).
3. Express humility by getting on your knees (see *Phil. 2:5-11*).
4. Ask the Holy Spirit to impress you with a way to deal with the temptation (see *Prov. 3:5-6*) and (*1 Cor. 10:13*).
5. Adopt God's attitude and choose His response toward the temptation.
6. Ask for God to walk with you past the temptation (*Heb. 7:25*).
7. Look for a Scripture to claim during the temptation (*Ps. 119:97-105*).
8. Ask God to help you focus on His will (see *Phil. 2:13*).
9. Acknowledge and ask forgiveness for thinking about the temptation (see *1 John 1:9*).
10. Obey God's commands, knowing that you are in spiritual warfare (see *Rom. 8:26-27*).

IN THE CARPENTER'S SHOP
Are you making progress in putting off the old self and replacing it with the new?

Yesterday you listed a behavior you wanted to reject in order to build Christlike character. Describe in the margin an instance in which you have already put aside that behavior.

Read *Philippians 2:5-11* during your quiet time. See how God speaks to you through this passage. Continue to meet your goal of having quiet times 21 consecutive days. Complete the Daily Master Communication Guide in the margin. If you miss a day begin over again and try to have a quiet time 21 days in a row.

DAY 4

Thinking Christ's Thoughts

Daily Master Communication Guide

Philippians 2:5-11

What God said to me:

What I said to God:

You may think: *Is it really possible for me—a sinful human being—to have the mind of Christ? I can imagine a well-known pastor being able to think Christ's thoughts, but someone like me? Isn't it improper to believe that I can think as Christ does?*

YOU HAVE THE MIND OF CHRIST

Believing that you can have the mind of Christ is not improper. The mind of Christ came to you when you were saved (see *1 Cor. 2:16* in the margin). God created you to be like Jesus. *Romans 8:29* says, *Those God foreknew he also predestined to be conformed to the likeness of his Son, that he might be the firstborn among many brothers. Hebrews 2:10* says that God is the process of *bringing many sons to glory.* The glory you are to have is the glory of being like God's perfect Son, Jesus Christ. *Philippians 2:5*, which you read yesterday as part of your daily Bible reading and quiet time, reminds you that you have Christ's mind. Would the Bible remind you that you have Christ's mind if engaging it and putting it to work for you were impossible? How, then, do you know how to think the thoughts of Christ? By knowing Christ, hearing Him, and learning His truth.

From what book can you know Christ, hear Him, and learn His truth?

Read *John 8:31-32* in the margin or quote it from memory. What does living in God's truth do for the enslaved mind?

Living in God's Word, the Bible, is the primary source of your knowledge about Christ. The Word reveals His truth. As you hold to, or remain in, the Word, He speaks to you through the Holy Spirit. One of the Holy Spirit's roles is to show you the truth. His truth sets the enslaved mind free.

 Live in His Word now by working on this week's Scripture-memory verses, *Romans 12:1-2*. Write them in the margin.

Circle the term that Jesus used in *John 8:31-32* to describe a person who holds to, or remains in, His Word?

    follower   **disciple**   **convert**   **sinner**

A person who holds to His Word is His disciple. These verses say that you will be His disciple indeed if you hold to, or remain in, His Word.

 Having your daily quiet time is a way you continue in His Word and shape your personality to be like Christ. Read *Luke 4:14-21*. Complete the Daily Master Communication Guide in the margin.

"Who has known the mind of the Lord that he may instruct him?" But we have the mind of Christ (1 Cor. 2:16).

"If you hold to my teaching, you are really my disciples. Then you will know the truth, and the truth will set you free" (John 8:31-32).

**Daily Master
Communication Guide**

Luke 4:14-21

What God said to me:

What I said to God:

The new quality Christ is adding to my life:_____.

Recognize that God is in the group.

Use the following questions to evaluate the degree to which your mind is being renewed daily. Are you really Jesus' disciple? ❑ Yes ❑ No If so, how do you know? Review *1 Corinthians 2:16* and *John 8:31* in the margin on page 131 and state in the space below how you know that you are Christ's disciple.

If you are Jesus' disciple, what source of power renews your mind daily?

Are you willing to commit to make God's Word a part of your daily life? ❑ Yes ❑ No If so, write a specific goal you have set for yourself.

I will _____.

IN THE CARPENTER'S SHOP

Does your character reveal that you have a renewed mind? Are you putting off the old self and developing a new character, with the Holy Spirit's help?

Yesterday you described a step you've taken to get rid of the old self. In the margin describe a new quality Christ is adding to your life.

PRAYING FOR CHRISTLIKE CHARACTER

One way to seek insight into building Christlike character is to ask others to pray with you about it. One of the most rewarding and effective ways to pray with others is conversational prayer.

Conversational prayer is a group talking together with God. In any group conversation each person says a few sentences, and then someone else adds something to the subject. When that subject comes to a natural conclusion, someone brings up another subject. The same process takes place in conversational prayer. The following guidelines can help you experience prayer in a new, exciting way.

Read the principles of conversational prayer that follow. Draw a star beside the part of conversational prayer you think you'll find most challenging. Ask God for help with that part.

PRINCIPLES OF CONVERSATIONAL PRAYER

1. Recognize that God is in the group and that you, as a group, are conversing with Him about matters of mutual interest. Some groups even place an empty chair in their midst to remind them that He is present.
2. Pray about one subject at a time. No one should begin praying about a new subject until everyone who wants to pray about the present subject has had an opportunity. Don't be afraid of silence. You can discern when it's time to move to another subject. Don't talk about the subject; don't make lists; just pray.

3. Pray brief prayers. One or two sentences by each person on one subject are usually sufficient. This allows everyone to be involved in the conversation.

4. Speak normally. Don't use formal terms of address or a closing such as Amen at the end of each short prayer. Though prayed by a group, it's still one continuous prayer.

5. Use the first-person singular pronoun whenever possible: *I* and *me* instead of *we* and *us*.

6. Be specific in requests and in confessions of sins. If you are specific, God helps other persons pray about the same need. One person in a group might say, "Help me with pride." Another says, "Lord, I have that problem, too." People don't recognize many answered prayers because they didn't pray specifically.

7. Continue the conversation as long as the group desires or the time limit allows. Someone may have to slip out for a few minutes. Bodily position is not important. Pray with your eyes open if that is comfortable. *John 11:41* implies that Jesus did. You may need to close your eyes in order to concentrate on the Lord. Let God talk to you as you talk to Him.

Be specific in requests and in confessions of sins.

 Pray with a friend, a family member, or your prayer partner and teach that person the principles of conversational prayer. Write a day and a time when you plan to do this:

Day:_____

Time:_____

Stop and ask God to help you with the challenging area beside which you drew a star in "Principles of Conversational Prayer." Ask Him to make conversational prayer a rewarding part of your life in the Spirit.

DAY 5

A Reminder of Who You Are

This week you've learned what the Bible says about the need to renew your mind. You've learned that you truly have the mind of Christ and can think His thoughts. But how does this ability apply to you in your school, in your family life, in your church relationships, and in daily challenges?

Read the following case studies and explain in the margin beside it how each person could renew his or her mind.

Linda and Amanda are best friends. Amanda's parents own a very successful business. Linda's parents work hard to barely make enough money to provide for Linda and her four brothers and sisters. Linda always wants designer clothes like Amanda wears. Linda sometimes uses her dad's credit card for expensive clothes, which her dad can't really afford. Now Linda is pressuring her mom and dad for a new car like the one Amanda got for her birthday. What could Linda do to renew her mind?

Tony's dad hasn't worked for six months. His dad's unemployment embarrasses him. One day after Tony angrily criticized his dad for not having a job, Tony was invited by some new friends to a party after school. Tony knew that alcohol and drugs would be available at the party. As he started home from school, Tony found himself thinking more and more about this party and how it could help him forget his anger and embarrassment over his dad's unemployment. What could Tony do to renew his mind?

Jeremy was involved in his youth group's evangelistic outreach. Recently, his team experienced much success in visiting non-Christian prospects and leading them to Christ. Each week for the past five weeks one or more persons have given their hearts to Christ during one of Jeremy's visits. Word of these conversions spread throughout Jeremy's church. One day during the sermon, his pastor commended him for his witness. Jeremy began thinking that his success in witnessing might help him be elected to the church youth council. Enjoying the attention the church gave him, Jeremy became proud. What could Jeremy do to renew his mind?

You may have answered something like this:

Linda could renew her mind by recognizing her temptation to be just like Amanda. She could replace thoughts of acquiring expensive and more by learning biblical teachings about material possessions and by developing a specific plan for helping her family financially.

Tony could renew his mind by avoiding his new friends so that he won't encounter a situation that could lead him to ruin his life. He could pray for the Holy Spirit to show him ways to help his attitude, such as talking honestly with his dad about their issues, and consulting a pastor or a professional Christian counselor to help the family through this stressful period.

Jeremy could renew his mind by asking the Holy Spirit to help him as he reads what the Bible says about the reason Christians witness: to obey Christ, not to gain others' favor. As he reads *Philippians 2:5-8,* he could let the mind of Christ teach him how to be humble.

REPLACING OLD THOUGHTS

Read in the margin what the Bible says about how your thoughts shape your desires and actions. When you replace harmful thoughts with ones you know will honor Christ, your entire concept of yourself can change. If you constantly tell yourself, I'm no good, you may begin to act out those thoughts as a self-fulfilling prophecy. If you remind yourself of Christ's love for you and of your worthiness in His sight, you'll begin to act like a person of worth. You can renew your mind by replacing negative thoughts about yourself with the reminder that Christ died for you. You can renew your mind by remembering who—and whose—you are.

Describe specific situations in which you need to renew your mind.

Identify actions you'll take to renew your mind. See the list in the margin for possibilities. Review your answers, as well as the suggested answers, to the case studies you read. Some of those may apply to you.

Pray, asking God to give you courage to take the action you described.

 Say aloud this week's memory verses, *Romans 12:1-2,* to someone who could benefit from them. Explain to that person how these verses encourage you to renew your mind.

Do you sometimes feel conflict in your heart when you try to have the thoughts, attitudes, and actions of Jesus? Why does such conflict arise to interfere with your commitment to have the mind of Christ? Another look at the Worldly Christian portion of the Disciple's Personality provides an answer.

LEARNING THE DISCIPLE'S PERSONALITY

Read *1 Corinthians 3:1-3* in the margin. Why did Paul say that the Corinthian Christians were worldly instead of mature?

Paul said the Christians at Corinth were not mature Christians because they were jealous and they quarreled among themselves. If you don't allow Christ continually to be the Master of your life through His Spirit, you are a worldly Christian. Although you've allowed Christ to enter your life, you still struggle to con-

As he thinketh in his heart, so is he (Prov. 23:7, KJV).

How to Renew Your Mind

Here is a quick reference for renewing your mind. Keep a copy in your Bible, wallet, or purse for ready access.

- **Sing songs of praise.**
- **Memorize applicable Scriptures.**
- **Pray.**
- **Bring every thought under Christ's control.**
- **Set your mind on things above.**
- **Demolish Satan's strongholds.**
- **Commit yourself to God as a living sacrifice.**
- **Talk to a friend.**
- **Help someone in need.**
- **Claim the mind of Christ.**

Brothers, I could not address you as spiritual but as worldly—mere infants in Christ. I gave you milk, not solid food, for you were not yet ready for it. Indeed, you are still not ready. You are still worldly. For since there is jealousy and quarreling among you, are you not worldly? Are you not acting like mere men? (1 Cor. 3:1-3).

**Daily Master
Communication Guide**

Genesis 50:15-21

What God said to me:

What I said to God:

trol your own life. The big *I* of the old, natural person still dominates you. Worldly Christians, though children of God, continually open the door of the flesh, allowing the old nature to decide what they think, do, and feel, rather than follow the Spirit of God. You saw this situation when you read about Linda, Tony, and Jeremy in the case studies. You may see it in yourself, too.

✝ **The part of the Disciple's Personality drawing you've learned is below. Write *1 Corinthians 3:1-3* under the heading *The Worldly Christian*. By the end of this study you'll be able to draw the complete Disciple's Personality and to explain it in your own words.**

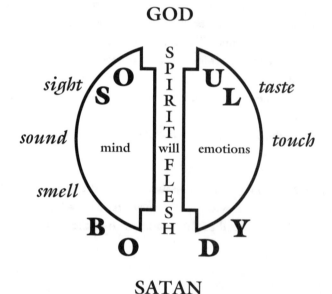

The Worldly Christian

GOD

sight ... *taste*

sound ... mind ... emotions ... *touch*

smell

SPIRIT will FLESH

SATAN

Setting aside old patterns can be challenging, but don't despair. Christ wants to be your Lord and to give you daily victory. The Holy Spirit will help you renew your mind.

Bob Dutton, a *MasterLife* teacher and conference leader, became aware of the worldly lives of many American Christians when he was in Russia. These Russian Christians sacrificed time and possessions to travel to the training. "I was ashamed," Bob said. "I was there to help dedicated Christians learn more about the Bible, and I had to admit that most Christians in America are more concerned with themselves than with following Christ. It was hard to admit that our government leaves God out of its decisions while I sat in a classroom in Russia teaching persons who have experienced persecution and oppression."

✝ **Read *Genesis 50:15-21* during your quiet time today. See how God speaks to you through this passage, which focuses on someone who replaced evil thoughts with good thoughts. Then complete the Daily Master Communication Guide in the margin.**

IN THE CARPENTER'S SHOP

How have you done this week getting rid of the old self and adopting new characteristics and behaviors?

Answer these questions about the area you identified on page 128.

A characteristic or behavior I have been getting rid of this week:

Something Christ has been adding to my character this week:

Stop and pray, thanking God for helping you in the areas you recorded. Ask Him to continue to give you the courage to make changes.

HAS THIS WEEK MADE A DIFFERENCE?

Review "My Walk with the Master This Week" at the beginning of this week's material. Mark the activities you have finished by drawing vertical lines in the diamonds beside them. Finish any incomplete activities. Think about what you'll say during your group session about your work on these activities.

As a result of your study of "Renew Your Mind," I hope that you understand ways being a worldly Christian holds you back from being all God wants you to be. I hope that the Worldly Christian part of the Disciple's Personality will help you identify areas of weakness or compromise in your life in the Spirit. The ability to think Christ's thoughts is crucial to your life in the Spirit. Allowing Christ-honoring thoughts to replace worldly, fleshly thoughts is a challenge for most Christians. The Holy Spirit is with you to help you renew your mind. You don't have to be a victim of Satan's efforts to have you adopt his destructive attitudes. Satan is defeated when you push his thoughts out of your mind and replace them with those that please Christ.

WEEK 9

Master Your Emotions

This Week's Goal

You will be able to use an ACTION plan to master your emotions.

My Walk with the Master This Week

You will complete the following activities to develop the six biblical disciplines. When you have completed each activity, draw a vertical line in the diamond beside it.

SPEND TIME WITH THE MASTER

◇ Have a daily quiet time each day, working toward the goal of having quiet times 21 consecutive days. Check the box beside each day you have a quiet time this week:

☐ Sunday ☐ Monday ☐ Tuesday ☐ Wednesday ☐ Thursday ☐ Friday ☐ Saturday

◇ During one day's quiet time, hold the nail your leader gave you in your group session for five minutes.

LIVE IN THE WORD

◇ Read your Bible every day. Write what God says to you and what you say to God.

◇ Memorize *Galatians 5:22-23.*

◇ Review *Philippians 2:13 and Romans 12:1-2.*

◇ Read "How to Listen to God's Word."

◇ Write important points from a sermon on the Hearing the Word form.

PRAY IN FAITH

◇ Pray for your family members and relatives.

FELLOWSHIP WITH BELIEVERS

◇ Spend some time with someone you don't like or with a person who doesn't like you.

WITNESS TO THE WORLD

◇ Read "Testimony Outline" and write information to use in your testimony.

MINISTER TO OTHERS

◇ Learn the Spiritual Christian part of the Disciple's Personality.

This Week's Scripture-Memory Verses

The fruit of the Spirit is love, joy, peace, patience, kindness, goodness, faithfulness, gentleness and self-control. Against such things there is no law (Gal. 5:22-23).

DAY 1

A Gift from God

My father often told about having a terrible temper when he was young. Even after becoming a Christian at age 19, he still exploded in anger. He struggled over and over again to remain calm and to have an attitude that would honor Christ.

After much prayer and Bible study my father began to notice a change in his responses to situations. One night a man stuck his fist in my dad's face and threatened him. But Dad refused to fight. He later said, "I knew I had won the battle over my temper when I did not respond as I had in the past."

Describe in the margin a situation in which your emotions got the best of you.

"If it feels good, do it!" seems to be today's motto. This self-centered thinking claims that your emotions are your master. Emotions make good servants but bad masters. Christ is to be your Master, even of your emotions. He wants to help you use your emotions in a responsible way. The Bible has a plan to help you deal with your emotions. This week you'll learn that plan and will understand how the Holy Spirit can help you take charge of your emotions. After this week's study you will be able to—
- relate your emotions to your values;
- list a six-step ACTION plan to deal with your emotions;
- apply the ACTION plan to an emotional experience.

WHAT ARE EMOTIONS?
Emotions are God-given feelings of pleasantness or unpleasantness. They are reactions to internal or external stimuli. Emotions aren't good or bad; you choose whether you use emotions to honor Christ or to harm yourself or others.

Emotions are an essential part of your personality. Life without emotions would be dull. If you didn't have emotions, you wouldn't experience anger or anxiety, but you also wouldn't experience the emotions of joy or love. God created you to experience a variety of emotions.

Read the verses in the margin and check the emotions Jesus experienced.   ❏ **anger**   ❏ **love**   ❏ **grief**   ❏ **joy**

Because Jesus was fully human, He experienced all of the emotions listed. The difference between Jesus and you is that He didn't sin when He experienced emotions.

THE SOURCE OF YOUR EMOTIONS
Emotions are responses to your values and beliefs. Because your values and beliefs are not exactly the same as any other person's, you may react to the same circumstances differently than someone else does.

He looked around at them in anger and, deeply distressed at their stubborn hearts, said to the man, "Stretch out your hand." He stretched it out, and his hand was completely restored (Mark 3:5).

"A new command I give you: Love one another. As I have loved you, so must love one another" (John 13:34).

Jesus wept (John 11:35).

"I am coming to you now, but I say these things while I am still in the world, so that they may have the full measure of my joy within them" (John 17:13).

Daily Master Communication Guide

Matthew 21:12-16

What God said to me:

What I said to God:

 During your quiet time today read *Matthew 21:12-16,* which describes ways Jesus used His emotions. Then complete the Daily Master Communication Guide in the margin.

Answer the following questions about *Matthew 21:12-16.*

The selling and buying in the temple caused different emotions in Jesus than in the chief priests and the teachers of the law. What emotions did Jesus feel, and why did He experience them?

What might have the chief priests and the teachers of the law felt and why?

The healing of the blind and lame man in the temple caused different emotions in the children than it did in the chief priests and the teachers of the law. What were the emotions the children felt, and why did they experience them?

What might have been the emotions of the chief priests and the teachers of the law and why did they experience them?

The same circumstances effect different people in different ways. You may have said that Jesus felt anger because He believed that the temple should be a house of prayer, while the chief priests and the teachers of the law might have felt indifference or perhaps joy because they believed that the temple was a place where people could buy sacrifices and keep the law. They were angry after Jesus drove out the money changers. The children may have felt joy because people were being healed and the Messiah had come, while the chief priests and the teachers of the law felt threatened because Jesus was proclaimed the Son of David (the Messiah).

Analyze *Luke 10:30-37,* in the margin on page 141. How did circumstances affect different persons in different ways?

The Levite seems to have felt indifferent. What value judgments do you think he made that produced this feeling?

The Samaritan evidently felt compassion and concern. What value judgments do you think he made that produced those feelings?

You may have answered that the Levite did not value the injured man as important or that he was in a hurry because he valued his work more than he valued the man. You may have said that the Samaritan valued the injured man enough to disrupt his plans and to contribute his resources to his healing.

Your values help you make the correct emotional response in a given situation. Too many people are glad, sad, or mad about the wrong things for the wrong reasons. If you can discern what makes you glad, sad, or mad, you can know your true values. A worldly Christian places his or her values on a self-centered life.

Think about the last time you were angry. Describe that experience.

What caused your anger? Check the items in the margin that were challenged.

Mentally check which listed items relate to the last time you felt fear, grief, joy, loneliness, anxiety, and embarrassment. Why did you feel these emotions? If you felt affirmed about the matters in the previous list, you probably experienced an emotion like joy. If you felt challenged about these matters, you probably experienced fear, anger, loneliness, or betrayal. Often, a person can't control emotions because they are narrowly focused on himself and arise from his worldly nature.

Read *I Corinthians 3:1-3* in the margin. Circle what Paul called these Christians who were controlled by the emotions of jealousy and strife.

You've studied the natural person and the worldly Christian (see *I Cor. 3:1-3*). This week you'll learn about the spiritual Christian, another part of the Disciple's Personality. Spiritual Christians have strong emotions, but they have learned to control their responses to emotions instead of letting emotions control their responses. A spiritual Christian relies on the Holy Spirit instead of the flesh.

RELYING ON THE SPIRIT

 Read your Scripture-memory verses, *Galatians 5:22-23*. What do these verses say about the Holy Spirit's role in self-control?

When the Holy Spirit transforms you, He is present in your life to give you the ability to control your emotions. The Holy Spirit can even influence you as you relate to persons whom you do not particularly like or who do not like you.

Spend time with someone you don't like or who doesn't like you. Share with the group what happened.

You may think: *I could never do something kind for or reach out to someone who dislikes me. If I tried, I'd lose my temper.* You may not be able to, but the Holy Spirit can give you that ability by influencing you and renewing your mind.

Ask the Holy Spirit to help you master your emotions and be willing to reach out to others in difficult situations.

"A man was going down from Jerusalem to Jericho, when he fell into the hands of robbers. They stripped him of his clothes, beat him and went away, leaving him half dead. A priest happened to be going down the same road, and when he saw the man, he passed by on the other side. So too, a Levite, when he came to the place and saw him, passed by on the other side. But a Samaritan, as he traveled, came where the man was; and when he saw him, he took pity on him. He went to him and bandaged his wounds, pouring on oil and wine. Then he put the man on his own donkey, took him to an inn and took care of him. The next day he took out two silver coins and game them to the innkeeper. 'Look after him,' he said, 'and when I return I will reimburse you for any extra expense you may have.'

"Which of these three do you think was a neighbor to the man who fell into the hands of robbers?" The expert in the law replied, "The one who had mercy on him." Jesus told him, "God and do likewise" (Luke 10:30-37).

❑ **My position or reputation**
❑ **My plans**
❑ **My possessions**
❑ **My rights**
❑ **My physical needs**
❑ **My identity**
❑ **My ideas**
❑ **My desires**

Brothers, I could not address you as spiritual but as worldly—mere infants in Christ. I gave you milk, not solid food, for you were not yet ready for it. Indeed, you are still not ready. You are still worldly. For since there is jealousy and quarreling among you, are you not worldly? Are you not acting like mere men? (1 Cor. 3:1-3).

Taking Positive Steps

Your emotions cause you to act, but you can also act your way into an emotion.

Acknowledge the emotion.
Consider why you have it.
Thank God that He will help you master it.
Identify the biblical response to it.
Obey the Holy Spirit's leading.
Nurture the appropriate fruit of the Spirit.

He took Peter and the two sons of Zebedee along with him, and he began to be sorrowful and troubled. Then he said to them, "My soul is overwhelmed with sorrow to the point of death. Stay here and keep watch with me" (Matt. 26:37-38).

❒ disappointed
❒ satisfied
❒ frightened
❒ jubilant
❒ betrayed
❒ hopeful
❒ lonely
❒ victorious
❒ helpless
❒ calm
❒ abandoned
❒ excited
❒ embarrassed
❒ assured
❒ confused
❒ validated
❒ other:_____
_____
_____

Sometimes you may believe that you can't master your emotions. You may feel that when they roll over you like a wave, you have no choice but to drift along with them. However, you are not helpless in learning to control your emotions. The Holy Spirit can help you when you are tempted to give in to your emotions.

I have written a specific course of action to help you master your emotions. It is known by the simple acrostic ACTION. Emotions are closely tied to actions. Your emotions cause you to act, but you can also act your way into an emotion. Read the acrostic in the margin showing what ACTION means. Begin learning each step.

Over the next few days you'll examine each element of this ACTION plan to learn how to deal with your emotions.

ACKNOWLEDGE THE EMOTION

Step one: Acknowledge the emotion. Denying or suppressing your emotions doesn't help. Have you heard someone shout through clenched teeth, "I am not angry!"? The words are entirely different from the emotion communicated. You can deal with an emotion only if you recognize it.

Read *Matthew 26:37-38* in the margin. What was the first thing Jesus did about His grief and distress as He faced the cross?

Jesus didn't try to deny or suppress His grief and distress as He faced the cross but admitted that He was sorrowful and began to pray. Burying an emotion can cause it to emerge in an unhealthy way later. Suppressing emotions can make you physically ill as well as add to the emotional load you carry.

Learning to identify your exact emotion will help you acknowledge your feelings. For example, you may think you are feeling sad about a matter when a closer look reveals that you actually feel lonely, abandoned, helpless, or overwhelmed. Giving an exact name to an emotion helps with the later steps of this action plan. Try this activity to identify emotions more accurately.

Reflect on the last time you felt a strong emotion. Check in the margin the feeling or feelings that most described you at that time.

CONSIDER WHY YOU HAVE THE EMOTION

Step two: Consider why you have the emotion. After you've acknowledged a feeling, it's important to understand why you are experiencing it. Doing this may not be as simple as you think. Sometimes an event that occurred hours or days before is still in your subconscious, causing an emotional reaction. Try this exercise.

Identify an emotion you had recently: _____

Why did you feel this way? Check all appropriate responses.

❑ **My physical condition**

❑ **My flesh (sinful desires)**

❑ **My relationship with God**

❑ **What someone did to me or for me**

❑ **What someone said to me or about me**

❑ **My thoughts**

❑ **My will**

❑ **Other:_____**

_____

_____

You may have identified that you felt confused because of something someone said to you. For example, when your coach questioned whether you have the skills to play, you were confused because you've trained and you thought that qualified you. Or maybe you identified feeling embarrassed about the physical condition of your body. Identifying the underlying cause of an emotion is a big step toward mastering your reaction to that emotion.

This week's memory verses, *Galatians 5:22-23,* emphasize self-control. The verses also list characteristics you'll have if the Spirit controls your life. In the margin list the nine fruit of the Spirit. Check your work by referring to page 138.

Learning the next portion of the Disciple's Personality will reinforce the first two steps you have studied for mastering your emotions.

LEARNING THE DISCIPLE'S PERSONALITY

Read the section "The Spiritual Christian" (p. 216) in the Disciple's Personality presentation.

Begin drawing the Spiritual Christian portion of the Disciple's Personality. The basic diagram is drawn for you below. Close the door of the flesh as you draw a cross in the center of the circle to encompass *spirit, flesh, mind, will,* and *emotions.* Write *crucified* across flesh. Above the circle write The Spiritual Christian. Refer to the Disciple's Personality presentation (pp. 212–18) if you need help. By the end of this study you'll be able to draw the complete Disciple's Personality and to explain it in your own words.

Identifying the underlying cause of an emotion is a big step toward mastering your reaction to that emotion.

Fruit of the Spirit

1.
2.
3.
4.
5.
6.
7.
8.
9.

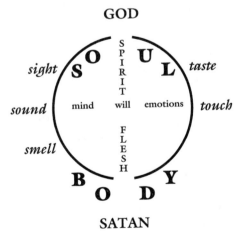

GOD

SATAN

I, _____, am crucified with Christ and I no longer live, but Christ lives in me. The life I live in the body, I, _____, live by faith in the Son of God, who loved me and gave Himself for me.

The World's Way

The acts of the sinful nature are obvious: sexual immorality, impurity and debauchery…I warn you, as I did before, that those who live like this will not inherit the kingdom of God (Gal. 5:19-21).

Now you must rid yourselves of all such things as these: anger, rage, malice, slander, and filthy language from your lips (Col. 3:8).

Do not let any unwholesome talk come out of your mouths, but only what is helpful for building others up according to their needs, that it may benefit those who listen (Eph. 4:29).

The Spirit's Way

The Fruit of the Spirit is love, joy, peace, patience, kindness, goodness, faithfulness, gentleness and self-control. Against such things there is no law (Gal. 5:22-23).

You have taken off your old self with its practices and have put on the new self, which is being renewed in knowledge in the image of its Creator (Col. 3:9-10).

Be imitators of God, therefore, as dearly loved children, and live a life of love, just as Christ loved us and gave himself up for us as a fragrant offering and sacrifice to God (Eph. 5:1-2).

Read *Galatians 2:20: I have been crucified with Christ and I no longer live, but Christ lives in me. The life I live in the body, I live by faith in the Son of God, who loved me and gave himself for me (Gal. 2:20).* **Can you make the statement Paul made? In the margin, write your name in the blanks in this adaptation of** *Galatians 2:20.*

Below are five statements. Write *S* beside the statements that describe the spiritual Christian.
___ **1. Puts aside the old selfish desires to death**
___ **2. Is promised victory over the world, the flesh, and the devil**
___ **3. Sets aside the lusts of the flesh**
___ **4. Has the Holy Spirit dwelling in his or her personality**
___ **5. Has God in control of both soul and body**

A spiritual Christian sets aside old ways. A spiritual Christian can do this because God promises victory over Satan, the world, the flesh, and the devil. The Holy Spirit, dwelling in a Christian's personality, gives God control of both soul and body. All five statements describe the spiritual Christian.

IN THE CARPENTER'S SHOP

Are you continuing to set aside, or tear down, the old self and to add new, Christ-like traits to your character?

Read the Scriptures in the margin, which relate to the improper use of language. From the verses marked "The World's Way" identify a specific behavior that you want to get rid of. From the verses marked "The Spirit's Way" identify an action you'll take to replace it. I've given you an example.

Here is an example.
Behavior I want to work on: saying hateful things about others
An action I'll take to put off the old self: stop being critical of my friends
An action I'll take to let the Holy Spirit make me more like Christ: consciously be loving in my conversations about and to others

Now you try it.
Behavior I want to work on:
An action I'll take to put off the old self:
An action I'll take to let the Holy Spirit make me more like Christ:

 In your quiet time today read *Galatians 2:11-21.* **Then complete the Daily Master Communication Guide on page 145.**

 Pray for your family members and relatives. Remember to keep a record of your prayers and answers to them on your Prayer-Covenant List (p. 205).

DAY 3

Giving Thanks in All Things

Sometimes people are unable to identify the causes of their emotions. Did you check one of the feelings listed on page 142 or wrote another one in the blank, but when you tried to determine the cause of it, you were clueless. Or perhaps you sensed that your emotion was out of proportion to the event that caused it.

For example, maybe you feel a deep sense of anger because your teacher overlooked you in your school's awards ceremony, but you're puzzled about why an innocent oversight like this caused such strong feelings. Or you may know that you feel lonely and abandoned when a friend forgets to meet you, but you don't understand why it's so hard to accept her apology for her mistake. If this is your situation, talk to your youth minister or to a Christian counselor or participate in a Christ-centered support group that helps people understand more about their emotions.[1] A person can take big steps toward mastering his or her emotions by discovering the deeper issues behind the strong feelings.

THANK GOD THAT HE WILL HELP YOU MASTER THE EMOTION
Step three: Thank God that He will help you master the emotion. Observe where this step fits into the ACTION acrostic.

Recall the key words in the first two steps in the ACTION acrostic.

A _____ the emotion.
C _____ why you have it.
T hank God that He will help you master it.
I dentify the biblical response to it.
O bey the Holy Spirit's leading.
N urture the appropriate fruit of the Spirit.

Read *Psalm 42*. Then complete the Daily Master Communication Guide in the margin on page 146. In *Psalm 42* what are the action steps David took when he felt strong emotion about his sin?

In grief about the death of his son and about his own spiritual condition, David took action steps that are good examples for us. David admitted that he was down, analyzed why he felt this strong emotion, and thanked God because he believed that God would help him.

You don't have to understand a situation to believe that God will work in it and to be grateful that He will do so.

Read *1 Thessalonians 5:18* in the margin. In which situations are you to give thanks?

Daily Master Communication Guide

Galatians 2:11-21

What God said to me:

What I said to God:

Give thanks in all circumstances, for this is God's will for you in Christ Jesus (1 Thess. 5:18).

We know that in all things God works for the good of those who love him, who have been called according to his purpose (Rom. 8:28).

About midnight Paul and Silas were praying and singing hymns to God, and the other prisoners were listening to them (Acts 16:25).

Read *Romans 8:28* in the margin. Why can a person of faith give thanks in everything?

Read *Acts 16:25* in the margin. How did Paul and Silas prevent their situation from producing harmful emotions?

You are to give thanks in all things, not just the ones you understand or the ones that please you. If you are a person of faith, you can do this because you believe that God will work all things together for good. Paul and Silas prayed and sang hymns to keep themselves from reacting harmfully to being jailed. When by faith you trust God to work in a situation and when you thank Him for doing so, your mind is open to consider the benefits that may result.

List benefits that might result from having the following emotions.

Fear:_____
Anger:_____
Loneliness:_____
Joy:_____
Jealousy:_____

Even though you may not like to think about feeling fear, anger, loneliness, or jealousy, these emotions can have good results. Fear may keep you from taking unnecessary risks. Anger might lead you to right a wrong or an injustice. Loneliness may cause you to rely on God to fill the emptiness in your life. Jealousy can make you realize that you need to work harder in a relationship. Joy may cause you to be kind to others or to praise God for a development in your life.

 Work on your memory verses, *Galatians 5:22-23*. Say them aloud to a friend. Share how the Holy Spirit is helping you learn to have self-control, the final fruit of the Spirit mentioned.

IN THE CARPENTER'S SHOP
What progress are you making in getting rid of the old self and adding new behaviors to your life?

Yesterday you identified a behavior you hoped to put away in order to build Christlike character in the way you use language. Today describe an instance in which you have acted to set aside the old behavior.____

Prayer and study of the Word often helps you make progress toward putting off the old self and adding Christlike thoughts and actions to your life. Besides reading the Word, you can also receive insight by hearing the Word preached or taught. Many times insight from a preacher, speaker, or Bible-study leader is the exact tool the Holy Spirit uses to help you meet your goal.

Daily Master Communication Guide

Psalm 42

What God said to me:

What I said to God:

Read "How to Listen to God's Word" and answer the questions.

HOW TO LISTEN TO GOD'S WORD

1. Evaluate what kind of hearer you are. Read *Matthew 13:3-23* and classify yourself as one of the following.

   a. *Apathetic hearer:* hears the word but is not prepared to receive and understand it (see *v. 19*).

   Do I let the message go in one ear and out the other? ❏ **Yes** ❏ **No**

   b. *Superficial hearer:* receives the word temporarily but does not let it take root in the heart (see *vv. 20-21*).

   Do I accept what is said without applying it to myself? ❏ **Yes** ❏ **No**

   c. *Preoccupied hearer:* receives the word but lets the worries of this world and the desire for things choke it (see *v. 22*).

   Do I remember to practice the message during the week, or do I let other priorities crowd it out? ❏ **Yes** ❏ **No**

   d. *Reproducing hearer:* receives the word, understands it, bears fruit, and brings forth results (see *v. 23*).

   Does the message yield maximal fruit in my life? ❏ **Yes** ❏ **No**

2. Be alert for a word from God: *Be quick to hear (Jas. 1:19,* RSV).

3. Remove sin so that the word can be planted in your heart (see *Jas. 1:21*).

4. Pay attention to what the Bible says about you, just as you would to your reflection in a mirror (see *Jas. 1:23*).

   a. Takes notes on the Hearing the Word form (see p. 220). List the date, place, speaker, text, and title of the message if given.

   b. Write the points of the message as the speaker presents them.

   c. Under each point write explanation, illustrations, and application.

   d. Write any specific statements the Spirit impresses on you.

   e. Summarize the main point the speaker wants you to do, be, and/or feel as a result of this sermon. Use the following questions to write your summary.

   • What did God say to me through this message? Write the specific point that you feel God wanted you to hear in the message.

   • How does my life measure up to this word? Look in the mirror of the Word and recognize ways you fall short of what God has said. Be specific.

   • What specific, immediate, measurable, timely, and attainable actions will I take to bring my life in line with this word?

   • What truth do I need to study further? The Lord may impress you to search the Scriptures for more information on a specific subject mentioned.

5. Do the Word, and you will be blessed in what you do (see *Jas. 1:25*). Check yourself several times in the days that follow to determine whether you have incorporated the message into your life and have begun to bear fruit from it.

 Write important sermon points on the Hearing the Word form on page 220. Copy the form to use with all sermons.

DAY 4

A Biblical Response

Step four: Identify the biblical response to the emotion. Review the steps in the plan.

IDENTIFY THE BIBLICAL RESPONSE TO THE EMOTION
Supply the key words in the first three steps you have studied.

A_____ **the emotion.**
C_____ **why you have it.**
T_____ **God that He will help you master it.**
Identify the biblical response to it.
Obey the Holy Spirit's leading.
Nurture the appropriate fruit of the Spirit.

Emotions are spontaneous, but the actions they produce don't have to be. The Bible teaches that you're responsible for how you choose to let your emotions cause you to behave. You can't escape responsibility by blaming your behavior on a negative feeling or on the person or circumstance causing that feeling.

You may believe that someone wronged you or that your family background programmed you to act a certain way. You may think: *I can't help that I act this way. He made me angry when he criticized me.* But can someone really make you angry and make you respond improperly? Regardless of what starts the event, the choice of how to respond is yours. You can sin in that response, or you can choose to honor Christ. One sin doesn't justify another.

In the following case studies underline each person's blaming response.

It was Carlene's brother's turn to clean the kitchen after dinner, but her parents told her to do it. In her haste to go on a date she carelessly stacked the dishes, causing several to fall and break. When her parents pointed out her carelessness, Carlene raged: "What about all of the wrong things you do? You're not perfect either, you know!"

Jed's father was an alcoholic. Jed didn't have a role model for dependability. As a teenager, Jed began drinking alcohol. When his teacher expressed concern, Jed yelled back: "It's all my father's fault! He never told me not to drink! This is just the way I am!"

Wanda's father beat her, and her mother never acted lovingly toward her. As an adult, Wanda was unforgiving and refused to communicate with her parents. She told her pastor, "I hate them for the way they treated me."

In each case the individual blamed someone else for his or her wrong actions.

Even though their home situations may have been bad Carlene, Jed, and Wanda had choices whether to sin or take responsibility for their actions. The Bible gives principles for responding to emotions. The better you know the Bible, the more easily you can apply it to deal with all emotions.

Read the Scriptures in the margin. Write in your own words biblical responses to the following emotions.

Hate *(Luke 6:27-28):*

Anxiety *(Phil. 4:6-7):*

Joy *(Phil. 4:4):*

Anger *(Eph. 4:25-26,31-32):*

Envy *(1 Pet. 2:1; 1 Cor. 13:4):*

For *hate* you may have written that the biblical response is to do good to those who hate you; for *anxiety*, that you are to pray to God and not to be anxious; for *joy*, that you are to acknowledge the source of goodness; for *anger*, that you are to avoid sinning from anger and to settle matters quickly; for *envy*, that you are to lay envy aside and to love others.

Based on the Scriptures you read in the previous exercise, describe in the margin, how the characters in the three case studies might have responded in a Christ-honoring way if they had sought biblical solutions for their emotions.

You might have answered something like this: Instead of turning on her parents in anger, Carlene could have set a Christian example by asking her parents to sit down with her and calmly listen to her concerns. Instead of blaming his family background and continuing the cycle of alcohol abuse, Jed could have reached out to a dependable adult family member. Jed could have talked to his youth minister, a school counselor, or professional Christian Counselor. Instead of harboring bitterness toward her parents, Wanda could have prayed that the Holy Spirit would help her forgive. She might have sought the help of a professional Christian counselor or a Christ-centered support group to learn positive ways to relate to her parents despite her painful past.

Say aloud from memory *Galatians 5:22-23.* **Choose one of the nine fruit of the Spirit and describe below how you plan to use it to master your emotions. Each fruit of the Spirit is not only an emotion but also a tool for mastering your emotions.**

"Love your enemies, do good to those who hate you, bless those who curse you, pray for those who mistreat you" (Luke 6:27-28).

Do not be anxious about anything, but in everything, by prayer and petition, with thanksgiving, present your requests to God. And the peace of God, which transcends all understanding, will guard your hearts and your minds in Christ Jesus (Phil 4:6-7).

Rejoice in the Lord always (Phil. 4:4).

Each of you must put off falsehood and speak truthfully to his neighbor, for we are all members of one body. "In your anger do not sin." Do not let the sun go down while you are still angry.
 Get rid of all bitterness, rage and anger, brawling and slander, along with every form of malice. Be kind and compassionate to one another, forgiving each other, just as in Christ God forgave you (Eph. 4:25-26, 31-32).

Rid yourselves of all malice and all deceit, hypocrisy, envy, and slander of every kind. Like newborn babies, crave pure spiritual milk, so that by it you may grow up in your salvation, now that you have tasted that the Lord is good (1 Pet. 2:1).

Love…does not envy (1 Cor. 13:4).

Carlene:

Jed:

Wanda:

**Daily Master
Communication Guide**

John 19:17-37

What God said to me:

What I said to God:

HOW WOULD CHRIST RESPOND?

As you think about ways Christ would have you master your emotions, you can remember His example on the cross—the ultimate example of a person's control of emotions. Think of the ways Christ could have responded to this event: He could have raged, threatened, blamed, or scolded. He could have called on angels to protect Him. Instead, He sought God's will in His responses, even to the end. Certainly, He expressed His sorrow, as you studied in day 2. He expressed His concern for His mother. He expressed His human physical need. But the ultimate mastery occurred when He surrendered everything to God's will, even when that meant suffering and dying on the cross.

 Read *John 19:17-37*, the passage describing Jesus' death on the cross, during your quiet time today. See how God speaks to you. Complete the Daily Master Communication Guide in the margin.

Also during your quiet time today hold the nail your leader gave you in your group session for five minutes. Feel and smell the nail. Press the point of the nail against your palm. Think about Christ's suffering for you and let the Holy Spirit show you the importance of Jesus' pain for you. Read aloud *Galatians 2:20* as you think about His suffering: *I have been crucified with Christ and I no longer live, but Christ lives in me. The life I live in the body, I live by faith in the Son of God, who loved me and gave himself for me.*

IN THE CARPENTER'S SHOP

If Christ is the Master of your life, you'll want to be like Him—even in your language. How is the Holy Spirit helping you tear down the old self and replace old behaviors with new ones?

List a new thought or action that replaced the one you tore down in the way you use language. How are you working to put this new thought or action in place of the old?

DAY 5

The Higher Calling

OBEY THE HOLY SPIRIT'S LEADING

Step five: Obey the Holy Spirit's leading.

In the margin write the action steps you have studied so far. Look at the way step five fits into the ACTION acrostic. This time I will supply the key word and will let you finish the statement.

Natural and worldly persons want to do what their emotions, mind, or will tells them. In contrast, spiritual persons obey the higher call to do what the Holy Spirit reveals. Doing what God says is right, rather than what you want to do, is a conscious act of the will. Christians understand their obligations to act rightly toward others even if they don't feel like doing so. If you wait until you feel like doing right, you may find yourself excusing your failure.

Read the following accounts. Write _E_ beside those that describe someone who used feelings as an excuse for irresponsibility. Write _R_ beside those in which the person acted responsibly.

_____ Jim slammed on his brakes and bore down on the horn while an elderly man crept across the street. Then Jim sped away so that he wouldn't miss the next light.

_____ When a fellow student shouted a curse word at Matt for getting too close to his car in traffic, he yelled back, "Same to you, jerk."

_____ A woman tried on many pairs of shoes in the store before announcing that she really couldn't afford to buy any. Then she asked directions to another shoe store. The teenage salesperson drew her a map and thanked her for stopping by.

You likely recognized that the person in the last illustration—the salesperson who went the extra mile—as the only one who dealt responsibly with emotions.

Not only do your feelings influence the way you act, but the way you act also determines how you feel. You can change your feelings by changing your actions, as the saying "Act your way into a new feeling" states. Jesus' solution for many emotional responses was to command an action rather than a feeling. Read _Matthew 5:24_ and _Matthew 7:1-2_ in the margin.

Read _1 Corinthians 13:4-7_ in the margin. When the Bible tells you to love your fellow Christians, love is described as (check one)—
  ❑ **an emotional feeling;** ❑ **a way of behaving.**

Love is something you do. Love manifests itself in the way you act. Acting lovingly toward someone even if you don't feel like doing so is the essence of love. The Holy Spirit can help you do this.

A _____
  _____.
C _____
  _____.
T _____
  _____.
I _____
  _____.
Obey _____
  _____.
<u>**Nurture the appropriate fruit of the Spirit.**</u>

"Leave your gift there in front of the altar. First go and be reconciled to your brother; then come and offer your gift" (Matt. 5:24).

"Do not judge, or you too will be judged. For in the same way you judge others, you will be judged, and with the measure you use, it will be measured to you" (Matt. 7:1-2).

Love is patient, love is kind. It does not envy, it does not boast, it is not proud. It is not rude, it is not self-seeking, it is not easily angered, it keeps no record of wrongs. Love does not delight in evil but rejoices with the truth. It always protects, always trusts, always hopes, always perseveres (1 Cor. 13:4-7).

He that is slow to anger is better than the mighty; and he that ruleth his spirit than he that taketh a city (Prov. 16:32, KJV).

A_____

_____.

C_____

_____.

T_____

_____.

I_____

_____.

O_____

_____.

Nurture the appropriate fruit of the Spirit.

❐ **love**
❐ **joy**
❐ **peace**
❐ **patience**
❐ **kindness**
❐ **goodness**
❐ **faithfulness**
❐ **gentleness**
❐ **self-control**

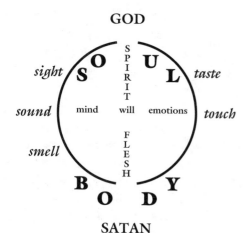

Read *Proverbs 16:32* in the margin. This verse says that a person who remains in control of self is stronger than the strong and mightier than the mighty. A person who declines to reply in anger, conquering his or her emotions, demonstrates more strength than does a person who conquers a city.

 During your quiet time today read *Matthew 26:57-68,* about a time when Jesus maintained self-control. Then complete the Daily Master Communication Guide in the margin on page 153.

NURTURE THE APPROPRIATE FRUIT OF THE SPIRIT
Step six: Nurture the appropriate fruit of the Spirit.

In the ACTION acrostic in the margin write the steps you've studied.

Each fruit of the Spirit is more than an emotion. Each is a stable trait of character. You develop each by having a close relationship with Christ through the Holy Spirit and by growing in maturity through experience.

 Say aloud your memory verses, *Galatians 5:22-23.* Then in the margin check which fruit of the Spirit you believe you most need to develop in mastering your emotions. You may check more than one. How do you plan to develop this trait or these traits of character?_____

_____

Ask God to help you develop this trait of character you identified and to help you make this a meaningful part of your life in the Spirit.

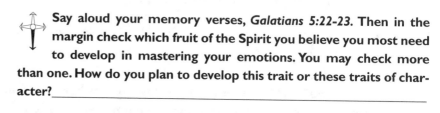 **Say again the verses you memorized in previous weeks, *Philippians 2:13* and *Romans 12:1-2.***

Before your next group session apply the ACTION steps to an emotion. Write the results at the end of this week's work, page 154. Be prepared to describe your experience to your fellow group members.

IN THE CARPENTER'S SHOP
Review the progress you have made this week in building Christlike character. How is the Holy Spirit helping you in your use of pure language?

Name the behavior you have put aside and what Christ has been adding to your character this week._____

LEARNING THE DISCIPLE'S PERSONALITY
Review the Disciple's Personality. The basic diagram has been drawn for you. Draw the elements of the spiritual Christian. Label the drawing *The Spiritual Christian* and write *Galatians 2:20* under the label. Refer to the Disciple's Personality presentation (pp. 212–19) if you need help.

An inmate in a penitentiary in Texas, told his MasterLife leader that concepts of the Disciple's Personality now keep him from reacting violently when people make him angry. "My old way was to react from my emotions," the inmate said. "When I was in control, if someone got in my face, I would go off. I would shoot him, stab him, whatever was convenient. Part of the game I would play was to be a tough guy, a bad guy. It's one way you think you win respect, but people don't respect you. They fear you. Respect is something you get from people when you show love and kindness and consideration."

A spiritual Christian develops Christlike character and shares the good news to help others have the assurance of knowing that through Christ they can master their emotions. How do you share your joy in Christ and your assurance that the Holy Spirit will help you maintain self-control?

 Read the following guidelines for writing your testimony. Complete the activities as you read.

TESTIMONY OUTLINE
Witness means "someone who gives evidence." You have evidence of a changed life through the indwelling Christ. You need to verbalize that witness—to tell others who Christ is, what He has done, and how much He means to you.

These guidelines will help you prepare a basic testimony of your salvation experience. During the next three weeks you'll learn to adapt your basic testimony to meet the needs of particular witnessing opportunities.

The apostle Paul verbalized his witness at every opportunity to everyone who would listen. In the margin read the words Paul wrote in *Romans 1:16*.

Even Christians who are skilled in giving their testimonies and in adapting their testimonies to specific situations begin with a basic testimony of conversion.

The Scriptures provide at least two detailed records of occasions when Paul verbalized his witness, *Acts 22:1-15* and *Acts 26:9-20*. In both cases Paul used his conversion experience as evidence for his witness. In both cases he mentioned four facts in the same order as they appear in the chart in the following activity.

Read *Acts 22:1-15* and *Acts 26:9-20* in your Bible. Use the following chart to analyze Paul's testimony and to identify the four necessary components of a salvation testimony. In the proper column write the references of two to five consecutive verses from *Acts 22* in which Paul told about each of four parts of his conversion experience. Then follow the same instructions when Paul verbalized his witness in *Acts 26*. You should be able to find each of these four components in from two to four verses, and all of these should come in the order the chart lists them. I have done the first one.

	Acts 22	Acts 26
1. Paul had not always followed Christ.	3–5	
2. God began to deal with Paul's rebellion.		
3. Paul received Christ as his Lord.		
4. Paul's new life was centered on Christ's purposes.		

Daily Master Communication Guide

Matthew 26:57-68

What God said to me:

What I said to God:

I am not ashamed of the gospel, because it is the power of God for the salvation of everyone who believes: first for the Jew, then for the Gentile (Rom. 1:16).

1. My life and attitudes before I followed Christ:

You may be amazed to discover that most unbelievers have never heard anyone share information of the type Paul shared in verbalizing his witness. Each conversion experience is different. Therefore, your testimony of how you came to know Christ is personal and unique and evidence that only you can give.

Although your conversion experience is unique, it can probably be outlined in much the same way Paul outlined his. In verbalizing your witness, share the same four types of information that Paul shared, even though the evidence itself will sound quite different.

In the margin write four facts about your conversion that should be shared with unbelievers.

2. How I realized that God was speaking to me:

You don't need to prepare enough material for a sermon. Witnessing is not preaching; it's giving evidence. If you can develop even a one-minute testimony of your conversion experience, you'll find opportunities to share it.

Check to see if you identified these verses on the chart of the components of Paul's testimonies: *Acts 22: verses 3-5,6-9,10-13,14-15. Acts 26: verses 9-12,13-18,19,19-20.*

HAS THIS WEEK MADE A DIFFERENCE?
Review "My Walk with the Master This Week" at the beginning of this week's material. Mark the activities you've finished by drawing vertical lines in the diamonds beside them. Finish any incomplete activities.

3. How I became a Christian:

Write the results of your applying the ACTION plan to an emotion.

4. What being a Christian means to me:

I hope that you feel more confident in your ability to act in Christ-honoring ways as the Holy Spirit helps you bring your emotions under control. You may not be able to achieve the ideal results instantly. Changing old patterns takes practice. Don't be discouraged if you occasionally revert to old, out-of-control behaviors. When you do, ask forgiveness and ask God to make you aware of the Holy Spirit's presence in your life to help you make better choices.

---

[1]The following Christ-centered support-group resources are recommended to help you understand more about your emotions:
McGee, Robert S. *The Search, Youth Life Support Edition.* Nashville: LifeWay Press, 1993.
Springle, Pat, and Susan Lanford. *Untangling Relationships, Youth Life Support Group Series.* Nashville: LifeWay Press, 1995.

2. Participation in the world—the way you act

3. Communication with others—the way you relate to others

Without a body you would have no contact with the physical world.

Give an example in the margin of how your body enables you to be involved in the world through each of the three functions.

You may have answered something like this: 1. No one is exactly like me. The way I look makes it possible for others to identify me. 2. I can experience the world, and I can do God's business. 3. Talking and body language are important in spreading the gospel.

Your body allows you to influence the created order. Because you have mobility, you can move from place to place to perform God's tasks. Because you have strength in your body, you can accept assignments for Him.

After reading *Genesis 1:27-28* in the margin, list three verbs that tell three different things God intended for human beings to do in the world.

God expected you to be fruitful and multiply, to subdue the earth and make it useful, and to master or rule over living creatures. Your body makes you feel at home in the created order.

How do your body's three functions help you do what God asks you to do in relating to the world? Write your answers in the margin.

Here are possible answers: Because of identification—the way I look—someone may be attracted to my unique identity and may want to get acquainted. If God leads us, marriage and a family may be the result. Participation—the way I act—gives me dominion over other creatures and the ability to be on mission with God in the world. Communication—the way I relate—makes it possible for me to lead, make decisions, and communicate them.

 Read aloud this week's memory verses, *1 Corinthians 6:19-20.* How does God intend for you to regard your body?

God intends for you to highly regard your body because it's the dwelling for His Spirit. You likely want to provide only the best dwelling for the Spirit of God.

Being disciplined isn't in my nature. The Holy Spirit can control what I can't control. I say again and again, "Lord, I can't control this; will You control it?" Then He takes over and controls the part of my life that my physical body might lead me to misuse or misapply.

Stop and ask the Holy Spirit to work in your life so that you have victory every day with God—in the control of your body and in other areas that come to mind.

---

1. Identification as a unique person: *clean*
1 in 1 million

2. Participation in the world: *Calm*

3. Communication with others: *like me anyone else*

God created man in his own image, in the image of God he created him; male and female he created them,. God blessed them and said to them, "Be fruitful and increase in number; fill the earth and subdue it. Rule over the fish of the sea and the birds of the air and over every living creature that moves on the ground" (Gen. 1:27-28).

Three Verbs

1. *Rule over*

2. *Increase*

3. _____

1. Identification—the way you look:

2. Participation—the way you act:

3. Communication—the way you relate to others:

The World's Way

Do not be foolish, but understand what the Lord's will is. Do not get drunk on wine, which leads to debauchery (Eph. 4:17-18).

The acts of the sinful nature are obvious: sexual immorality, impurity, and debauchery…I warn you, as I did before, that those who live like this will not inherit the kingdom of God (Gal. 5:19-21).

Put to death, therefore, whatever belongs to your earthly nature: sexual immorality, impurity, lust, evil desires and greed, which is idolatry (Col. 3:5).

The Spirit's Way

Instead, be filled with the Spirit (Eph. 5:18).

Live by the Spirit, and you will not gratify the desires of the sinful nature (Gal. 5:16).

Since, then, you have been raised with Christ, set your hearts on things above, where Christ is seated at the right hand of God. Set your minds on things above, not on earthly things. For you died, and your life is now hidden with Christ in God (Col. 3:1-3).

IN THE CARPENTER'S SHOP

One way to gain control over your body by developing your character. The Holy Spirit can help change your character when you are in Christ. How are you working to put off the old person and to put on the new?

Read the Scriptures in the margin that relate to abusing the body. From the verses marked "The World's Way" identify a specific behavior you want to get rid of. From the verses marked "The Spirit's Way" identify an action you'll take to replace it. I have given you an example. Each day this week you will record your progress in working on this behavior. If this matter is too personal to write about here, you may write about it elsewhere, but please address this critical change.

Here is an example.
Behavior I want to work on: drinking substances that are harmful to me as a way of dealing with emotional pain
An action I will take to put off the old self: inquire about a support group that helps persons overcome alcohol dependency
An action I will take to let the Holy Spirit make me more like Christ: face my pain and rely on Christ's power to help me through difficult issues

Now you try it.
Behavior I want to work on:

An action I will take to put off the old self:

An action I will take to let the Holy Spirit make me more like Christ:

Read *James 3:1-12*, which discusses the power of the tongue, in your quiet time today. Then complete the Daily Master Communication Guide in the margin on page 156.

How are you progressing in writing your testimony? Preparing your testimony and the encouragement of your *MasterLife* group can help you become bolder in your efforts to witness. Tell a Christian friend how you began to prepare your testimony in week 9. Explain what you wrote in the outline and how you plan to expand it.

DAY 2

Doing Things Your Own Way

Adam and Eve failed to do what God asked. Instead of being partners with God in ruling the world, they decided to do things their own way. The result was chaos. The good bodies of those two were invaded by a sinful nature.

What is another word for *body* that also means "the sinful nature"?

The words translated *flesh* in the Bible have two distinct meanings: "the physical body" and "the sinful nature."

WHAT GOD EXPECTS

God created the physical body to be good, but when people sinned, the body was affected. Although the body itself is not evil in itself, it is weak and susceptible to the flesh (the sinful nature). God expects you to honor Him through your physical body and to decline to let the flesh, or the sinful nature, take over. The body has the capacity to do good if the flesh isn't in control.

Read in the margin the Scriptures that show the possibility of using the body for good. Match the references with the statements below.

B 1. *Genesis 1:31*   a. Jesus compared His church to His body.

A 2. *John 1:14*   b. Human bodies were created as good and were pleasing to God.

C 3. *Romans 8:23*   c. Your body will be redeemed.

D 4. *Ephesians 1:22-23*   d. Jesus was incarnated in a human body.

Your body can be used for good. The fact that Jesus was incarnated in a human body testifies to the fact that God looked with favor on the physical body. You won't always have this body but will someday redeem it for a form that Jesus wants you to have in heaven. The correct answers are 1. b, 2. d, 3. c, 4. a.

You've studied three facts about the nature of your body. Write in the margin what the statements mean to you.

You may have answered similar to this: 1. Because God created my body as good, He expects me to take care of it. 2. Because I've sinned, my body likes the ways of the flesh, and I must be on guard against worldly ways. 3. God can do anything, even use my weak body for His good.

To review what you learned earlier, list in the margin, the three functions your body performs that involve you in the world.

If you had difficulty recalling the three functions, refer to yesterday's lesson.

God saw all that he had made, and it was very good. And there was evening, and there was morning—the sixth day (Gen. 1:31).

The Word became flesh and made his dwelling among us. We have seen his glory, the glory of the One and Only, who came from the Father, full of grace and truth (John 1:14)

Not only so, but we ourselves, who have the firstfruits of the Spirit, groan inwardly as we wait eagerly for our adoption as sons, the redemption of our bodies (Rom. 8:23).

God placed all things under his feet and appointed him to be head over everything for the church, which is his body, the fullness of him who fills everything in every way (Eph. 1:22-23).

1. God created the body as good.

2. Something happens to the body when flesh takes over.

3. God created the body for His use.

Idetification

Participation

communication

IN THE CARPENTER'S SHOP

What progress are you making in allowing the Holy Spirit to help you put off the old self and replace it with the new?

One way to keep your body from being susceptible to un-Christlike ways is to know who you are in Christ, to stand firm in that identity, and to share your convictions with others. You grow in your faith when you give your Christian testimony. Today you'll receive specific help for writing your testimony.

 Read the following guidelines for writing your testimony and write on a separate sheet of paper information that will help you write an expanded testimony.

GUIDELINES FOR WRITING YOUR TESTIMONY

Various situations will call for you to give your testimony differently. Because each situation is unique, your testimony will be unique to each situation.

Your testimony will probably always include the four points from your basic testimony that you wrote last week. But a situation may call for you to say more about one point than the others. Or the person to whom you're witnessing identifies more closely with different examples.

This material will prepare you to write an expanded version of the basic testimony you've already developed. Place your original basic testimony where you can see it. Write each heading on a separate sheet of paper. Make notes on each sheet as you study the following material. Your goals are to—
• be certain you said all you needed to say about each part of your testimony;
• develop background information for adapting or emphasizing each part of your testimony when the occasion calls for it.

MY LIFE AND ATTITUDES BEFORE I FOLLOWED CHRIST

When you tell what your life was like before you became a Christian, share the good things as well as the bad. This allows others to identify with what you say.

Share interesting details about yourself that will make you come across as an ordinary person. Write and be prepared to talk about—
• where you lived before you became a Christian;
• what you did before you became a Christian;
• your interests and hobbies before you became a Christian;
• your priorities before you became a Christian.

Share details about your life indicating that you truly needed greater meaning and purpose. Your purpose is not to confess your evil life but to tell your story.

HOW I REALIZED THAT GOD WAS SPEAKING TO ME

Write notes explaining how God showed you His love while you were still an unbeliever. Generalize so a person can identify with your description. How, when, and where did God get through to you? What person(s) or things did He use?

HOW I BECAME A CHRISTIAN

Write how you trusted your life to Christ. Let the Bible be your authority rather than what someone said to you: Say, "Here is a Bible verse that made me realize what Jesus did for me: ..." Be sure to state that you prayed to receive Christ.

You might be inclined to use "church language" here. Be sensitive to those who will not understand the meanings of such words or who may have been frightened away by high-pressure. Review what you have written and replace church words with everyday words.

Write in your own words short statements about four important facts:
• Sin is an I-controlled life. It's failing or refusing to be what God wants you to be.
• Sin's penalty is separation from God in this life and for eternity.
• Christ paid the penalty for sin when He took your sin to the cross, accepted the judgment for it, and made it possible for you to be accepted by the Father.
• Receiving Christ is acknowledging to Him that you are a sinner, accepting forgiveness from Him, inviting Him to enter your life as your Savior and Lord, and trusting Him to do for you the things you could never do for yourself.

Check your testimony to be certain you have at least one sentence about each of these facts.

WHAT BEING A CHRISTIAN MEANS TO ME

Be careful not to give the impression that becoming a Christian automatically solved all of your problems. Describe your lifestyle as a Christian. You may not realize how different your lifestyle is from that of an unbeliever. Many things you take for granted will be significant to a non-Christian. Describe briefly the changes that have taken place in your life in the following areas.
• Relationships with family
• Use of money
• Purpose of life
• Attitude toward death
• How you deal with problems or failure
• Value of Christian friends

SUGGESTIONS FOR GIVING YOUR TESTIMONY

When you give your testimony to someone, follow these guidelines:
1. Keep it short so that your listener will not become uncomfortable.
2. Tell what happened to you. It's your story that others want to hear. Don't say "you"; say "I" and "me."
3. Avoid negative remarks. Don't criticize religious groups or a specific church.
4. Ask yourself, *If I were an unbeliever, what would this mean to me?*
5. Eliminate religious words. Lost people don't understand religious words like *repented, made a decision for Christ, invited Jesus into my heart, walked the aisle, joined the church, saved,* and *was baptized.*

IF YOU ACCEPTED CHRIST WHEN YOU WERE A CHILD

If you are from a Christian home and accepted Christ as a child, don't feel that your conversion isn't dramatic enough to share. It's always significant for an unbeliever to learn the way God enters human lives.

 Read *Acts 16:25-34*, the passage in which Paul and Silas witnessed to the jailer, in your quiet time today. Then complete the Daily Master Communication Guide in the margin.

Daily Master Communication Guide

Acts 16:25-34

What God said to me:

What I said to God:

I know that nothing good lives in me, that is, in my sinful nature. For I have the desire to do what is good, but I cannot carry it out. For what I do is not the good I want to do; no, the evil I do not want to do—this I keep on doing. Now if I do what I do not want to do, it is no longer I who do it, but it is sin living in me that does it. So I find this law at work: When I want to do good, evil is right there with me. For in my inner being I delight in God's law; but I see another law at work in the members of my body, waging war against the law of my mind and making me a prisoner of the law of sin at work within my members (Rom. 7:18-23).

What the law was powerless to do in that it was weakened by the sinful nature, God did by sending his own Son in the likeness of sinful man to be a sin offering. And so he condemned sin in sinful man (Rom. 8:3).

We know that our old self was crucified with him so that the body of sin might be done away with, that we should no longer be slaves to sin—because anyone who has died has been freed from sin (Rom. 6:6-7).

If the Spirit of him who raised Jesus from the dead is living in you, he who raised Christ from the dead will also give life to your mortal bodies through his Spirit, who lives in you (Rom. 8:11-13).

Who Is the Master of Your Body?

A newscast showed an award-winning athlete helping physically challenged young people. A few seconds later in the newscast another athlete was reported to have used illegal drugs to enhance his performance in the Olympics. Are you the master of your body or does something else control you?

THE STRUGGLE FOR CONTROL

The potential for your body to be used in positive, Christ-honoring ways is tremendous. However, in reality, your body is still subject to sin and death.

Read *Romans 7:18-23* in the margin. Under the verses, describe an experience in which you desired to do good yet did the opposite.

Maybe you answered like this: I hurt my family with my filthy speech, but I keep doing it. Overeating isn't good for me, but I do it in spite of my good intentions.

In the previous exercise you saw that the flesh tends to use the senses and the normal desires of your body to master you. Check the pursuits that have become your masters at one time or another:

❑ **food**　　　　❑ **sex**　　　　　❑ **work**　　　❑ **money**
❑ **education**　❑ **recreation**　❑ **clothing**　❑ **sports**
❑ **religion**　　❑ **others' approval**　❑ **beauty**　❑ **television**
❑ **other:**

Were you surprised to see religion in the list? If you are attending church and involving yourself in the fellowship of believers to obtain others' approval, you are motivated by the wrong reason. You can become enslaved by this worldly desire, forgetting that God calls you to serve from obedience to Him.

Read the verses in the margin. Write three primary actions Christ took to free you from bondage to the flesh.

Christs ___coming___ **condemns sin in the flesh (Rom. 8:3).**
Christs ___crucifixion___ **frees you from the bondage of the body of sin (Rom. 6:6-7).**
Christs ___ressurection___ **gives you life through the Spirit so that you can put to death the deeds of the body (Rom. 8:11-13).**

Christ's coming to earth as a human being—His incarnation—condemns sin, His crucifixion frees you from sin's bondage, and His resurrection gives you life through the Spirit. The Holy Spirit takes these three actions of Christ and makes them real in your life. Life in the Spirit applies that work of Christ to your life.

1. Say aloud this week's memory verse. 2. Continue working on *1 Corinthians 6:19-20,* by saying it aloud. 3. Ask God how He wants you to glorify Him with your body. 4. Check below commitments you will make to honor Christ with your physical body.

I will—
❑ watch my intake of empty calories that don't add to my nutrition;
❑ begin an exercise program;
❑ increase the amount of rest I get each day;
☑ look at my eating patterns and stop eating from anxiety or tension rather than from hunger;
❑ cut down on substances like caffeine that may make me irritable;
☑ stop using substances such as nicotine, alcohol, or other drugs that harm my body.

IN THE CARPENTER'S SHOP
In the previous exercise you checked commitments you'll make. Was one of these commitments similar to the step you described yesterday to get rid of a behavior? Today describe what Christ is adding to your life to replace that part of your old self. Read the verses on page 158.

You may be interested in noting how many sermons you hear in the next few weeks focus on honoring Christ with your body instead of allowing fleshly, sinful concerns to take control. Begin paying particular attention to encouragement you receive from sermons about this matter.

Continue to use the Hearing the Word form on page 220 to take notes on sermons. Especially note any sermon references that address the subjects you are studying this week.

In your quiet time today read *Judges 16:15-30,* about an Old Testament character who used his body for both good and evil. Complete the Daily Master Communication Guide in the margin.

Daily Master Communication Guide

Judges 16:15-30

What God said to me:

What I said to God:

DAY 4

Useful to the Master

I_____

C_____

R_____

We know that our old self was crucified with him so that the body of sin might be done away with, that we should no longer be slaves to sin (Rom. 6:6).

You died, and your life is now hidden with Christ in God. When Christ, who is your life, appears, then you also will appear with him in glory (Col. 3:3-4).

Those who belong to Christ Jesus have crucified the sinful nature with its passions and desires. Since we live by the Spirit, let us keep in step with the Spirit (Gal. 5:24-25).

"I have been crucified with Christ and I no longer live, b ut Christ lives in me. The life I live in the body, I live by faith in the Son of God, who loved me and gave himself for me" (Gal. 2:20).

What positive steps can you take when you find yourself doing things that are the opposite of what you know is right? You can apply to your everyday life the three actions Christ took for your salvation.

To review, in the margin list the three actions you learned in day 3.

Christ's incarnation condemns sin, His crucifixion frees you from sin's bondage, and His resurrection gives you life through the Spirit.

 Say aloud this week's memory verses, *1 Corinthians 6:19-20*. How does Christ's incarnation in you through the Holy Spirit apply to your body?

You may have written something like this: The Holy Spirit lives in me. I am God's, and my body exists to glorify God. I can use my body for His purposes.

Christ's incarnation—His coming to earth as a human being—led to His crucifixion. Christ was crucified for you.

Read the verses in the margins. Below the verse answer this question about each: How does your acceptance of Christ's crucifixion as the substitute for your crucifixion apply to your body?

You may have answered this way: 1. Because my old self was crucified with Christ, I am no longer a slave to the body of sin. I'm a new creature in Christ and can act accordingly. 2. Because I have died with Christ, I am to consider my bodily members dead to the deeds of the flesh (or I am to put to death the deeds of the flesh). 3. My sinful nature, with its lusts and desires, has been put to death; so I can walk in the Spirit as He directs my thoughts and actions.

Paul said, *If we died with Christ, we believe that we will also live with Him (Rom. 6:8).* Christ rose and gave you new birth.

INSTRUMENTS OF RIGHTEOUSNESS

Read *Galatians 2:20* in the margin. How does your participation in Christ's resurrection through the new birth and His living in you apply to your body?

Read *Romans 6:11-14* in the margin and write under it the answer to this question, How does your participation in Christ's resurrection through the new birth and His living in you apply to your body?

You may have answered similar to: 1. My life now is not my own but Christ's. He reigns in my body. 2. I'm alive to God. I'll let Him reign in my body by yielding members of my body to Him as instruments of right living.

Your body won't be perfect until it's completely redeemed at Christ's return. In the meantime your identification with Christ's incarnation, crucifixion, and resurrection gives you potential for righteous living. You still have potential for unrighteous living. Scripture urges you to put to death the deeds of the flesh.

How often does Christ expect you to take up your cross?_____ How, then, can you live victoriously as you take up your cross daily? Through the Disciple's Personality presentation you've learned how to let God take control of your mind, will, emotions, and therefore your soul and body.

LEARNING THE DISCIPLE'S PERSONALITY
Read the section "Steps to Victorious Living" (p. 216) in the Disciple's Personality presentation.

 On the Disciple's Personality illustration below write the components of the spiritual Christian. Then write *Philippians 2:13* under *will*, *Ephesians 5:18* above *Spirit*, *Romans 12:2* under *mind*, *Galatians 5:22-23* under *emotions*, *Romans 6:12-13* under *flesh*, *1 Corinthians 6:19-20* on one side of the circle, and *Romans 12:1* on the other side. Refer to the Disciple's Personality presentation (pp. 212-18) if needed.

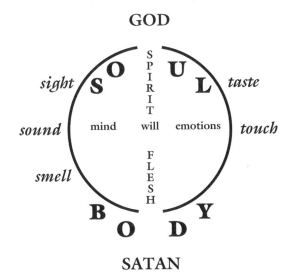

Read *John 20:1-18*, the passage that describes Jesus' resurrection, during your quiet time today. Complete the Daily Master Communication Guide in the margin.

In the same way, count yourselves dead to sin but alive to God in Christ Jesus. Therefore do not let sin reign in your mortal body so that you obey its evil desires. Do not offer the parts of your body to sin, as instruments of wickedness, but rather offer yourselves to God, as those who have been brought from death to life; and offer the parts of your body to him as instruments of righteousness. For sin shall not be your master, because you are not under law, but under grace (Rom. 6:11-14).

Daily Master Communication Guide

John 20:1-18

What God said to me:

What I said to God:

Therefore, I urge you, brothers, in view of God's mercy, to offer your bodies as living sacrifices, holy and pleasing to God—this is your spiritual act of worship. Do not conform any longer to the pattern of this world, but be transformed by the renewing of your mind. Then you will be able to test and approve what God's will is–his good and pleasing will (Rom. 12:1-2).

Hands:

Eyes:

Feet:

Stomach:

Sex organs:

Ears:

Tongue:

1. Identification as a distinct personality:

2. Participation in the world:

3. Communication with others:

A Living Sacrifice

Romans 12:1 says that you are to present your body as a living sacrifice. What does that mean? Think about the days before Christ when people presented animal sacrifices. Christ came to change that practice when He died on the cross as the ultimate sacrifice. Christ wants you in His service not as a dead sacrifice but as a living one. He wants not material things sacrificed but lives sacrificed on the altar of service to Him. He wants a life fully invested in Him.

If you present your body as a living sacrifice, what does that mean you will do?

You might have answered: If I present my body as a living sacrifice for the Master's use, it means that I will do more than give lip service to my faith. I'll sacrifice every area of my life to Him and will commit my body to holy, righteous living.

COMMITTING TO CHRIST'S SERVICE
In day 1 I told you about the missionary, who regularly prayed a prayer committing every part of His body to Christ's service. Will you do that, too?

Write in the margin how you will use each part of your body as you present it to God for His glory.

Draw a star beside the area in which you feel you need the most help in surrendering to God.

Stop and ask God to help you remove barriers to surrendering that member of your body to the Master's service. Ask Him to help you by making you aware of the Holy Spirit's presence when you are tempted to use that part of your body in wrong living.

In the margin, write one way you will commit to use your body for each of the three functions in God's service.

With the relationship of your body and your spiritual life in mind, answer this question: If you were to present your body as a living sacrifice for God's glory, how would your body make you feel?
❑ glad   ❑ sad   ❑ mad

Presenting your body to God can be the most freeing, gratifying, and joyful feeling in the world. You have a choice about how your body responds to situations. Recall that in the illustration of the Disciple's Personality, your will is located in a position to decide between the spirit and the flesh. If you choose to close the door of the flesh, the door will close. The decision to present your body as a living sacrifice means that you close the door of the flesh. With the Holy Spirit's help, you can change harmful habits and yield *all* of your life to the Master.

Will you present your body as a living sacrifice for God's glory?
❑ **Yes** ❑ **No** **If so, tell Him so in a prayer right now.**

LEARNING THE DISCIPLE'S PERSONALITY

✝ **Read "Who Are You?" (p. 218) in the Disciple's Personality presentation, then answer the questions in the margin.**

Read *I Thessalonians 5:23-24* **in the margin. What do these verses tell you about the support you have for living blamelessly?**
❑ **Living a holy life is too difficult; it's all up to me, and I can't handle it.**
❑ **The Lord Jesus Christ who calls me will empower me to use my body, soul, and spirit in right living.**

These verses assure you that the Lord who calls you to serve Him is faithful to help you act in the right way. He has sent the Holy Spirit to help you in this daily challenge.

✝ **In the space below is the spiritual-Christian illustration with blanks for you to add the Scripture references that go with it, as you learned yesterday. Many of these are memory verses you have learned in this study. Say them aloud as you write the references on the illustration. Refer to the Disciple's Personality presentation (pp. 212–18) if you need help.**

• **Are you a natural person whose spirit is dead? Do your bodily senses and your natural desires control you?** ❑ **Yes** ❑ **No**
• **Are you a worldly Christian who has allowed Christ to enter your life but is still being mastered by the desires of the flesh? Is the big I still in control?** ❑ **Yes** ❑ **No**
• **Are you a spiritual Christian who has been crucified with Christ and is being controlled by the Holy Spirit?** ❑ **Yes** ❑ **No**

May God himself, the God of peace, sanctify you through and through. May your whole spirit, soul and body be kept blameless at the coming of our Lord Jesus Christ. The one who calls you is faithful and he will do it (I Thess. 5:23-24).

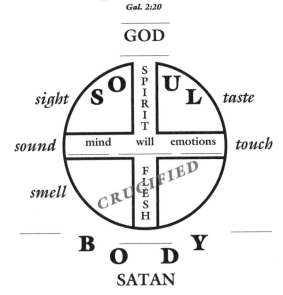

The Spiritual Christian
Gal. 2:20

GOD

sight   S O U L   taste
SPIRIT
sound   mind   will   emotions   touch
FLESH
smell   CRUCIFIED

B O D Y
SATAN

**Daily Master
Communication Guide**

Philippians 1:19-26

What God said to me:

What I said to God:

The Disciple's Personality presentation has been used many times to win someone to faith in Christ. A Florida pastor was visiting a couple he had visited several times before. The wife was a Christian, but the husband, an unbeliever, had always been unwilling to listen to a traditional gospel presentation. This time the pastor used the Disciple's Personality to confront the man with his spiritual condition. Drawing the natural-person and spiritual-Christian diagrams, he asked the man, "Which are you?" The husband pointed to the natural person. David asked, "Which would you like to be?" He pointed to the spiritual-Christian diagram and replied, "I've always wanted to be a Christian." David then led the man to pray to receive Christ as Savior and Lord.

After the prayer the wife spoke up: "I am not either one," and the pastor replied, "I may have a diagram that represents you." When he drew the worldly-Christian diagram, she immediately said, "That's me!" he then led her to rededicate her life to Christ.

After learning the Disciple's Personality, you will be able to use it not only to lead persons to salvation but also to help others—
- deal with their emotions;
- close the door to Satan;
- renew their minds;
- find assurance that they can say no to temptation.

IN THE CARPENTER'S SHOP
Review your work this week and recall your efforts to get rid of the old self and to put on new actions and thoughts. How has the Holy Spirit helped you become more Christlike? Answer these questions about the area of change you identified on page 166:

Something I have been getting rid of this week:

Something Christ has been adding to my character this week:

Stop and pray. Thank God for helping you in the ways you listed. Ask Him to continue giving you the courage to make changes.

 In your quiet time today read *Philippians 1:19-26*, which describes the priority Paul placed on exalting Christ in his body. Then complete the Daily Master Communication Guide in the margin.

HAS THIS WEEK MADE A DIFFERENCE?
Review "My Walk with the Master This Week" at the beginning of this week's material. Mark the activities you have finished by drawing vertical lines in the diamonds beside them. Finish any incomplete activities. Think about what you will say during your group session about your work on these activities.

As you complete your study of "Present Your Body," I hope that you have gained new insights about why you sometimes take actions that contradict your good intentions. I hope that you've committed each part of your body to the Lord's service and that you will let the Holy Spirit help you when you are tempted to make wrong choices.

WEEK 11

Be Filled with the Spirit

This Week's Goal

You will be able to allow the Holy Spirit to fill you.

My Walk with the Master This Week

You will complete the following activities to develop the six biblical disciplines. When you have completed each activity, draw a vertical line in the diamond beside it.

SPEND TIME WITH THE MASTER

◇ Have a daily quiet time, working toward the goal of having quiet times 21 consecutive days. Write the number of minutes you spend in your quiet time each day.

__ Sunday __ Monday __ Tuesday __ Wednesday __ Thursday __ Friday __ Saturday

LIVE IN THE WORD

◇ Read your Bible every day. Write what God says to you and what you say to God.
◇ Memorize *Ephesians 5:18*.
◇ Review *Philippians 2:13*; *Romans 12:1-2*; *Galatians 5:22-23*; and *1 Corinthians 6:19-20*.
◇ Using the Hearing the Word form, write notes from a sermon or a Bible study to apply to your life this week.

PRAY IN FAITH

◇ Pray for people you know and influence.

FELLOWSHIP WITH BELIEVERS

◇ Share with a Christian friend what God is doing in your life—struggles as well as victories.

WITNESS TO THE WORLD

◇ Write your testimony, using the ideas in "How to Write Your Testimony." Be ready to share it at the next group session.

MINISTER TO OTHERS

◇ Explain how to apply the Disciple's Personality, using *James 4:1-8*.

This Week's Scripture-Memory Verse

"Do not get drunk on wine, which leads to debauchery. Instead, be filled with the Spirit" (Eph. 5:18).

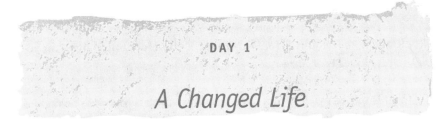

A Changed Life

As a freshman in college, the Holy Spirit created in me an overwhelming desire to witness to others. He helped me overcome my shyness. I witnessed to many people each week, but I wasn't successful in leading anyone to Christ. I memorized Scripture, read witnessing books, and prayed. But something was missing.

I had a burning desire to be used by God, but no one could tell me how. Finally, a friend lent me the book *The Holy Spirit: Who He Is and What He Does* by R. A. Torrey. For the first time I realized that the Holy Spirit is a person who possesses us instead of a power, an influence, or an attitude we possess. I learned that the Holy Spirit, who lives in me, wants to fill me for service.

By the next evening I had finished the book and was ready to follow its instructions to be filled with the Spirit. I confessed all of my sins, presented myself fully to God, and asked in faith for the Holy Spirit to fill me. As I confessed my sins, I realized how much the Holy Spirit loved me and had been grieved by my ignoring Him. Then I presented my body, will, emotions, mind, and spirit to be used by God in any way. I accepted by faith the filling of the Holy Spirit without an outward sign or manifestation. I told God, "I'll accept the fact that I'm filled with the Spirit on the basis of faith in your Word, no matter what happens after." I immediately sensed a deep awareness of the Spirit's love, which has grown stronger through the years as my relationship with God has deepened.

The next evening I witnessed to a boy on the street, and he accepted Christ as his Savior. Two nights later, two teenagers accepted Christ. The following night a man professed faith in Christ; the night after, another man did.

I said to a friend: "Every night when I witness, someone accepts Christ." That night no one did. I asked forgiveness for daring to think I had won those persons to Christ myself. God refilled me with His Spirit after I confessed my sin, yielded to Him, and asked in faith. Again people to whom I witnessed accepted Christ.

Since then the Holy Spirit has taught me that the secret is to be filled for each task of service. Thousands of times when I've sinned, I've asked Him to refill me, and He has done so. The filling of the Spirit empowers different gifts in different persons, but always the result brings glory to Christ and attracts others to Him.

In the previous account what was the turning point at which God was able to do as He desired in my life?

The turning point in my story was when I asked in faith for the Holy Spirit to fill me after I had confessed my sins and had yielded myself to God. Until then I had not allowed Him to work through me in His fullness.

Every person who has been born of the Spirit has the Holy Spirit living in his or her heart. *Romans 8:16* says, *The Spirit himself testifies with our spirit that we are God's children.* However, not everyone is filled with the Spirit and equipped for service (see *Rom. 8:9*).

Daily Master Communication Guide

Acts 2:1-21

What God said to me:

What I said to God:

Look again at *Romans 8:16*. Do you have the Holy Spirit living in you? ☑Yes ❏ No ❏ Not sure

If you have given your life to Christ, He lives in you through His Spirit. However, you may or may not be filled with the Spirit at the present time.

Read *Ephesians 5:18: Do not get drunk on wine, which leads to debauchery. Instead, be filled with the Spirit.* Are you filled with the Spirit right now? ❏ Yes ❏ No ☑Not sure

God wants your personality to be overflowing with His Spirit. As you yield yourself to God, He takes control of your personality. Your inner self is integrated, and you experience constant fellowship with Him.

WHAT IT MEANS TO BE FILLED

A distinct difference exists between having the Spirit of God in you and being filled with the Spirit. Peter is an example of this difference. Even before Pentecost Peter had the Spirit of Christ. *John 20:22* says, *With that he* [Christ] *breathed on them and said, "Receive the Holy Spirit."* In this verse Jesus breathed the Spirit into the disciples. This allowed the disciples to take up His mission, which they could accomplish only under the Spirit's leadership. Even though Peter had the Spirit of Christ in him already, at Pentecost a major change occurred in his life. When the Holy Spirit came in His fullness on the church, Peter was filled with the Spirit.

Before Pentecost Peter was cowardly and denied Jesus. Hot-tempered, he cut off a soldier's ear with a sword. After Pentecost we see no evidence of instability or superficiality in Peter. He became a different person. He preached boldly, he allowed God to work miracles through him, he proclaimed Christ while he risked his life, and he spoke with power and faith.

EXPERIENCING THE SPIRIT'S POWER

Everyone who has accepted Christ has the Spirit of Christ living in him or her. Read *2 Corinthians 1:21-22* in the margin.

But a distinct difference exists between having water in a river and having the water fill or overflow its banks. That's why Jesus spoke of the Spirit's overflowing you. Read *John 7:38-39* in the margin. The Holy Spirit wants to flow through you like the living water Jesus mentioned. Whenever the disciples in the Book of Acts encountered persons who were not filled with the Spirit, they prayed for them to be filled. Then God would move in their lives.

 ***Ephesians 5:18* is this week's Scripture-memory verse. Turn to page 170 and read it aloud to begin learning it.**

Today's Christians face the same problem the disciples faced—trying to fight spiritual battles with human resources. A majority of Christians live and serve as if Pentecost never happened. They try to obey Christ's commands in their own strength; yet they wonder how Satan so often outsmarts and overpowers them. They ignore the mission of the Holy Spirit, who came to continue Jesus' roles of

It is God who makes both us and you stand firm in Christ. He anointed us, set his seal of ownership on us, and put his Spirit in our hearts as a deposit, guaranteeing what is to come (2 Cor. 1:21-22).

"Whoever believes in me, as the Scripture has said, streams of living water will flow from within him" By this he meant the Spirit, whom those who believed in him were later to receive (John 7:38-39).

inspiring, empowering, and guiding them. For them, the third member of the Trinity—the Holy Spirit—is almost "the unknown God." They think of Him as an influence, an attitude, or a way to express the fact that God is everywhere.

Is the Holy Spirit a personal, intimate friend who fills your life?
☑ Yes ❑ No ❑ Not sure

You may have tried to witness or teach a Bible study without relying on the Holy Spirit's power. You may have tried to solve a problem in your personal life without asking God to fill you with His Spirit.

The solution to your inadequacy lies in experiencing the Holy Spirit's presence and power as the disciples did at Pentecost. Pentecost can't be repeated any more than Calvary can be repeated. However, Christians can experience the power of Pentecost just as they can experience the redemption of Calvary.

IN THE CARPENTER'S SHOP
One work of the Holy Spirit is to help you be like Jesus. Today you'll choose an area of your life in which you want to be more Christlike.

Read the Scriptures in the margin that relate to anger and similar behaviors. From the verses marked "The World's Way" identify a specific behavior you want to get rid of. From the verses marked "The Spirit's Way" identify an action you will take to replace it. I have given you an example. Each day this week you will record your progress in working on this behavior.

Here is an example.
Behavior I want to work on: saying things in anger that I later regret
An action I will take to put off the old self: ask the Holy Spirit to teach me how to let Him control me and my tongue even in anger
An action I will take to let the Holy Spirit make me more like Christ: be more loving and kind in all of my relationships

Now you try it.
Behavior I want to work on: _Procrastination_
An action I will take to put off the old self: _____
An action I will take to let the Holy Spirit make me more like Christ:
_____

Stop and pray that you will constantly be filled with the Spirit and that He will work through you.

 Share with a Christian friend your struggles and victories. Share with that person the area of your life you selected for the Holy Spirit to help you change. Ask them to hold your accountable.

 Read *Acts 2:1-21* during your quiet time today. Complete the Daily Master Communication Guide on page 170.

The World's Way
Now you must rid yourselves of all such things as these: anger, rage, malice, slander, and filthy language from your lips (Col. 3:8).

The acts of the sinful nature are obvious: sexual immorality, impurity and debauchery… I warn you, as I did before, that those who live like this will not inherit the kingdom of God (Gal. 5:19-21).

Get rid of all bitterness, rage and anger, brawling and slander, along with every form of malice (Eph. 4:31).

The Spirit's Way
As God's chosen people, holy and dearly loved, clothe yourselves with compassion, kindness, humility, gentleness and patience (Col. 3:12).

The fruit of the Spirit is love, joy, peace, patience, kindness, goodness, faithfulness, gentleness and self-control (Gal. 5:22-23).

Be kind and compassionate to one another, forgiving each other, just as in Christ God forgave you (Eph. 4:32).

The man without the Spirit does not accept the things that come from the Spirit of God, for they are foolishness to him, and he cannot understand them, because they are spiritually discerned (1 Cor. 2:14).

"When he comes, he will convict the world of guilt in regard to sin and righteousness and judgment: in regard to sin, because men do not believe in me; in regard to righteousness, because I am going to the Father, where you can see me no longer; and in regard to judgment, because the prince of this world now stands condemned" (John 16:8-11).

The Holy Spirit convicts people of _____ because they don't believe in Jesus.

The Holy Spirit convicts the world of _____ by His sinless life.

The Holy Spirit convicts the world of _____ by condemning and judging Satan. Anyone who follows Satan is also condemned.

It is written: "No eye has seen, no ear has heard, no mind has conceived what God has prepared for those who love him" but God has revealed it to us by his Spirit (1 Cor. 2:9-10).

We have not received the spirit of the world but the Spirit who is from God, that we may understand what God has freely given us (1 Cor. 2:12).

"The Counselor, the Holy Spirit, whom the Father will send in my name, will teach you all things and will remind you of everything I have said to you" (John 14:26).

DAY 2

Your Spirit and God's Spirit

When you're born of the Spirit, your spirit is made alive, and you're able to respond spiritually. The Holy Spirit helps you (1) understand spiritual things; (2) allows God to work through you.

SPIRITUAL UNDERSTANDING
Read 1 Corinthians 2:14 in the margin. What can people understand without the Spirit's help? Check the correct answer.
☐ **The deep things of God**
☒ **The basic truths of God**
☐ **No spiritual truths**

Without the Spirit a person can understand nothing about God.

Read John 16:8-11 in the margin and in the blanks following the verses write ways the Holy Spirit convicts the world.

The answers are *sin, unrighteousness,* and *judgment.*
The Holy Spirit helps you understand the truths of God. Read *1 Corinthians 2:9-10* in the margin. I've heard this verse applied to what is in heaven, but it clearly says that God, through His Spirit, has already revealed truths that were not previously known by humankind.

Read 1 Corinthians 2:12 and John 14:26 in the margin. What is the Spirit trying to teach you?

The Holy Spirit helps you recall Christ's teachings. He will teach you all things (see *John 16:15*) and guide you into His truth.

THE SPIRIT WORKS THROUGH YOU
Not only does the Holy Spirit make you aware of the truth, but He also does God's work through you and other believers.

Read Acts 1:8 in the margin on the next page. What does the Spirit enable you to do?

The Holy Spirit enables you to be Christ's witness. *Zechariah 4:6* says, *"Not by might nor by power, but my spirit, says the Lord Almighty."*

Read Acts 4:8 and Acts 4:31 in the margin on the next page and underline the words showing that the filling of the Spirit was the key element in God's speaking or working through persons.

Did you underline such words as *Peter, filled with the Holy Spirit, said* in the first verse and *they were all filled with the Holy Spirit and spoke* in the second verse.

Review by listing the two things the Spirit enables you to do. Check your answers by looking at the list on page 174.

1.   **2.**

LETTING THE SPIRIT ENTER

The Spirit of God and the human spirit are different. God is divine; you are human. God's Spirit enters your personality through your human spirit. You are responsible for letting the Spirit of God come in or for shutting Him out.

Read *Revelation 3:20* in the margin. How does this verse picture Jesus?

Jesus is outside the door of your heart and gently asking for entrance. When you open your life to Him and invite Him to come in, God's Spirit enters your life and brings peace to your soul. In this verse He was talking to Christians who were shutting Him out of their church.

 Pray for people you know—for acquaintances and close friends. Pray for opportunities to share God's love and His availability to them. Write their names on your Prayer-Covenant List.

A CONTINUAL FILLING

A true disciple lets the Spirit of God continually fill and control his or her entire personality, as this week's Scripture-memory verse instructs.

 Stop and say aloud your memory verse, *Ephesians 5:18*.

Read *Acts 4:29*. In the margin write what the apostles asked for.

When they were threatened, the apostles didn't ask for release or safety. They asked to be able to speak the Word with great boldness, and God filled them with His Spirit and gave them boldness. As a result, many people came to Christ.

Ask the Holy Spirit to fill you and to give you boldness for Christ.

IN THE CARPENTER'S SHOP

How is the Holy Spirit working to change you into the image of Christ? What progress are you making in developing Christlike character?

You've listed a behavior related to anger that you hoped to get rid of to be more like Jesus. Describe in the margin an instance in which you have already worked to set aside that behavior.

 Read *Acts 4:13-31* during your quiet time today. Then complete the Daily Master Communication Guide on page 176.

"You will receive power when the Holy Spirit comes on you; and you will be my witnesses in Jerusalem, and in all Judea and Samaria, and to the ends of the earth" (Acts 1:8).

Peter, filled with the Holy Spirit, said to them: "Rulers and elders of the people! If we are being called to account today for an act of kindness shown to a cripple and are asked how he was healed, then know this, you and all the people of Israel: It is by the name of Jesus Christ of Nazareth, whom you crucified but whom God raised from the dead, that this man stands before you healed" (Acts 4:8).

After they prayed, the place where they were meeting was shaken. And they were all filled with the Holy Spirit and spoke the word of God boldly (Acts. 4:31).

"Here I am! I stand at the door and knock. If anyone hears my voice and opens the door, I will come in and eat with him, and he with me" (Rev. 3:20).

"Now, Lord, consider their threats and enable your servants to speak your word with great boldness" (Acts 4:29).

**Daily Master
Communication Guide**

Acts 4:13-31

What God said to me:

What I said to God:

*May God himself, the God of peace,
sanctify you through and through. May
your whole spirit, soul and body be kept
blameless at the coming of our Lord
Jesus Christ (1 Thess. 5:23).*

Filled Without Limit

You've learned that true disciples let the Spirit of God continually fill and control their entire personalities. However, not all Christians allow God to control their lives. Worldly Christians still struggle with the big *I* of the natural person.

Based on what you learned as you studied the Disciple's Personality, describe in your own words why the Spirit of God does not fill everyone's personality.

You may have answered something like this: Not everyone has opened the door of his or her spirit to God's Spirit. You must first open the door before the Spirit of God can fill your personality.

CONTROLLED BY THE SPIRIT

You have the Spirit of Christ dwelling in you if you belong to Jesus. You may treat Him as a guest, a servant, a tenant, or Lord and Master—the owner of the property. But the Spirit will not fill you completely until you acknowledge Christ's lordship and submit to His personal and divine authority. *First Thessalonians 5:23*, in the margin, describes what God does in your personality.

***Sanctify* means to "set apart" or "to cleanse." Write *T* beside the statement that best expresses the truth of *1 Thessalonians 5:23*.**
___ **God sets apart or cleanses your entire personality.**
___ **God cleanses your spirit only.**

Your entire personality is cleansed as God's Spirit controls your spirit. When God sanctifies your entire personality, He and you enjoy mutual fellowship.

Although you have the Holy Spirit living in you, you might not be giving Him His rightful place. Check the box that best describes how the Holy Spirit would say that you treat Him.
❏ **As a guest**
❏ **As a servant**
❏ **As a tenant**
❏ **As Master—the owner of the property**

What relationship should exist between God's Spirit and your spirit? Check the correct answer.
❏ **Your spirit should control God's Spirit.**
❏ **God's Spirit and your spirit should be on equal terms.**
❏ **God's Spirit should control your spirit.**

God's will is that you be completely controlled by His Spirit. This week's Scripture-memory verse, *Ephesians 5:18*, tells how this occurs.

 Say aloud this week's Scripture-memory verse, *Ephesians 5:18*, as you continue to memorize it.

OCCUPIED WITH CHRIST

John 3:34, in the margin, states that Jesus was filled with God's Spirit without limit. Jesus had the Spirit filling Him constantly and empowering Him in everything He did. I urge you to open your entire life to the Holy Spirit.

What would be required for you to follow totally the Holy Spirit's guidance in everything you do? Check the following statements that apply.

I would have to—
❑ confess and forsake sin in my life;
❑ spend more time in **Bible study** to hear the **Spirit** speaking to me;
❑ spend more time in prayer asking for the **Spirit** to reveal God's will to me;
❑ ask the **Spirit** to fill me;
❑ turn to God first when a crisis occurs rather than as the last resort;
❑ be alert and open to opportunities to witness;
❑ seek the **Christ-honoring** solution to situations rather than my solutions;
❑ take this action: _____.

In his book, *The Full Blessing of Pentecost*, Andrew Murray lists these main points about a Christian's being filled with the Holy Spirit.

As you read the following quotation by Andrew Murray, underline troublesome areas that limit your being filled with the Holy Spirit.

1. It is the will of God that every one of His children should live entirely and unceasingly under the control of the Holy Spirit.
2. Without being filled with the Spirit, it is utterly impossible that an individual Christian or a church can ever live or work as God desires.
3. Everywhere and in everything we see the proofs, in the life and experience of Christians, that this blessing is but little enjoyed in the Church, and alas! is but little sought for.
4. This blessing is prepared for us and God waits to bestow it. Our faith may expect it with the greatest confidence.
5. The great hindrance in the way is that the self-life, and the world, which it uses for its own service and pleasure, usurp the place that Christ ought to occupy.
6. We cannot be filled with the Spirit until we are prepared to yield ourselves to be led by the Lord Jesus to forsake and sacrifice every thing for this pearl of great price.[1]

"The one whom God has sent speaks the words of God, for God gives the Spirit without limit" (John 3:34).

**Daily Master
Communication Guide**

Luke 24:13-53

What God said to me:

What I said to God:

Now read the following quotation by L. L. Letgers. As you read, think about ways your life resembles or does not resemble this description.

Your evidence that you are filled with the spirit is that Jesus becomes everything to you. You see Him. You are occupied with Him. You are fully satisfied with Jesus. He becomes real, and when you witness about Him, the Holy Spirit witnesses with you regarding the truth about Him. ... Jesus is your Lord and Master and you rest in His Lordship. ... The real evidence of a Spirit-filled life is ... first, that others see the Holy Spirit working in your life the character of Christ, the fruit of the Spirit, and second, that you in your own private life see in the Book the things of Jesus, and that you are personally rejoicing in Him, and are occupied with Him.[2]

List below in the correct column the phrases in this quotation that—

MY LIFE RESEMBLES	MY LIFE DOES NOT RESEMBLE
1.	1.
2.	2.
3.	3.
4.	4.
5.	5.

Which of the following best reflect your response to the quotations you read about being filled with the Spirit? Check all that apply.
❑ **I have never known the kind of life described.**
❑ **Lord, I have wandered from You. I want to return.**
❑ **I have not yet arrived, but I'm working on living in this manner.**
❑ **Lord, please fill me so that I may experience this kind of life.**
❑ **Lord God, I praise You for the mighty work You have done in my life.**
❑ **Other:**_____

One help to being occupied with Jesus is to apply the Word you hear preached or taught. Genuinely looking forward to the times you hear God's Word preached can help you discern its relevance for you and can make you receptive to the Holy Spirit as He speaks to you through it. The next activity will help you look for the Holy Spirit's work in your life.

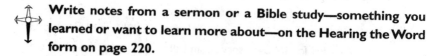 **Write notes from a sermon or a Bible study—something you learned or want to learn more about—on the Hearing the Word form on page 220.**

Read *Luke 24:13-53*, **the passage that describes Jesus' ascension into heaven, during your quiet time today. See how God speaks to you through this passage. Then complete the Daily Master Communication Guide in the margin.**

DAY 4

How to Be Filled

If you still have questions about how to be filled with the Holy Spirit, this week's Scripture-memory verse contains several clues about how this occurs. It gives four important facts about the directive "Be filled with the Spirit."

✝ **Before you read about these important facts, say aloud this week's Scripture-memory verse, *Ephesians 5:18,* three times from memory. Also take this opportunity to review the other verses you have memorized since you began this study.**

We can learn a great deal by looking at the meaning of this verse in its original language. The phrase *be filled* is—

- passive voice. *Passive* means that you can't do something yourself. Someone has to do it to you. Only God can fill you. You can't fill yourself or cause yourself to be filled.
- present tense. You're to be filled now.
- continuous action. Present tense in Greek indicates continuous action. It means *keep on being filled*. Although your conversion was a one-time experience, the filling of the Spirit is not. It needs to keep on happening. Think about a pipe through which water passes at all times. If the Spirit is filling you, He is always going through you as He works to minister to others.
- imperative mood. "Be filled" is an order, a command to all Christians. It's not just an option or something you can dismiss because you don't understand it. It's a teaching of God's Word. My understanding of being filled was greatly affected by my personal experience of being filled with the Holy Spirit, years after my conversion, which I related in day 1. However, the Bible teaches that some Christians are filled when they are saved, like Cornelius in *Acts 10.*

Go back and draw a star beside the fact you most need to be reminded of. Why do you need this reminder?

THE SPIRIT FLOWS THROUGH YOU

How can someone personally experience the filling of the Holy Spirit? If you belong to Jesus, His Spirit already dwells in you. But His purpose is to fill you continually and to flow through you to others. You are not to be a container but a conduit or a channel for Him. The filling of the Spirit enables God to communicate His message to others through you.

A Christian must take three steps to be filled and controlled by the Spirit:

1. Confess your sin, disobedience, emptiness, and need for God's cleansing. Read 1 John 1:9 in the margin.
2. Present every member of your body to be made a righteous instrument in God's hands. Recall *Romans 12:1,* one of your Scripture-memory verses.

If we confess our sins, he is faithful and just and will forgive us our sins and purify us from all unrighteousness (1 John 1:9).

"If you then, though you are evil, know how to give good gifts to your children, how much more will your Father in heaven give the Holy Spirit to those who ask him!" (Luke 11:13).

Speak to one another with psalms, hymns and spiritual songs. Sing and make music in your heart to the Lord (Eph. 5:19).

Always giving thanks to God the Father for everything, in the name of our Lord Jesus Christ (Eph. 5:20).

Submit to one another out of reverence for Christ (Eph. 5:21).

"You will receive power when the Holy Spirit comes on you; and you will be my witnesses in Jerusalem, and in all Judea and Samaria, and to the ends of the earth" (Acts 1:8).

After they prayed, the place where they were meeting was shaken. And they were all filled with the Holy Spirit and spoke the word of God boldly (Acts 4:31).

3. Ask God to fill, control, and empower you, as *Luke 11:13*, in the margin, promises. Believe that God has answered your prayer.

What steps do you need to take to experience the filling of God's Spirit? Bow your head now and open your spirit to the Spirit of God. Follow the three steps listed above. Write what you experienced by faith.

 Stop and pray. Say aloud *Ephesians 5:18*, this week's Scripture-memory verse. Thank God for the gift of His fullness.

In the verses in the margin find three results of being filled with the Spirit.
1. ***Ephesians 5:19:***
2. ***Ephesians 5:20:***
3. ***Ephesians 5:21:***

Christians today can be like those in the early church, in which Spirit-filled members learned to worship God with thanksgiving for everything. These early Christians often expressed thanksgiving through music. You may have responded like this: 1. speaking to one another and singing to the Lord, 2. giving thanks, 3. submitting to one another.

GOD'S PURPOSES IN FILLING YOU
God has a double purpose in filling you with His Spirit. First, God wants to develop Christlike character in you. In *1 Thessalonians 5:23*, Paul prayed that your personality would be found blameless: *May God himself, the God of peace, sanctify you through and through. May your whole spirit, soul and body be kept blameless at the coming of our Lord Jesus Christ.* Second, God wants to empower you to do His work.

Read *Acts 1:8* and *Acts 4:31* in the margin. Explain what the Holy Spirit enables you to do.

The Holy Spirit provided power for witnessing with boldness. The disciples, timid and fearful earlier, now preached fearlessly. The Holy Spirit empowers ordinary people to testify boldly even under difficult circumstances. You need the power of the Spirit to enable you to witness. Being bold doesn't mean that you are never nervous or that you never fear an opportunity to witness. It means that you have the courage to do it even when you are afraid.

I hope that you also look forward to the time when you can share your prepared testimony with people around you.

APPLYING THE DISCIPLE'S PERSONALITY
Each week of this study you've learned a different component of the Disciple's Personality. Now that you have learned the entire presentation, you may wonder how to use this knowledge in everyday situations.

The Disciple's Personality contains many Bible truths that apply to a variety of situations:

1. Use it to evaluate your spiritual growth.

2. Apply its teachings to gain victory in your personal life:

a. Use it to overcome the world, the flesh, and the devil when you face temptation..

b. Use it in prayer as you dedicate your total personality to the Master. Pray about each part of your personality.

c. Use it to review the Scripture-memory verses related to the victorious life.

d. Use it to review Bible teachings about each part of your personality.

3. Draw it to help others evaluate whether they are natural, worldly, or spiritual persons and to explain how they can apply it to their lives.

4. Use it with an unsaved person to explain how to become a disciple of Christ. First draw and explain the Natural Person. Next draw and explain the Spiritual Christian. If the person accepts Christ, draw the Worldly Christian to show how not to live. If he or she doesn't accept Christ, you may need to draw and explain the Worldly Christian to explain why some Christians don't live victorious lives. Otherwise, don't present the Worldly Christian to this person.

✝ Practice explaining in your own words how to apply the Disciple's Personality, using the basic drawing below. Your leader showed you in the previous group session how to apply the illustration, using *James 4:1-8*. Close the door of the flesh as you draw a cross in the center of the circle to encompass *spirit, flesh, mind, will,* and *emotions*. Write *crucified* across flesh. Now write *submit* above the circle. Write *Draw near to God* and draw an arrow toward God. Write *God will draw near to you* and draw an arrow from God toward the circle. Write *resist* below the circle and draw an arrow toward Satan. Write *will flee from you* below Satan and draw a downward arrow. See page 219 if you need help with your drawing.

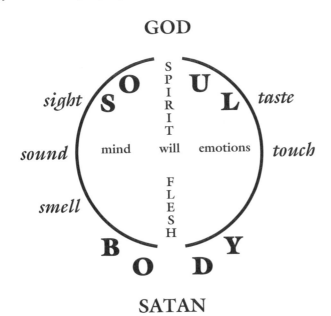

Daily Master Communication Guide

Acts 10

What God said to me:

What I said to God:

Now use *James 4:1-8* to explain this application of the presentation in your own words.

Have you already used the Disciple's Personality? ❑ Yes ❑ No If so, describe your experience below. If not, be open to ways the Holy Spirit reveals to you.

IN THE CARPENTER'S SHOP
How is the Holy Spirit guiding your efforts to put off the old self and to replace it with the new?

In day 2 you recorded your progress in tearing down old habits related to anger. Today describe what you see Christ adding to your life to replace that old habit.

During your quiet time today read *Acts 10*, describing Cornelius's salvation and the filling of the Holy Spirit. Let God speak to you through this passage. Then complete the Daily Master Communication Guide in the margin.

DAY 5

Accomplishing God's Purposes

You've learned that God wants to accomplish two purposes in the life of a Spirit-filled Christian: • To develop Christlike character; • To equip you for ministry.

DEVELOPING CHRISTLIKE CHARACTER

The first purpose, developing Christlike character, is achieved through the fruit of the Spirit and the second through the gifts of the Spirit. Let's look at the way the fruit of the Spirit produces Christlike character.

Review the fruit of the Spirit in *Galatians 5:22-23*. **Read 2 Peter 1:5-8 in the margin, in which Peter named the building blocks of Christian character. Underline these qualities. Why did Peter say that you need these qualities?**

Peter said you need these qualities so that you will be effective and productive in the Christian life. A person who has life in the Spirit bears fruit for Christ.

IN THE CARPENTER'S SHOP

How has the Holy Spirit worked in you this week to build Christlike character? Are you getting rid of the old self and adding new behaviors to your life?

Answer the questions about the area related to anger that you identified on page 173.
Something I have been getting rid of this week:

Something Christ has been adding to my character this week:

EQUIPPING FOR MINISTRY

The Holy Spirit accomplishes the second purpose, equipping you for ministry, by giving gifts of the Spirit. He empowers you to minister to others through these gifts. When you see persons who are filled with the Spirit, you immediately see that they want to minister. They want to let God work through them and to join God on His mission. Only the continual filling and refilling of the Spirit can produce this desire. Fruit produces character, and gifts produce effective ministry.

Some gifts of the Holy Spirit are listed in *1 Corinthians 12:7-11* **and** *Romans 12:6-8*, **which are in the margin. Read the verses and write below them any gift(s) you believe the Holy Spirit has given you.**

To what extent have you developed the gift(s) you have been given? Write the number(s) beside the gift(s) you listed above. 1. none 2. some 3. much

For this very reason, make every effort to add to your faith goodness; and to goodness, knowledge; and to knowledge, self-control; and to self-control, perseverance; and to perseverance, godliness; and to godliness, brotherly kindness; and to brotherly kindness, love. For if you possess these qualities in increasing measure, they will keep you from being ineffective and unproductive in your knowledge of our Lord Jesus Christ (2 Pet. 1:5-8).

To each one the manifestation of the Spirit is given for the common good. To one there is given through the Spirit the message of wisdom, to another the message of knowledge by means of the same Spirit, to another faith by the same Spirit, to another gifts of healing by that one Spirit, to another miraculous powers, to another prophecy, to another distinguishing between spirits, to another speaking in different kinds of tongues, and to still another the interpretation of tongues. All these are the work of one and the same Spirit, and he gives them to each one, just as he determines (1 Cor. 12:7-11).

We have different gifts, according to the grace given us. If a man's gift is prophesying, let him use it in proportion to his faith. If it is serving, let him serve; it it is teaching, let him teach; if it is encouraging, let him encourage; if it is contributing to the needs of others, let him give generously; if it is leadership, let him govern diligently; if it is showing mercy, let him do it cheerfully (Rom. 12:6-8).

God's first purpose:

How He accomplishes it:

God's second purpose:

How He accomplishes it:

CHRONOLOGICAL

1. Before I met Christ
2. How I realized my need
3. How I became a Christian
4. What being a Christian means to me

THEMATIC

1. A theme, a need, or a problem
2. How I became a Christian
3. What being a Christian means to me

Stop and ask God to help you surrender your gifts to Him and to help you find ways to develop your gifts to their fullest.

Christlike character and effectiveness in ministry are possible only through the continual filling of the Spirit. It's impossible to achieve it by your own effort. Develop your spiritual gifts so that you can minister as the Spirit desires.

To summarize what you've learned about God's purposes in filling you with the Spirit, fill in the blanks in the margin.

HOW TO WRITE YOUR TESTIMONY

This material will help you compile the facts of your Christian life in a clear, concise testimony. Here are reasons for writing your testimony.
• To clarify experiences in your mind
• To allow your leader to give feedback so that you can sharpen your testimony
• To develop a standard testimony you can adapt to specific situations
• To practice your testimony so that you are ready to use it anytime
Follow these guidelines to write your testimony.
1. Use the testimony you wrote in week 9 and the notes you made in week 10 as resources for your first draft. After the first draft is evaluated, you may rewrite it in a more polished version. Write the way you talk. Use *I* and *me*. Don't worry about formal rules of grammar. You'll communicate your testimony verbally by sharing, not preaching.
2. Choose one of the following approaches to write the testimony.
   a. Chronological (see in margin). This approach is better when enough significant experiences happened before your conversion to distinguish clearly between your life before and after conversion.
   b. Thematic (see in margin). This approach is the better choice when you were saved as a child and/or do not remember enough significant events before your conversion that the other person can identify with. Begin by focusing on an experience, problem, issue, or feeling, such as a fear of death, a desire for success, a basic character flaw, a search for identity, or a crisis.

If you use the thematic approach, you may begin with a brief testimony about your current situation such as I've discovered how not to worry, I've discovered a purpose for living, I've overcome loneliness, or I've overcome my fear of death.

State the theme and tell how you solved your problem. This flashback technique can take the place of telling your experience before conversion. The date of your conversion isn't as important as your personal relationship with Christ. Many people have full assurance that they are saved, but they have trouble identifying the exact time of their conversion. If you have doubt about your salvation, talk with your MasterLife leader or pastor who can help you find assurance of salvation. The flashback technique allows you to give the facts without detailing when they happened. Even though you may not remember consciously thinking through each of the four facts of the gospel (sin, sin's penalty, Christ's payment, and receiving Christ) at conversion, you can mention them in the flashback approach, since you have become aware of them and believe them now.

Check in the margin the approach above that you intend to use.

☐ **CHRONOLOGICAL**
☐ **THEMATIC**

3. Write an interesting introduction about your life and attitudes before following Christ. Help the person see you as an ordinary person. Give a few brief facts about your early life to set the scene. Use facts that the person can identify with or that help him or her see you as a normal person. Don't dwell on details that would be unimportant to a stranger. Use concrete words and word pictures to describe the situation. Be brief.

4. Highlight the events that led to your salvation (how you realized your need for Christ). Avoid using the name of your church, your specific age, or the date of conversion unless the person hearing your testimony has the same background. Keep these facts general to make it easier for others to identify with you. Don't use church words that might not be understood by persons with limited or different religious backgrounds.

Summarize the events that led you to realize your need for Christ.

5. Summarize the facts of salvation (how you became a Christian).

a. *Chronological.* Tell how you became aware that sin involves living an "I-controlled" life. State how you felt when you realized the penalty of sin and how you knew that Christ paid the penalty for your sin. Explain how you received Christ. Emphasize repentance and faith in Christ as the way to salvation.

b. *Thematic.* Even if you can't remember each of the previous stages clearly, you can state your realization without referring to the time you realized each. However, state with confidence that you received Christ and are following Him as your Lord.

State with confidence that you received Christ and are following Him as your Lord.

Sometimes a personal testimony is a good way to begin a witnessing encounter. If you use your testimony to introduce a presentation of the gospel, you may omit the next point and tell how to receive Christ through the gospel presentation.

6. Share the results of knowing Christ as Lord and Savior (what being a Christian means to you). Quickly summarize the difference Christ has made in your life. Give concrete examples.

a. Mention how you continue to struggle so that you don't give the impression that you think you're perfect. For example, "Being a Christian doesn't mean that I don't have problems, but now Christ helps me through them."

b. Don't spend too much time on this point. Many Christians tend to focus on what has happened since conversion. Mention it, but the non-Christian needs to know how you reached this point. He should relate more to the beginning experience than to later experiences. Focus your testimony on salvation.

7. Close your testimony in a way that leads to further conversation about salvation. Use questions such as:

a. Has anything like that ever happened to you?

b. Does that make sense to you?

c. Have you ever thought that you would like to have such peace (assurance, joy, experience, and so on)?

d. Do you know for certain that you have eternal life and that you will go to heaven when you die?

Close your testimony in a way that leads to further conversation about salvation.

Lord Jesus, I'm a sinner. I need You. I want You to be my Savior and Lord. I accept Your death on the cross as the payment for my sins, and I now entrust my life to Your care. Thank You for Your resurrection from the grave. Thank You for forgiving me and for giving me a new life. Please help me grow in my understanding of Your love and power so that my life will bring glory and honor to You. Amen.

Signed_____

Date_____

Daily Master Communication Guide

Romans 12:1-8

What God said to me:

What I said to God:

8. Check your testimony by using the following questions. Revise your rough draft as needed. You'll rewrite your testimony after it has been evaluated during your next group session.
   a. Does it have a clear story line that ties everything together?
   b. Are all four parts of your testimony developed proportionally?
   c. In explaining how you became a Christian, did you include the four doctrinal truths of the gospel (see p. 161)?
   d. Is your testimony too brief? Too long? Does it need details?
   e. Does the testimony end with a sentence that leads to further conversation?
   f. Does the testimony sound conversational, formal, or preachy?

9. Writing your testimony may be difficult. The time required to write it will depend on its complexity and on the number of times you've given it before. Thinking about unpleasant events in your life may be upsetting. You may discover the need to be sure that you've been saved. Satan doesn't want you to prepare a testimony. Ask God to help you.

   If you have any question about if you are saved, you can receive Jesus Christ now by invitation. *Romans 10:13* says, *"Everyone who calls on the name of the Lord will be saved."* You may use the prayer in the margin to express your commitment.

 Write your testimony, using "How to Write Your Testimony." Be ready to share it at the next group session. It should be only three minutes long. That is equal to about one page, typed and double-spaced, or two pages handwritten.

 During your quiet time today read *Romans 12:1-8*. Complete the Daily Master Communication Guide in the margin.

HAS THIS WEEK MADE A DIFFERENCE?
Review "My Walk with the Master This Week" at the beginning of this week's material. Mark the activities you've finished by drawing vertical lines in the diamonds beside them. Finish any incomplete activities. Think about what you'll say in your group session about your work on these activities.

As you complete your study of "Be Filled with the Spirit," consider the following statements and check the boxes beside those that apply.
❑ **I'm more aware than ever of the gift of the Holy Spirit living in me.**
❑ **I desire to be filled with the Spirit and will take steps to be filled.**
❑ **The filling of the Holy Spirit in me is already motivating me to use my gifts to minister to others.**
❑ **The Holy Spirit has helped me build more Christlike character this week by tearing down old thoughts and actions and by replacing them with new ones.**

¹Andrew Murray, *The Full Blessing of Pentecost* (Port Washington, Pa.: Christian Literature Crusade, 1954), 7.
²L. L. Letgers, *The Simplicity of the Spirit-Filled Life* (Farmingdale, N.Y.: Christian Witness, 1968), 51–52.

WEEK 12

Live Victoriously

This Week's Goal

You'll be able to explain how you became a Christian and how to live a life of victory in the Spirit.

My Walk with the Master This Week

You will complete the following activities to develop the six biblical disciplines. When you complete each activity, draw a vertical line in the diamond beside it.

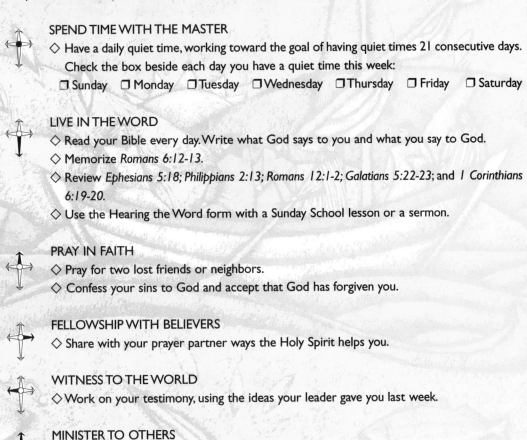

SPEND TIME WITH THE MASTER

◇ Have a daily quiet time, working toward the goal of having quiet times 21 consecutive days. Check the box beside each day you have a quiet time this week:

❑ Sunday ❑ Monday ❑ Tuesday ❑ Wednesday ❑ Thursday ❑ Friday ❑ Saturday

LIVE IN THE WORD

◇ Read your Bible every day. Write what God says to you and what you say to God.
◇ Memorize *Romans 6:12-13*.
◇ Review *Ephesians 5:18*; *Philippians 2:13*; *Romans 12:1-2*; *Galatians 5:22-23*; and *1 Corinthians 6:19-20*.
◇ Use the Hearing the Word form with a Sunday School lesson or a sermon.

PRAY IN FAITH

◇ Pray for two lost friends or neighbors.
◇ Confess your sins to God and accept that God has forgiven you.

FELLOWSHIP WITH BELIEVERS

◇ Share with your prayer partner ways the Holy Spirit helps you.

WITNESS TO THE WORLD

◇ Work on your testimony, using the ideas your leader gave you last week.

MINISTER TO OTHERS

◇ Practice giving your testimony.
◇ Draw and explain the Disciple's Personality.
◇ Explain how to apply the Disciple's Personality, using *Galatians 5:16-25*.

This Week's Scripture-Memory Verse

Do not let sin reign in your mortal body so that you obey its evil desires. Do not offer the parts of your body to sin, as instruments of wickedness, but rather offer yourselves to God, as those who have been brought from death to life; and offer the parts of your body to him as instruments of righteousness (Rom. 6:12-13).

Everyone born of God overcomes the World. This is the victory that has overcome the world, even our faith. Who is it that overcomes the world? Only he who believes that Jesus is the Son of God (1 John 5:4-5).

What I do is not the good I want to do; no, the evil I do not want to do—this I keep on doing. Now if I do what I do not want to do, it is no longer I who do it, but it is sin living in me that does it. So I find this law at work: When I want to do good, evil is right there with me. For in my inner being I delight in God's law; but I see another law at work in the members of my body, waging war against the law of my mind and making me a prisoner of the law of sin at work within my members. What a wretched man I am! Who will rescue me from this body of death? (Rom. 7:19-24).

The mind of sinful man is death, but the mind controlled by the Spirit is life and peace; the sinful mind is hostile to God. It does not submit to God's law, nor can it do so. Those controlled by the sinful nature cannot please God (Rom. 8:6-8).

❑ 1. The worldly mind is God's enemy.
❑ 2. The worldly mind is life and peace.
❑ 3. The worldly mind doesn't submit to God's law.
❑ 4. The worldly mind can't please God.

Thanks be to God that, though you used to be slaves to sin, you wholeheartedly obeyed the form of teaching to which you were entrusted. You have been set free from sin and have become slaves to righteousness (Rom. 6:17-18).

Victory Over Sin

Learning how your personality works helps you understand how to live a victorious life. Just understanding these concepts does not stop sin in the world. Satan is always at work, seeking to devour anyone he can. Knowledge is power, but the real power is the Holy Spirit. By learning how easily you can slip and how easily you can leave open the door of the flesh, you can stay on guard against thoughts and actions that are part of the old self and can put Christlike traits in their place.

When Jesus died on the cross and rose from the grave, He won the victory over sin. He promised that His disciples would share in His victory (see *1 John 5:4-5* in the margin). A victorious Christian life is a Spirit-filled life.

INTERNAL CONFLICT

In every person a war rages between the forces of Satan and the forces of God. Every person is made in God's image. He or she has God's moral law stamped into his or her being. Yet this person's fallen bodily senses and fleshly desires are in control. Read about this person's dilemma in *Romans 7:19-24* in the margin.

Think about the passage you just read and write in the margin a brief summary of what Paul described.

You may have written a response similar to this: I want to do good, but I can't because of sin. I'm captive to the law of sin.

The worldly Christian is in a constant state of tension. Because the door of the flesh is still open and because the big *I* is still in control, evil desires enter and work to crowd out the Holy Spirit.

Read in the margin what Paul said about the worldly mind in *Romans 8:6-8*: Then check the correct responses below the verse.

God isn't pleased with a mind that yields itself to sin. He considers it an enemy. It operates outside God's law. It brings the exact opposite of life and peace. The correct answers to the margin exercise are 1, 3, and 4.

CHOOSING CHRIST DAILY

The spiritual Christian is not perfect. But daily this Christian crucifies the flesh and consciously allows the Spirit to fill him or her. When this person is tempted, he or she closes the door to Satan and opens the door to Jesus.

First read *Romans 6:17-18* in the margin; then, check below the way a person who is a servant of sin can be made free from sin.
❑ 1. By obeying God's Word   ❑ 2. By refusing to be tempted

Obeying God's Word is the way you can refrain from being a slave to sin. The

Word contains everything you need for life and peace. It contains every instruction you need for living. You can recall the Word when you need a reminder of how you are to think and act. The correct answer is 1. See *2 Peter 1:3*.

Memorizing Scripture helps you resist temptation. This week's Scripture-memory verses are *Romans 6:12-13*. Turn to page 187 and read them aloud. Write how memorizing these verses will help you resist temptation.

You may have said that these verses remind you to use your body for good and not evil. Recalling them in a time of temptation can help you resist Satan and can remind you to ask God to help you.

IN THE CARPENTER'S SHOP

What are practical ways you can replace evil with good? Today look at another area of your life in which you want to be more Christlike.

Read the Scriptures in the margin that relate to greed. Underline the words or phrases related to greed. From the verses marked "The World's Way" identify a specific behavior you want to get rid of. From the verses marked "The Spirit's Way" identify an action you will take to replace it. I have given you an example. Each day this week you will record your progress in working on this behavior.

Here is an example.
Behavior I want to work on: <u>overspending</u>
An action I'll take to put off the old self: no longer buy designer brands I can't really afford because that's what my friends wear
An action I'll take to let the Holy Spirit make me more like Christ: be content with what I have and control my material desires; memorize *Hebrews 13:5* to help me do this

Now you try it.
Behavior I want to work on: _____
An action I'll take to put off the old self:_____
An action I'll take to let the Holy Spirit make me more like Christ:
_____

Share with your prayer partner how the Holy Spirit helps you. Tell that person about the area you wish to change and ask him or her to pray with you that the Holy Spirit will help you set aside this behavior. Give the person the right to ask you about how you are doing in this area. Be accountable.

During your quiet time today read *Ephesians 5*. Then complete the Daily Master Communication Guide on page 190.

His divine power has given us everything we need for life and godliness through our knowledge of him who called us by his own glory and goodness (2 Pet. 1:3)

The World's Way

Among you there must not be even a hint of sexual immorality, or of any kind of impurity, or of greed, because these are improper for God's holy people (Eph. 5:3).

Put to death, therefore, whatever belongs to your earthly nature: sexual immorality, impurity, lust, evil desires and greed, which is idolatry (Col. 3:5).

The acts of the sinful nature are obvious: sexual immorality, impurity and debauchery...I warn you, as I did before, that those who live like this will not inherit the kingdom of God (Gal. 5:19-21).

The Spirit's Way

Be imitators of God, therefore, as dearly loved children and live a life of love, just as Christ loved us and gave himself up for us as a fragrant offering and sacrifice to God (Eph. 5:1-2).

Set your minds on things above, not on earthly things (Col. 3:2).

The fruit of the Spirit is love, joy, peace, patience, kindness, goodness, faithfulness, gentleness and self-control. Against such things there is no law (Gal. 5:22-23).

**Daily Master
Communication Guide**

Ephesians 5

What God said to me:

What I said to God:

The sinful nature desires what is contrary to the Spirit, and the Spirit what is contrary to the sinful nature. They are in conflict with each other, so that you do not do what you want (Gal. 5:17).

Do not love the world or anything in the world. If anyone loves the world, the love of the Father is not in him (1 John 2:15).

Be self-controlled and alert. Your enemy the devil prowls around like a roaring lion looking for someone to devour (1 Pet. 5:8).

DAY 2

Alert to the Enemy

Victorious living involves being aware of Satan's potential hold on you and keeping the enemy at a distance. Even though the human personality is God's highest creation, an individual's personality is damaged when he or she follows Satan and chooses to sin. Satan's weapons are powerful. Only a foolish Christian fails to take Satan seriously.

THE FORCES YOU FACE
Read the verses in the margin. Record the forces mentioned that are fighting against the Spirit of God within you.

*Galatians 5:17:*_____
*1 John 2:15:*_____
*1 Peter 5:8:*_____

These verses make clear that the enemy is alive and vigilant in seeking to destroy Christians. He constantly looks for a weak point in your personality so that he can cause you to stumble. Your sinful nature, the world, and the devil are the forces that fight against the Spirit of God within you.

In each of the following case studies, underline the point at which Satan is fighting against the Spirit of God within the person.

Julie needed an afternoon and weekend job to help with the family finances. Although she made good grades in school and would work hard, she was still unemployed after a six-month search. Her dad's medical bills went even higher, and the family financial picture looked bleak. Julie, a Christian, had trusted God with her job search but was beginning to doubt that God was aware of her distress.

Ken, suffered serious injuries when a drunk driver hit him. At first he vowed that fighting the disabilities would not get him down, but the treatments and his discomfort were taking an emotional and physical toll. The time away from school because of the injuries was endangering his graduation. Having been faithful in his Christian walk, Ken wondered why God didn't heal him quickly.

Ray had worked hard in his landscape business and was successful. As his income grew, he bought many material possessions. Ray had always been active in his church, but his increased work schedule, as well as his interest in his new boat, began taking more of his time. Soon he began to tell himself that he didn't have time for church because he was such a busy, important person.

Satan attacked each individual at a point of weakness. When Julie questioned whether God was aware of her distress and when Ken questioned why God did not intervene in his suffering, they gave Satan an entry point in their lives. When Ray thought that he could make it on his own without the fellowship of other believers, he became vulnerable to the enemy.

Satan looks for moments of distress, doubt, fear, and pain to gain a foothold in your life. He sees these as opportunities to destroy your trust in God. The Holy Spirit can help you rest in the Lord and exercise self-control while you wait for God's help.

As you read the case studies, could you identify with any of them? Has Satan attempted to destroy you in a weak or anxious moment? If so, draw a star beside the illustration that is similar to the way you have been challenged. Identify a weak area of your life now or in the recent past. Briefly describe your struggle.

 This week's Scripture-memory verses address the challenges you face when sin attempts to reign in your life. Try to write Romans 6:12-13 from memory.

What the law was powerless to do in that it was weakened by the sinful nature, God did by sending his own Son in the likeness of sinful man to be a sin offering. And so he condemned sin in sinful man (Rom. 8:3).

"I have told you these things, so that in me you may have peace. In this world you will have trouble. But take heart! I have overcome the world" (John 16:33).

He who does what is sinful is of the devil, because the devil has been sinning from the beginning. The reason the Son of God appeared was to destroy the devil's work (1 John 3:8).

THE VICTORY HAS BEEN WON

What has Jesus done to secure victory for you over sin that fights against the Spirit of God within you? The three verses in the margin answer this question.

Read the verses in the margin and describe below what Jesus has done to conquer the enemy.

*Romans 8:3:*_____

*John 16:33:*_____

*1 John 3:8:*_____

What a victory! You're not alone when you sustain Satan's attacks. Christ has gone before you to provide victory for you. In Christ's death on the cross He condemned sin in the flesh, He overcame the world, and He destroyed the devil's work. He has also given you the Holy Spirit to strengthen you in times of temptation.

Doesn't this marvelous news make you long for everyone you know to have this kind of power? Can you think of persons in your circles of influence who yield to temptation because they have never accepted Jesus? Perhaps you see them sinning as the devil takes control of them, and you want them to know the One who has crushed Satan and has overcome the world.

Daily Master Communication Guide

Galatians 5

What God said to me:

What I said to God:

Pray for two people at school or for two neighbors who don't know Jesus.

IN THE CARPENTER'S SHOP
How well are you withstanding Satan's attacks in your life? The Holy Spirit will help you put off or lay aside a harmful thought or action and put on more Christlike character.

In day 1 you listed a behavior you hope to tear down to become more Christlike. Today describe an instance in which you have already begun to set aside that behavior.

During your quiet time today read *Galatians 5,* another chapter you've been reading for instructions on Christlike behavior. Then complete the Daily Master Communication Guide in the margin.

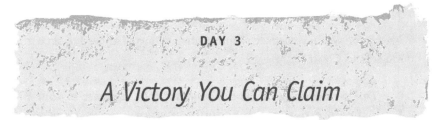

DAY 3

A Victory You Can Claim

Yesterday you learned that Jesus has already provided the victory for you when Satan tries to catch you at a weak moment and to turn your trust away from God. Picture the scene of Jesus dying on the cross for you. Do you know why He was there? So that you can participate in His victory over sin. Under the law no forgiveness of sins could occur without the shedding of blood. Jesus' death and resurrection make possible your righteousness before God. His sinless perfection is the only acceptable offering for your atonement. Without the shedding of Jesus' blood, no removal of sins could happen. Read *Hebrews 9:22* in the margin.

Read the verses in the margin that describe Jesus' victory over sin. Match each verse with the correct summary statement.

___ 1. *Hebrews 9:26*   a. **You are dead to sin through Jesus.**

___ 2. *Romans 6:11*   b. **Jesus' blood cleanses you from sin.**

___ 3. *1 Corinthians 15:56-57*   c. **Jesus purified us from sin by His sacrifice.**

___ 4. *1 John 1:7*   d. **You have victory over sin through Jesus.**

The blood of our sinless Savior is the source of your cleansing from sin. It is as though you are dead to the power of sin. Sin is no longer your master. Jesus has provided a way out. The correct answers are 1. c, 2. a, 3. d, 4. b.

A LIFE OF VICTORY

Jesus' victory can be yours. *Galatians 2:20* states two inseparable dynamics of victory: *I have been crucified with Christ and I no longer live, but Christ lives in me. The life I live in the body, I live by faith in the Son of God, who loved me and gave himself for me.* One of those dynamics is death—the rejection of your own selfish desires. The other is new life—the complete commitment to Christ's lordship and God's will.

Complete this verse with the words that describe these two dynamics in action. Check your work by looking in the previous paragraph.

"I have been _____ with Christ and I no longer _____."

Death to self produces a life that is victorious over the world, the flesh, and the devil. This theme is repeated in *Romans 6:11,* which appears in the margin.

Read *Romans 6:11* in the margin. Write in your own words what this verse means.

In fact, the law requires that nearly everything be cleansed with blood, and without the shedding of blood there is no forgiveness (Heb. 9:22).

Then Christ would have had to suffer many times since the creation of the world. But now he has appeared once for all at the end of the ages to do away with sin by the sacrifice of himself (Heb. 9:26).

Count yourselves dead to sin but alive to God in Christ Jesus (Rom. 6:11).

The sting of death is sin, and the power of sin is the law. But thanks be to God! He gives us the victory through our Lord Jesus Christ (1 Cor. 15:56-57).

If we walk in the light, as he is in the light, we have fellowship with one another, and the blood of Jesus, his Son, purifies us from all sin (1 John 1:7).

**Daily Master
Communication Guide**

Colossians 3

What God said to me:

What I said to God:

Maybe you wrote something like this: I think of myself as dead to sin but alive through Jesus Christ.

The verse you wrote about, *Romans 6:11,* appears in your Bible just before this week's Scripture-memory verses, *Romans 6:12-13.* Practice saying aloud your memory verses and review the other verses you've memorized.

How do you feel about the fact that Jesus' victory over sin can be yours? Check the statement or statements that apply:
❏ I have a difficult time believing that this is possible. Sin and the devil are too powerful to be overcome.
❏ I want to believe that I have victory over sin, but I feel unworthy.
❏ I don't deserve this kind of love, but I believe God's Word when it says that this is a precious gift to me, and I accept it freely.
❏ Other: _____

Christ's victory over sin is a popular theme in sermons and lessons in churches. Using the Hearing the Word form on page 220, write what you've learned from a Sunday School lesson or a sermon this week, especially anything related to victorious living.

IN THE CARPENTER'S SHOP
How are you claiming Christ's victory in your efforts to put off the old self and to replace it with the new? Yesterday you wrote about progress you are making in tearing down old habits in areas related to greed. Today describe something new Christ is adding to your life to replace the old.

During your quiet time today read *Colossians 3,* that's about living a Christlike life. Let God speak to you through this passage. Then complete the **Daily Master Communication Guide** in the margin.

DAY 4

Resisting Temptation

Victory in Jesus Christ may seem easy enough to claim when you're listening to a good sermon at church or when you're having a meaningful quiet time at home. But what about when you're on the job, in a family conflict, or in a personal struggle? How do you experience victory in the heat of daily circumstances?

STRENGTH TO WITHSTAND TEMPTATION

To understand how to experience this victory, first study how sin takes root in your life. Sin begins with temptation. The Bible says that Jesus was tempted in every way you are tempted; yet He did not sin (see *Heb. 4:15* in the margin). How reassuring it is to realize that He knows and understands when you find yourself on the verge of falling into Satan's traps. Because Jesus understands, He can help you when you're tempted (see *Heb. 2:18* in the margin).

Read *1 Corinthians 10:13* in the margin. Based on what you read, explain what's wrong with this statement: Some temptations are so strong that they can't be resisted.

We do not have a high priest who is unable to sympathize with our weaknesses, but we have one who has been tempted in every way, just as we are—yet was without sin (Heb. 4:15).

Because he himself suffered when he was tempted, he is able to help those who are being tempted (Heb. 2:18).

No temptation has seized you except what is common to man. And God is faithful; he will not let you be tempted beyond what you can bear. But when you are tempted, he will also provide a way out so that you can stand up under it (1 Cor. 10:13).

No temptation is too strong to withstand. For every temptation God provides a way of escape.

What impact does prayer have on temptation? Read *Matthew 26:41* in the margin. Then check the correct answer.
❏ **If you pray, you will not be tempted.**
❏ **Through prayer you can resist temptation.**

"Watch and pray so that you will not fall into temptation. The spirit is willing, but the body is weak" (Matt. 26:41).

The verse from *Matthew* that you read contains words spoken by Jesus when He was in the garden of Gethsemane with the disciples. He knew that they would need more than willing spirits to withstand the temptation ahead of them. He knew that they needed to be strengthened with prayer. Prayer doesn't prevent temptation. Temptation will always occur. Prayer can give you the spiritual strength to resist temptation.

FLEEING TEMPTATION

Evil thoughts and desires may pass through a person's mind. That is temptation. Temptation itself is not sin. Dwelling on those thoughts—letting the mind entertain the idea—is sin. When a worldly Christian "window-shops" for sin, the devil comes to the door and invites the worldly Christian in. The worldly Christian responds, "Oh, no, just looking." Yet this person's openness to temptation often leads to sin.

What does the Bible warn a spiritual Christian to do about temptation? Read *2 Timothy 2:22* in the margin. A spiritual Christian is warned to—
❑ **run away from temptation;**
❑ **seek it.**

What does the same verse say that a spiritual Christian is to pursue?

Flee the evil desires of youth, and pursue righteousness, faith, love and peace, along with those who call on the Lord out of a pure heart (2 Tim. 2:22).

A spiritual Christian is to pursue righteousness, faith, love, and peace. If right living; faith in God; and loving, peaceful relationships are the goals, a spiritual Christian has an arsenal of weapons to use in times of temptation.

Reread the case studies on page 190. Describe the steps each Christian could take to withstand temptation.

Julie:

Ken:

Ray:

Julie is a prime candidate for Satan's attack because of her discouragement. She could resist Satan by admitting her frustration in her job hunt while remembering God's faithfulness to her in the past and seeking assurance from Scripture that He cares about His children. She could ask other Christians to give her tips for finding a job. She should ask others to pray that God will provide for her family.

Resisting temptation during physical pain like Ken's takes strength of character that only the Holy Spirit makes possible. Ken could lay his physical condition and his future at the foot of the cross, believing that he can trust the days ahead to

the God who created him and took care of him until this time. He could acknowledge his feelings of loneliness and helplessness. He could pray about his options,
including other courses of treatment or other medical opinions. He could check
with his school administrators for possibilities to help him graduate such as cor-
respondence courses, tutors, or a "home-bound" teacher until his health
improves.

Ray's arrogance and self-importance are ways Satan is gaining a foothold in his
life. The Holy Spirit can convict Ray of sin in his life and can bring him to seek forgiveness. Ray could reexamine his use of time and resources. Besides returning to
regular fellowship with believers, he could spend some of his leisure time in ministry programs of the church. Instead of placing self-gratification at the center of
his life, he could focus on Christ as his main priority.

**Everyone, even a spiritual person, sins. What should you do when the
Holy Spirit convicts you of sin in your life? Read _1 John 1:9-10_ in the
margin and write _true_ beside the correct statement:**

_____ **1. You should say that you have not sinned.**
_____ **2. You should confess your sin.**
_____ **3. You should punish yourself for your sin.**

_If we confess our sins, he is faithful and
just and will forgive us our sins and purify
us from all unrighteousness. If we claim
we have not sinned, we make him out to
be a liar and his word has no place in
our lives (1 John 1:9-10)._

No one is above sin. God wants you to confess sin. Confession enables God
to keep His promise to forgive you. The correct statement is 2.

Whom do you know who needs to hear the healing message that God forgives sin? Many people you know live in the bondage of sin, not knowing that they
can claim God's promise to wipe away their sins. Your testimony can help you
share that good news.

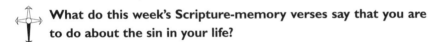 **Continue to work on your testimony, using the ideas your leader
gave you last week. Remember to limit it to three minutes. Be
ready to give your testimony at the Testimony Workshop that
follows this study.**

**What do this week's Scripture-memory verses say that you are
to do about the sin in your life?**

**Say aloud this week's Scripture-memory verses. Then review the vers-
es you memorized during the previous weeks of this study.**

**During your quiet time today read _Job 1_, which describes Job's
refusal to sin in the face of discouragement. See how God speaks
to you through this passage. Then complete the Daily Master
Communication Guide on the next page.**

**Daily Master
Communication Guide**

Job 1

What God said to me:

What I said to God:

APPLYING THE DISCIPLE'S PERSONALITY

Practice explaining in your own words how to apply the Disciple's Personality, using *Galatians 5:16-25.* Your leader should have explained how to do this in your previous group session. On the basic diagram below, close the door of the flesh as you draw a cross in the center of the circle to encompass *spirit, flesh, mind, will,* and *emotions.* Write *crucified* across *flesh.* Now write *walk, led,* and *live* above the circle and draw an arrow above these words pointing up. Write *fruit of the Spirit* above the arrow and draw above these words another upward arrow pointing to God. Then write *lusts* and *desires* below the circle with an arrow pointing down toward *works of the flesh.* Draw another arrow that points down toward Satan. See page 219 if you need help with your drawing.

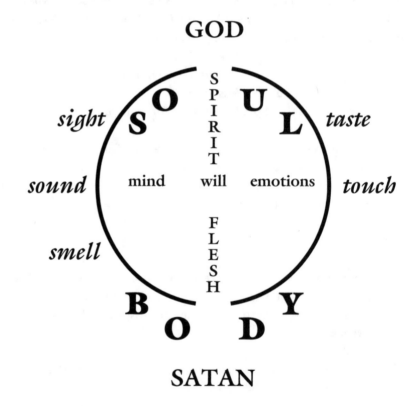

Now write your explanation here.

DAY 5

Victory in Jesus

A young woman told my wife and I one of the most amazing stories about victorious living that I've ever heard. Her life began as anything but victorious.

The young woman was one of six children of an alcoholic father. By the age of 13 she was living on the street on her own. From there her life spiraled downward until she was living with her boyfriend. Yet through determination she graduated from college, and started teaching in elementary school. One of her students, a nine-year-old girl, seemed different. After school she helped erase the chalkboard and clean the room, and the two became good friends. The student asked the woman if she went to church. The woman answered that she used to go to confession with her mother. The girl asked her teacher to help her learn Scripture verses she needed to learn before being baptized. The first Scripture was *John 3:16.* When the woman read it, she cried. "I couldn't imagine that God loved me after what I had done," the woman recalled.

The woman then attended a church service and cried all the way through it. "I talked to my live-in boyfriend and told him that we needed to change," she said. One day when he was away, she returned home to find a man in her apartment searching for money. When she couldn't give him any money, he raped her. The woman recounted what happened next: "After it was over, I opened the Bible to *John 3:16,* which was the only verse I knew. Then he said that he knew what he had done was wrong but that his mother was sick and needed money. He asked me to forgive him. I responded, 'If God is willing to forgive me for all I've done, how can I refuse to forgive you?' We knelt, and he asked for forgiveness. Asking forgiveness for my sinful lifestyle, I turned over my life to Christ. Two weeks later I went back to church and made my profession of faith. My boyfriend would not change, so I moved out."

The woman then began praying for her parents' salvation. Six years later, they gave their lives to Christ. She began serving at church, then went on mission trips to Mexico and Belize. Now she serves as a missionary in a country closed to the gospel. She concluded her story: "I praise God for His goodness and His love. I'm thankful that I can show His love to people who don't know anything about Him."

As she walked away, I thought to myself: *O the depth of riches both of the wisdom and knowledge of God! how unsearchable are his ... ways (Rom. 11:33,* KJV). After I heard the way Christ had graciously forgiven her and had helped her become a fervent, bright witness for Him, I understood even more clearly the victory we have in Christ.

Because of the cross, God forgives and accepts you, just like this woman in the above paragraphs. Therefore, you have no need to try to make things right yourself or to give up in despair. From the cross Jesus gives you His righteousness as you are crucified and resurrected with Him.

Jesus assures His disciples that those who suffer with Him will someday reign with Him (see *2 Tim. 2:11-13* in the margin). His victory points to the future, but it is also present tense.

*If we died with him,
we will also live with him;
if we endure,
we will also reign with him.
If we disown him,
he will also disown us;
if we are faithless,
he will remain faithful,
for he cannot disown himself
(2 Tim. 2:11-13).*

1. Something I have been getting rid of this week:

2. Something Christ has been adding to my character this week:

Steps I Need to Take:

IN THE CARPENTER'S SHOP

How has the Holy Spirit been working in you this week to build Christlike character? How are you progressing in getting rid of the old self and in letting the Spirit add new behaviors to your life?

Complete the two statements in the margin as you think about the changes related to greed that you identified earlier this week.

Stop and thank God for the gift of the Holy Spirit to help mold you into Christlikeness.

Meditate on the moral and spiritual victories Jesus has won for you during the past few weeks. Identify areas of your life in which you are still suffering defeat.

Review the seven steps to Christlike character listed at the end of the Disciple's Personality presentation (p. 218). Write in the margin what steps you need to take to achieve victory in every area of your life?

APPLYING THE DISCIPLE'S PERSONALITY

✝ **Now that you're approaching the end of this *MasterLife* study, you're asked to demonstrate your knowledge of the Disciple's Personality, which you've been learning throughout this study. Draw and explain in your own words the Disciple's Personality to another group member. Say the verses that go with it. See pages 212–19 if you need help.**

I hope that you've found your Scripture memory worthwhile during this study. You have memorized six Scriptures that accompany various parts of the Disciple's Personality. Nothing you have done in this study has been without an investment of time. I hope that this process has helped you hide God's Word in your heart so that you can use it, along with the concepts of the Disciple's Personality, in a variety of situations.

✝ **Write the verses you've memorized during this study. See how well you can remember them without looking back. Be prepared to say them to a partner at the Testimony Workshop.**

Romans 6:12-13:

Ephesians 5:18:

Philippians 2:13:

Romans 12:1-2:

Galatians 5:22-23:

1 Corinthians 6:19-20:

THE TESTIMONY WORKSHOP

As you've participated in this study, you've learned essential elements for writing your Christian testimony, which you should be ready to present at the Testimony Workshop that follows this study. I hope that this will be a meaningful experience for you.

 Practice giving your testimony to others as you prepare to present it during the Testimony Workshop at the end of this study. Limit it to three minutes. Be prepared to present it in a variety of situations—to a skeptical person, to someone who is eager to hear, to someone who believes that he or she can earn salvation, and so on.

During your quiet time today read *2 Timothy 2,* in which Paul instructed Timothy about claiming victory in Christ. Then complete the Daily Master Communication Guide in the margin.

HAS THIS WEEK MADE A DIFFERENCE?

Review "My Walk with the Master This Week" at the beginning of this week's material. Mark the activities you've finished by drawing vertical lines in the diamonds beside them. Finish any incomplete activities.

Congratulations on completing your study of *MasterLife, Student Edition.* I hope that the concept of life in the Spirit has new meaning for you after these weeks of study. Examining the warring components of your personality is challenging, often requiring that you admit your weaknesses and temptations even though you like to think of yourself as someone who doesn't easily stumble. I pray that this process has made you more aware of the vulnerable areas of your life so that you can be more alert to times when you need to close the door of sin. May the Holy Spirit strengthen you as you claim victory in Christ.

What a great time of fellowship and growth you have to look forward to when you attend the Testimony Workshop! By now your leader has probably given you details about this workshop. I predict that you'll be moved in ways you can't imagine when you hear reports of ways the Holy Spirit has worked in group members' lives. Most importantly you will be empowered and motivated as you refine and polish your own three-minute testimony and prepare to share it with persons that need to hear it. The workshop will give you strength and courage to bear witness that you never thought you could experience. I hope you have great days ahead as a disciple of Jesus Christ!

Daily Master Communication Guide

2 Timothy 2

What God said to me:

What I said to God:

The Disciple's Cross

The Disciple's Cross is the focal point for all you learn in *MasterLife: The Disciple's Cross*. The cross provides an instrument for visualizing and understanding your opportunities and responsibilities as a disciple of Christ.

Following are step-by-step instructions for presenting the Disciple's Cross to another person. Each week of this study you learn a portion of the Disciple's Cross and the Scripture that accompanies it. As you learn the cross and review it in the future, you may find it helpful to refer to this step-by-step explanation and to the completed drawing on page 204. Don't attempt to memorize this presentation. You'll learn how to present it in your own words. Don't feel overwhelmed by the amount of material involved. You'll learn it in weekly segments. By the end of the study you will be able to explain the entire cross and to say all of the verses that accompany it.

To explain the cross to someone, use a blank, unlined sheet of paper to draw the illustration developed here in stages. Instructions to you are in parentheses. The following material is the presentation you make to the other person.

A disciple of Christ is a person who makes Christ the Lord of his or her life. (Quote *Luke 9:23* and write the reference and the three commitments in the upper right corner of the page: *deny, cross, follow.*) A disciple's first commitment is to deny yourself. That doesn't mean to reject your identity but to renounce the self-centered life. To do that, a disciple of Christ learns the following six disciplines of the Christian life.

SPEND TIME WITH THE MASTER

(In the center of the page draw a circle.) The empty circle represents your life. It pictures denying all of self for Christ. You can't be a disciple of Christ if you're not willing to deny self. If this circle represents your life, Christ should fill the entire circle as you focus on Him. (Write the word *Christ* in the circle.) Christ is to have priority in everything. Life in Christ is Christ living in you.

(Write *John 15:5* under the word *Christ* in the circle and quote the verse from memory.) What can you do without abiding in Christ? Nothing! Christ said that He is the Vine and that we are the branches. The branches are part of the Vine. You are part of Christ. He wants to live His life through you. Is this the kind of life you would like to have?

Luke 9:23
Deny
Cross
Follow

In addition to denying yourself, you need to take up your cross. The Disciple's Cross pictures the resources Christ gives us to help us live in Him. (Draw the cross around the circle.)

LIVE IN THE WORD

The way to have life in Christ is to have His Word in you. (Write *Word* and *John 8:31-32* on the lower crossbar and quote these verses from memory.) The Word is your food. You cannot grow closer to Christ unless you regularly stay in the Word. You receive the Word in many ways: by listening to someone preach it, by reading it, by studying it, by memorizing it, by meditating on it, and by applying it. Making Christ Lord means that you want to study, meditate on, and apply the Word regularly.

PRAY IN FAITH

Part of life in Christ and of having a relationship with Him is praying in faith. (Write *prayer* and *John 15:7* on the upper crossbar and quote the verse from memory. Point to the words *Christ, Word,* and *prayer* as you quote the corresponding parts of the verse.) If you abide in Christ and His Word abides in you, you can ask what you want, and God will do it. Notice that the vertical bar of the cross, representing the Word and prayer, highlights your relationship with God, the basic ways you communicate with God, and the basic ways He communicates with you.

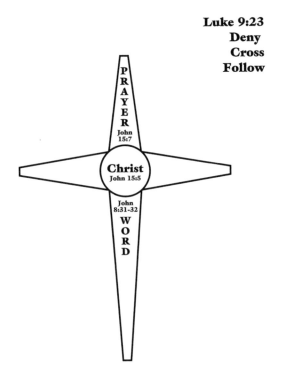

FELLOWSHIP WITH BELIEVERS

Life in Christ means that you live in fellowship with your brothers and sisters in Christ. (Write *fellowship* and *John 13:34-35* on the right crossbar and quote these verses from memory.) Jesus said the way to show that you are His disciple is to love one another. God provided the ideal place for you to grow—His church. A church is not a building or an organization, although it uses both of these. A church is a body of baptized believers who have agreed to carry out Christ's ministry in the world. A committed Christian stays in fellowship with a local body of believers in order to grow in Christ. The church is the body of Christ! If you have life in Christ, you realize how important living in His body, the church, is.

WITNESS TO THE WORLD

Life in Christ includes witnessing to others. It involves following Him, another commitment of a disciple. Witnessing is shar-

ing with others about Christ and your relationship with Him. (Write *witness* and *John 15:8* on the left crossbar and quote the verse from memory.) If you abide in Christ, you will bear fruit. Fruit can be the fruit of the Spirit or a new Christian. *Galatians 5:22-23* lists the fruit of the Spirit as love, joy, peace, patience, kindness, goodness, faithfulness, gentleness, and self-control. Fruit does not always grow quickly, but it grows continually and bears in season. Fruit bearing is the normal, natural result when you have Christ at the center of your life. Jesus said the way to show that you are His disciple is to bear much fruit. This includes witnessing. Witnessing is the natural outgrowth of living in Christ. If you are spending time with the Master, living daily in the Word, praying in faith, and fellowshipping with God's people, you naturally share with others the Christ who lives in your heart.

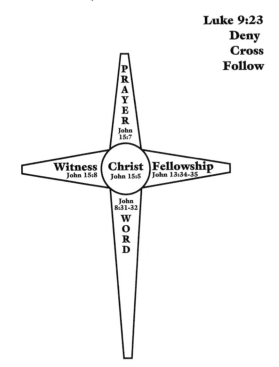

MINISTER TO OTHERS

As the fruit of the Spirit grows in your life in Christ, you also reach out to others through ministry. You take up your cross in service to others, which is another commitment of a disciple. Cross bearing is voluntary, redemptive service for others.

Look again at the circle in the center of the cross. Your life in Christ should continue to grow and expand. (Make circular broken lines that move out from the center of the circle.)

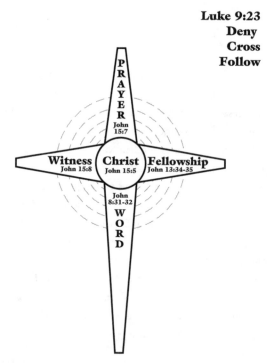

Luke 9:23
Deny
Cross
Follow

As you grow in Christ, you reach out to others through all kinds of ministry and service. (Add pointed arrows to the ends of the crossbars.) The arrows indicate that your growth in Christ should express itself in ministries. Living in the Word leads to a ministry of teaching or preaching. (Write *ministry of teaching/preaching* below the cross.)

Praying in faith leads to a ministry of worship or intercession. (Write *ministry of worship/intercession* above the cross.)

Fellowshipping with believers leads to a ministry of nurture to other believers. (Write *ministry of nurture* to the right of the cross.)

Witnessing to the world leads to a ministry of evangelism. (Write *ministry of evangelism* to the left of the cross.)

Your witness and your fellowship lead to Christian service to other persons. (Write *ministry of service: John 15:13* above the horizontal bar and quote the verse.) Notice that the horizontal bar of the cross, representing witness and ministry, highlights your relationships with others.

These five ministry areas compose the ministry of a disciple and of Christ's church. The goal of discipleship is expressed in *2 Timothy 2:21: If a man cleanses himself from the latter, he will be an instrument for noble purposes, made holy, useful to the Master and prepared to do any good work.* You need to grow in all spiritual disciplines and ministries to master life and to be prepared for the Master's use. If you develop all of these disciplines, your life will be balanced and fruitful.

(As you present the following, write the number and the first word following the number in the upper left corner of the page.) To remember this illustration, notice that you have—

1 Lord as the first priority of your life;

2 relationships: a vertical relationship with God and horizontal relationships with others;

3 commitments: deny self, take up your cross daily, and follow Christ;

4 resources to center your life in Christ: the Word, prayer, fellowship, and witness;

5 ministries that grow from the four resources: teaching/preaching, worship/intercession, nurture, evangelism, and service;

6 disciplines of a disciple: spend time with the Master, live in the Word, pray in faith, fellowship with believers, witness to the world, and minister to others.

By practicing these biblical principles, you can abide in Christ and can be useful in the Master's service.

Cross Diagram D

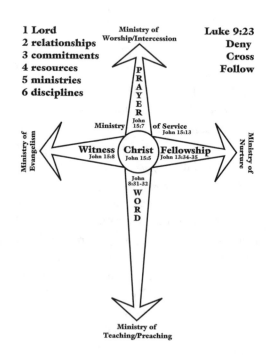

Prayer-Covenant List

Request	Date	Bible Promise	Answer	Date

MasterTime Worksheet

1. List major goals that you believe God has given you. Group them by year, month, week, and day.

2. List your daily and weekly responsibilities.

3. List your daily and weekly appointments

4. Rank the above goals, responsibilities, and appointments according to your priorities and time necessary.

5. Rank the goals long-term, year, month, week, day. Complete a MasterTime form for each.

6. Plan your task schedule for today keeping in mind your immediate commitments and responsibilities as well as your long-term goals. Write these on the Mastertime form. Continue each morning to complete your task schedule on a MasterTime form.

MasterTime
My Walk with the Master

Day _____   Date _____

Priority	Daily Tasks to Do	Minutes
	Daily Quiet Time	

Weekly Tasks to Do

Planning Ahead—Long-term Goals

Discipleship Inventory

This Discipleship Inventory[1] measures the functional discipleship level of individuals, groups, and churches. By using the inventory, believers can assess their development by considering 30 characteristics of a New Testament disciple in the categories of attitudes, behavior, relationships, ministry, and doctrine.

Follow these directions to complete the inventory:

• Respond to each statement as honestly as possible. Select an answer that most clearly reflects your life as it is, not as you would like it to be.

• Choose one answer for each statement.

• Don't spend too much time on any one question.

You will receive instructions for scoring your inventory at the Growing Disciples Workshop that follows this study.

How true is each of the following statements of you? Choose from these responses:

> 1 = never true   4 = often true
> 2 = rarely true   5 = almost always true
> 3 = sometimes true

1. I try to live by the Bible's moral and ethical teachings. **12345**

2. Reading and studying the Bible has made significant changes in the way I live my life. **12345**

3. My faith shapes how I think and act each day. **12345**

4. I talk with other persons about my beliefs in Christ as Savior and Lord. **12345**

5. I take time for prayer each day. **12345**

6. Because God has forgiven me, I respond with a forgiving attitude when others wrong me. **12345**

7. While interacting with others in everyday contacts, I seek opportunities to speak out about Jesus Christ. **12345**

8. My classmates and friends know that I am a Christian. **12345**

9. I go out of my way to show love to people I meet. **12345**

10. When I realize that I have disobeyed a specific teaching of the Bible, I correct the wrongdoing. **12345**

11. I pray for God's help when I have needs or problems. **12345**

12. I share personal feelings and needs with Christian friends. **12345**

13. I hold a grudge when treated unfairly. **12345**

14. I devote time to reading and studying the Bible. **12345**

15. I like to worship and pray with others. **12345**

16. I use my gifts and talents to serve others. **12345**

17. When I realize that I've offended someone, I go to him or her to admit and correct my wrongdoing. **12345**

18. I pray for the salvation of friends and acquaintances who are not professing Christians. **12345**

19. I work to remove barriers or problems that develop between me and my friends. **12345**

20. I feel too inadequate to help others. **12345**

How often, if ever, do you do each of the following? Choose from these responses:

> 1 = seldom or never   4 = several times a week
> 2 = about once a month   5 = once a day or more
> 3 = about once a week

21. Pray with other Christians, other than during church. **12345**

22. Participate in a small-group Bible study, other than Sunday School. **12345**

23. Pray or meditate, other than at church or before meals. **12345**

24. Memorize verses or passages of the Bible. **12345**

25. Study the Bible on my own. **12345**

26. Pray specifically for missions and missionaries. **12345**

Indicate how much you agree or disagree with each of the following statements. Choose from these responses:

> 1 = definitely disagree   4 = tend to agree
> 2 = tend to disagree   5 = definitely agree
> 3 = not sure

27. It is my personal responsibility to share the gospel message with non-Christians in my life. **12345**

28. Once a person is saved, he can't lose his salvation. **12345**

29. I often accept other Christians' constructive criticism and correction. **12345**

30. I believe that the Holy Spirit is active in my life. **12345**

31. If a person sincerely seeks God, she can obtain eternal life through religions other than Christianity. **12345**

32. I know how to explain the gospel clearly to another person without relying on an evangelistic tract. **12345**

33. A Christian should consider himself accountable to other Christians. **1 2 3 4 5**

34. A Christian should regularly find ways to tell others about Jesus. **1 2 3 4 5**

35. Salvation is available only through receiving Jesus Christ. **1 2 3 4 5**

36. My Christian life is no one else's business. **1 2 3 4 5**

37. The Holy Spirit comes into a person the moment she accepts Jesus as Savior. **1 2 3 4 5**

38. A literal place called hell exists. **1 2 3 4 5**

39. I believe that I have a personal responsibility to help the poor and hungry. **1 2 3 4 5**

40. The complete indwelling of the Holy Spirit occurs through an experience that is usually separate and distinct from the conversion experience. **1 2 3 4 5**

How many hours during the past month have you done each of the following through church, other organizations, or on your own? Don't count time spent in a paid job. Choose from these responses:

3 = 3–5 hours

1 = 0 hours   4 = 6–9 hours

2 = 1–2 hours   5 = 10 hours or more

41. Donated time helping persons who are poor, hungry, sick, or unable to care for themselves (don't count family members). **1 2 3 4 5**

42. Visited those who have visited my church. **1 2 3 4 5**

43. Helped friends or neighbors with problems. **1 2 3 4 5**

44. Been involved in a missions-related ministry or cause (for example, teaching about missions, raising money for missions, missions volunteer work). **1 2 3 4 5**

45. Visited persons in the hospital. **1 2 3 4 5**

46. Volunteered time at my church to teach, lead, serve on a committee, or help with a program or event. **1 2 3 4 5**

47. Visited in the homes of Christian friends. **1 2 3 4 5**

48. Visited the elderly or the homebound. **1 2 3 4 5**

How true is each of the following statements for you? Choose from these responses:

1 = absolutely false   4 = mostly true

2 = somewhat false   5 = absolutely true

3 = not sure

49. I am open and responsive to Bible teachers in my church. **1 2 3 4 5**

50. I readily receive and forgive those who offend me. **1 2 3 4 5**

51. I see myself as loved and valued by God. **1 2 3 4 5**

52. I express genuine praise and gratitude to God even in the midst of difficult circumstances. **1 2 3 4 5**

53. I avoid close relationships with others who hinder the expression of my Christian values and principles. **1 2 3 4 5**

54. I am consciously aware that God placed me on earth to contribute to the fulfillment of His plans and purposes. **1 2 3 4 5**

55. I recognize that everything I have belongs to God. **1 2 3 4 5**

56. My life is filled with stress and anxiety. **1 2 3 4 5**

57. I believe that God will always provide my basic needs in life. **1 2 3 4 5**

58. I am somewhat hesitant to let others know that I am a Christian. **1 2 3 4 5**

59. I avoid situations in which I might be tempted by sexual immorality. **1 2 3 4 5**

60. I am presently struggling with an unforgiving attitude toward another person. **1 2 3 4 5**

61. I feel very inferior to others in my church. **1 2 3 4 5**

62. I seek God first in expressing my values and setting my priorities. **1 2 3 4 5**

63. I am able to remain confident of God's love and provision even during very difficult circumstances. **1 2 3 4 5**

64. I forgive those who offend me even if they do not apologize. **1 2 3 4 5**

65. Being a Christian is a private matter and doesn't need to be discussed with others. **1 2 3 4 5**

Last year what percentage of your income did you contribute to each of the following? Choose from these responses:

1 = 0%   4 = 6–9%

2 = 1–2%   5 = 10% and above

3 = 3–5%

66. To my church. **1 2 3 4 5**

67. To other religious groups or organizations. **1 2 3 4 5**

68. To charities or social-service organizations. **1 2 3 4 5**

69. To international missions (through my church and denomination). **1 2 3 4 5**

For the following question choose from these responses:

1 = none   4 = the majority

2 = a few   5 = all

3 = several

70. How many of your closest friends do you consider to be unbelievers? 12345

How often have you done each of the following during the past year? Choose from these responses:

1 = never   4 = 6–9 times

2 = once   5 = 10 times or more

3 = 2–5 times

71. Clearly felt God's presence in my life. 12345

72. Shared with someone how to become a Christian. 12345

73. Invited an unchurched person to attend church, Bible study, or another evangelistic event. 12345

74. Experienced the Holy Spirit's providing understanding, guidance, or conviction of sin. 12345

75. Met with a new Christian to help him grow spiritually. 12345

76. Told others about God's work in my life. 12345

77. Helped someone pray to receive Christ. 12345

78. Gave a gospel tract or similar literature to an unbeliever. 12345

Indicate how much you agree or disagree with each of the following. Choose from these responses:

1 = strongly disagree   4 = agree

2 = disagree   5 = strongly agree

3 = not sure

79. It is very important for every Christian to serve others. 12345

80. One day God will hold me accountable for how I used my time, money, and talents. 12345

81. All Christians are to follow Bible teachings. 12345

82. The Bible is the authoritative source of wisdom for daily living. 12345

83. A Christian must learn to deny herself to serve Christ effectively. 12345

84. I have a hard time accepting myself. 12345

85. I have identified my primary spiritual gift. 12345

86. Following death, an unbeliever goes to a place called hell. 12345

87. Jesus' teachings are binding for the modern Christian. 12345

88. Giving time to a specific ministry in the church is necessary for a Christian's spiritual welfare. 12345

89. Regardless of my circumstances, I believe God always keeps His promises. 12345

90. Without the death of Jesus, salvation would not be possible. 12345

91. The Bible is a completely reliable revelation from God. 12345

Indicate how well-trained and prepared you believe you are in these areas. Choose from these responses:

1 = not trained at all   4 = adequately trained

2 = somewhat trained   5 = well-trained

3 = average

92. Presenting the plan of salvation. 12345

93. Individually following up or helping a new Christian grow and develop spiritually. 12345

94. Leading someone to pray to receive Christ. 12345

95. Visiting a prospect for my church. 12345

96. Leading a small-group Bible study. 12345

97. Sharing my personal testimony about how I became a Christian. 12345

How often during the past two or three years have you done each of the following? Choose from these responses:

1 = never   4 = weekly

2 = a few times   5 = daily

3 = monthly

98. Read the Bible by myself. 12345

99. Consciously put into practice the teachings of the Bible. 12345

100. Prayed by myself. 12345

101. Provided help to needy persons in my town or city. 12345

102. Read and studied about the Christian faith. 12345

103. Participated in Bible studies, religious programs, or groups outside my church. 12345

104. Made the necessary changes when I realized, as a result of exposure to the Bible, that an aspect of my life was not right. 12345

105. Shared an insight, idea, principle, or guideline from the Bible with others. 12345

106. Experienced the care, love, and support of other persons in a church. 12345

107. Directly tried to encourage someone to believe in Jesus Christ. 12345

108. Intentionally spent time building friendships with non-Christians. 12345

How true is each of these statements for you? Choose from these responses:

   1 = never true   4 = often true
   2 = rarely true   5 = almost always true
   3 = sometimes true

109. I feel God's presence in my relationships with other persons. 12345

110. I treat persons of the opposite sex in a pure and holy manner. 12345

111. When convicted of sin in my life, I readily confess it to God as sin. 12345

112. Through prayer I seek to discern God's will. 12345

113. I readily forgive others because of my understanding that God has forgiven me. 12345

114. I help others with their religious questions and struggles. 12345

115. I have learned through my faith and the Scriptures how to sacrifice for the good of others. 12345

116. I share my faults and weaknesses with others whom I consider to be close to me. 12345

117. I am generally the same person in private that I am in public. 12345

118. When God makes me aware of His specific will in an area of my life, I follow His leading. 12345

119. I regularly find myself choosing God's way over my way in specific instances. 12345

120. I am honest in my dealings with others. 12345

121. I regularly pray for my church's ministry. 12345

How often do you attend the following activities?

Choose from these responses:

   1 = never   4 = weekly
   2 = a few times   5 = more than once a week
   3 = monthly

122. Worship services at my church. 12345

123. Sunday School class. 12345

124. Bible studies other than Sunday School. 12345

125. Prayer groups or prayer meetings. 12345

Indicate how much you agree or disagree with each of these statements. Choose from these responses:

   1 = definitely disagree   4 = tend to agree
   2 = tend to disagree   5 = definitely agree
   3 = not sure

126. God fulfills His plan primarily through believers within a local-church context. 12345

127. Christ designated local churches as His means and environment for nurturing believers in the faith. 12345

128. A new believer should experience believer's baptism by immersion prior to acceptance by a local church as a member. 12345

129. Baptism and the Lord's Supper are local church ordinances and should not be practiced outside the gathered church. 12345

130. Each person born into the world inherited a sinful nature as a result of Adam's fall and is thereby separated from God and is in need of a Savior. 12345

131. Each local church is autonomous, with Jesus Christ as the Head, and should work together with other churches to spread the gospel to all people. 12345

132. There is only one true and personal God, who reveals Himself to humanity as God the Father, God the Son, and God the Holy Spirit. 12345

133. Christ will return a second time to receive His believers, living and dead, unto Himself and to bring the world to an appropriate end. 12345

134. Jesus Christ is God's Son, who died on the cross for the sins of the world and was resurrected from the dead. 12345

135. Jesus Christ, during His incarnate life on earth, was fully God and fully man. 12345

136. How religious or spiritual would you say your 3 or 4 best friends are? **123**

    1 = not very religious

    2 = somewhat religious

    3 = very religious

137. How many of your closest friends are professing Christians? **12345**

    1 = none   4 = the majority

    2 = a few   5 = all

    3 = several

138. Are you male or female?   **Male**   **Female**

139. Indicate your age group: **123**

    1 = 12–15

    2 = 16–19

    3 = 20 and over

140. I have been an active member of a local church. **12345**

    1 = never   4 = a large part of my life

    2 = a short time   5 = most of my life in my life

    3 = about half of my life

141. How long have you been a Christian? **12345**

    1 = less than 1 year   4 = 6–10 years

    2 = 1–3 years   5 = 11– 20 years

    3 = 4–5 years

142. Identifying as a member of a local church wherever I live is—**12345**

    1 = unnecessary   4 = of great value

    2 = of little value   5 = imperative

    3 = of some value

143. Have you ever been involved in discipleship training (an organized, weekly discipleship group)? **Yes No**

If so, which discipleship-training program were you involved in?

144. *MasterLife, Student Edition*   Yes   No

145. *Disciple Youth*   Yes   No

146. *Survival Kit*   Yes   No

147. *Tm 412*   Yes   No

148. *The Youth Disciple*   Yes   No

If other, please provide the name: _____

149. How many weeks were you involved in this discipleship training? **12345**

    1 = 0–5 weeks   4 = 16–25 weeks

    2 = 6–10 weeks   5 = More than 25 weeks

    3 = 11–15 weeks

150. When were you involved in this training? **From** _____ **to** _____

151. Was this discipleship training sponsored by your church? **Yes No**   If not, what group or organization sponsored the training?_____

152. Have you ever been discipled one-to-one by another Christian? **Yes No**

_____

James Slack and Brad Waggoner, "The Discipleship Inventory" (Richmond: The International Mission Board of the Southern Baptist Convention). Used by permission.

The Disciple's Personality

The Disciple's Personality is the focal point for all you learn in weeks 6-12. This presentation provides an instrument for understanding why you think, feel, and act as you do and explains how to become more Christlike in character and behavior.

Following are step-by-step instructions for presenting the Disciple's Personality to another person. Each week of this study you learn an additional portion of the presentation and the Scripture that accompanies it. As you learn the Disciple's Personality and review it in the future, you may find it helpful to refer to this step-by-step explanation and to the drawings.

Do not attempt to memorize this presentation. You'll learn how to present it in your own words. Don't feel overwhelmed by the amount of material involved. You will learn it in weekly segments. By the end of the study you'll be able to explain the entire Disciple's Personality and to say all of the verses that accompany it.

To explain the Disciple's Personality to someone, use blank, unlined sheets of paper to draw the illustrations shown. Instructions to you are in parentheses. The material that follows is the presentation you make to the other person. The words in bold type indicate when to add to your drawings.

Perhaps you sometimes wonder why you think, feel, and act as you do. May I draw an illustration that helped me understand myself? This drawing illustrates biblical teachings about your personality. It shows you how to make Christ Master of your life and how to master life.

A UNIFIED PERSONALITY

(Draw an incomplete circle in the center of a blank sheet of paper, leaving spaces at the top and the bottom of the circle as shown below. Write the word *God* above the circle.) **God** created you as a physical and spiritual being. The physical part

came from the earth. The spiritual part originated in God's Spirit. The circle represents you—your total personality. The Bible describes you as a unity. That's why I drew one circle to represent your personality. I will add each element of your personality as I explain it. When you understand each element of your personality and how it functions, you'll discover how to integrate your personality under the lordship of Christ.

Body

(Write *body* beneath the circle. Write the five senses on each side of the circle as illustrated below.) The Bible pictures you

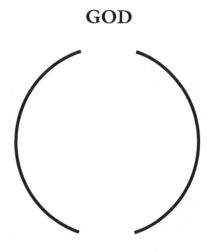

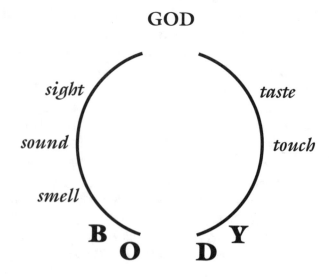

as a **body.** God made your body from the earth to serve several functions. Through your body you are able to participate in the physical world. Your **five senses** relate you to the rest of God's creation. Your body makes it possible to communicate with the world around you and with other living creatures. Your body gives you a physical identity that makes you a distinct, unique personality. God created your body good.

Soul

(Write the word *soul* inside the circle as illustrated. Write the words *mind, will,* and *emotions* as illustrated. Write the word *spirit* as illustrated below.) The Bible also pictures you as a **soul.** You do not just have a soul; you are a soul. *Genesis 2:7* says that the first human being became a living soul when God breathed into his nostrils the breath of life. God imparted His life to the person He had made. The words for *soul* in the Bible

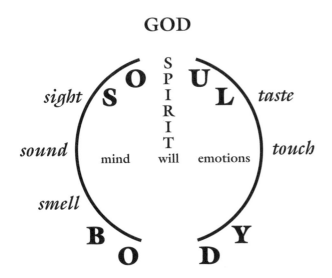

generally mean "life" or "the total self." When the Bible says that a person's soul is saved or lost, it refers to the total person. Sometimes the word for *soul* means "heart" or "the seat of the will, desires, and affection—the inner human being." The word *psyche* originates from the Greek word for *soul.* The soul's ability to think, will, and feel provides additional evidence that human beings are created in the image of God. These three elements—**mind, will,** and **emotions**—help form your distinctive personality.

Spirit

The Bible also pictures you as **spirit.** Your spirit directly relates you to God's image. It gives you the capacity to be aware of yourself and to fellowship and work with God. People and God are able to communicate directly. When God finished creating the first person, *Genesis 1:31* says, *It was very good.*[1]

THE NATURAL PERSON

The Flesh

(Write *Satan* beneath the circle.) Soon after the creation another spiritual being entered God's good creation. Humanity succumbed to **Satan's** temptation and disobeyed God. A different aspect of the spiritual nature entered the personality of human beings. That aspect is called the flesh. The Bible uses the word *flesh* in two ways. The general meaning is "body," referring to the physical body. The other meaning is symbolic, referring to the lower nature. It refers to the human capacity to sin and to follow Satan instead of God.

(Draw two open doors on the inside of the circle. Draw a handle inside each door.) Notice that the illustration has two doors. The top door, **the door of the spirit,** allows you to relate to God. The bottom door, **the door of the flesh,** allows you to relate to Satan. God created human beings with

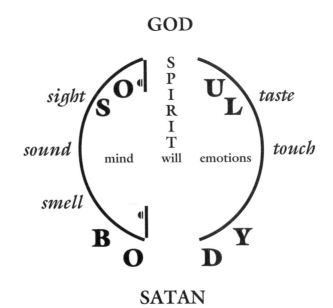

free will. Notice that the will stands between the door of the spirit and the door of the flesh and that the door handles are on the inside. Unfortunately, when Adam and Eve, the first human beings, were tempted by Satan, they chose to turn from God's leading to follow Satan's leading. At that moment the human being's ego, the big *I*, took over. (Draw lines between the two doors to form an *I* as illustrated below. Close the door of the spirit by completing the circle at the top. Draw a line through the word *spirit* as shown. Write *flesh* as illustrated. Leave the door of the flesh open.) The door of the **spirit** closed, and humanity died spiritually. The door of the **flesh** opened, and the sinful nature became the spiritual part of human personality. The results were terrible. The flesh came alive, causing the mind, will, and emotions to degenerate. The entire personality—body, soul, and spirit—was infiltrated by evil and death.

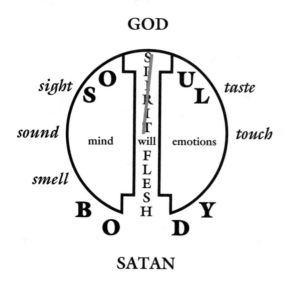

Through Satan's temptation humanity transgressed God's command and fell from its original innocence. Consequently, the descendants of the first sinful human beings inherit a nature and an environment inclined toward sin. As soon as they are capable of moral action, they become transgressors and are responsible to God for closing the door of the spirit and for shutting Him out.

The Condition of the Natural Person Today

(Write *The Natural Person* and *1 Corinthians 2:14* above the drawing.) **The natural person** is centered in himself or herself and is open to Satan's temptation and power. This person is unable to relate to God properly. **First Corinthians 2:14** says, *The man without the Spirit does not accept the things that come from the Spirit of God, for they are foolishness to him, and he cannot understand them, because they are spiritually discerned.*

Your thoughts are influenced by evil; your emotions control you; your will is weak. Even strong-willed and disciplined persons are not able to overcome the effects of the flesh. No matter how many good things you do, the Bible says that a natural person cannot please God. People can come to God only as the Holy Spirit draws them.

God loves you even though you have sinned. He sent His only Son to pay for your sins so that you would not perish but have eternal life. Jesus died on the cross to save you from sin and death and to bring you to God. After His resurrection He sent the Holy Spirit to earth to draw you to God.

The Holy Spirit can speak to a natural person even though the door of the spirit is closed. When you open the door of the spirit, the Spirit of God enters your personality, and your spirit is born again.

(If you are using this illustration with a lost person, move directly to the section "The Spiritual Christian." If you are talking with a Christian, proceed with "The Worldly Christian.")

THE WORLDLY CHRISTIAN
(Draw the illustration shown below. It is the same as the previous one without the line through *spirit* and with both doors left open. Write *The Worldly Christian* and *1 Corinthians 3:1-3* above the diagram.) Now I will draw the same **circle** to illustrate the worldly Christian. This person has **opened the door of the spirit** but has also **left open the door of flesh.** This person still lives in the flesh even though he or she

has been born again. At some point this person realized that Christ could give him or her eternal life. This person opened the door of the spirit and was born again by the power of the Holy Spirit. This Christian was made alive and became a partaker of the divine nature but failed to grow as he or she should.

Second Peter 1:3-4 says: His divine power has given us everything we need for life and godliness through our knowledge of him who called us by his own glory and goodness. Through these he has given us his very great and precious promises, so that through them you may participate in the divine nature and escape the corruption

in the world caused by evil desires. This passage then lists character traits a Christian needs to add as he or she grows: *Make every effort to add to your faith goodness; and to goodness, knowledge; and to knowledge, self-control; and to self-control, perseverance; and to perseverance, godliness; and to godliness, brotherly kindness; and to brotherly kindness, love (2 Pet. 1:5-7).* If the person does not do this, he or she will be ineffective, unproductive, nearsighted, and blind. The person will have *forgotten he has been cleansed from his past sins (2 Pet. 1:8-9).* These characteristics describe the worldly Christian. Christians who are not taught how to grow and live in the Spirit remain as they were when they were born again. They are still babies in the faith, although they may have been believers for many years. **First Corinthians 3:1-3** describes this person's immature spiritual life: *Brothers, I could not address you as spiritual but as worldly—mere infants in Christ. I gave you milk, not solid food, for you were not yet ready for it. Indeed, you are still not ready. You are still worldly.*

(Trace over the letter s with a capital S as shown below.) I will trace over the letter s in *spirit* with a **capital S** to show that the Holy Spirit is eternally a part of your spirit when you are born again. The worldly Christian's big mistake is having left open the door of the flesh. Satan still has access to this person, because the flesh dominates his or her thoughts, will, and emotions. The word *worldly* means "fleshly" or "carnal." This type of Christian is more likely to follow the physical senses and fallen nature than the spiritual nature he or she received at conversion.

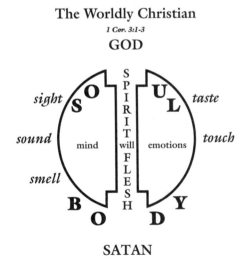

No doubt you sometimes feel conflict in your heart when you try to have the thoughts, attitudes, and actions of Jesus. Why does such conflict arise? If you do not allow Christ continually to be the Master of your life through His Spirit, you are a worldly Christian. Although you have allowed Christ to enter your life, you still struggle to control your own life. The big *I* of the old, natural person still dominates you. Worldly Christians continually open the door of the flesh, allowing the old nature to determine what they think, do, and feel, rather than follow the Spirit of God.

Competing influences cause this conflict in your personality. You hear Satan's voice through your flesh, and you hear God's voice as His Spirit speaks to your spirit. You hear the voice of self through your mind, will, and emotions. You become a battleground. How can you have victory in this kind of situation? Do not despair. Christ wants to be your Lord and to give you daily victory.

THE SPIRITUAL CHRISTIAN

(Draw another circle with the labels you used previously. Add the cross in the center as shown below. Leave the door of the spirit open and close the door of the flesh. Write *The Spiritual Christian* and *Galatians 2:20* above the circle as illustrated. Write *crucified* across *flesh*.) I will draw the **circle** once more to illustrate the spiritual Christian. As Christ's disciple, you are promised victory over the world, the flesh, and the devil. Here is how. Notice that your **will** is located between **the door of**

the spirit and the door of the flesh. The door of the spirit is open, while the door of the flesh is closed. When you are willing to let Christ master your life, His death on the cross and His resurrection give you a life of victory. You can say, as the apostle Paul did in *Galatians 2:20: I have been crucified with Christ and I no longer live, but Christ lives in me. The life I live in the body, I live by faith in the Son of God, who loved me and gave himself for me.*

The way to have victory is to consider your flesh **crucified.** Because this is an ongoing act of your will, the indwelling Christ helps you keep the door of the spirit open and the door of the flesh closed. As you put your old self to death, the Spirit of God gives you life daily to live in victory. When you do this, you are filled with the Spirit of God. You are able to live in the Spirit. God takes control of your mind, your will, your emotions, and therefore your soul and body.

Now you can see the contrast between the natural person and the worldly Christian. You can also see that the **spiritual Christian** walks in the Spirit so that he or she will not yield to the desires of the flesh.

STEPS TO VICTORIOUS LIVING

(Write *Philippians 2:13* under *will*. Write *Ephesians 5:18* above *Spirit.* Write *Romans 12:2* under *mind.* Write *Galatians 5:22-23*

The Spiritual Christian
Gal. 2:20
GOD

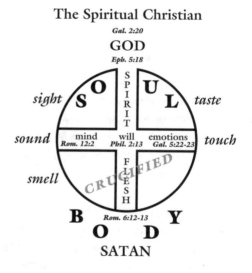

under *emotions*. Write *Romans 6:12-13* under *flesh*. Read or quote these Scriptures as you write.) Your victory is not automatic. As long as you live in your body, you continually fight the good fight of faith. But God promises you victory. Let me explain in practical terms how to let Christ master your total personality and how to let Him enable you to live in the Spirit.

Philippians 2:13 says, *It is God who works in you to will and to act according to his good purpose.* God helps you want to do His will and then gives you the ability to do it. By an act of your will, claim *Galatians 2:20* as your own experience.

Ephesians 5:18 says, *Be filled with the Spirit.* Ask the Holy Spirit to fill your personality and to keep filling you so that He can guide you, teach you, and give you the power to be a spiritual person.

Romans 12:2 says: *Do not conform any longer to the pattern of this world, but be transformed by renewing of your mind. Then you will be able to test and approve what God's will is—his good, pleasing and perfect will.*

Galatians 5:22-23 says: *The fruit of the spirit is love, joy, peace, patience, kindness, goodness, faithfulness, gentleness and self-control. Against such things there is no law.* As you allow the Spirit of God to fill you, He produces in you the fruit of the Spirit. The fruit of the Spirit helps produce the right emotions in you and helps you control your emotions.

Romans 6:12-13 says: *Do not let sin reign in your mortal body so that you obey its evil desires. Do not offer the parts of your body to sin, as instruments of wickedness, but rather offer yourselves to God, as those who have been brought from death to life; and offer the parts of your body to him as instruments of righteousness.* Your body is God's gift to you so that you can have an identity, participate in this world, and communicate with others. It is not evil in itself; only the flesh or your sinful nature is evil. Jesus came to live in your body to make it an instrument of righteousness instead of an instrument of sin. Present your body and all of its members to God to do good.

(Write *1 Corinthians 6:19-20* on one side of the circle and *Romans 12:1* on the other side of the circle.) The idea of punishing the body because it is evil is not a Christian idea. **First Corinthians 6:19-20** says: *Do you not know that your body is a temple of the Holy Spirit, who is in you, whom you have received from God? You are not your own; you were bought at a price. There-*

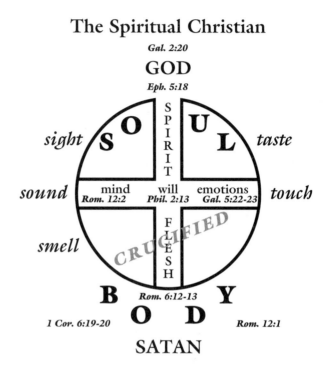

The Spiritual Christian
Gal. 2:20
GOD
Eph. 5:18

sight — *taste*
sound — mind *Rom. 12:2* — will *Phil. 2:13* — emotions *Gal. 5:22-23* — *touch*
smell — CRUCIFIED
BODY
Rom. 6:12-13
1 Cor. 6:19-20 — *Rom. 12:1*
SATAN

fore honor God with your body. **Romans 12:1** says, *I urge you, brothers, in view of God's mercy, to offer your bodies as living sacrifices, holy and pleasing to God—this is your spiritual act of worship.* Christ's incarnation in a human body shows its potential for being restored to its original condition when Christ returns again and gives you a spiritual body like His.

As you fully yield yourself to God, the Holy Spirit helps you master your mind, your will, your emotions, your body, and your soul through the power of Christ. The life you live now, you live *by faith in the Son of God,* as *Galatians 2:20* says. As you obey Christ and His commands, He lives in you and you in Him. Christ lives in the world through you. Your inner self is integrated, and you experience peace. You are continually being filled with the Holy Spirit, and you overflow with joy, love, peace, praise, and thanksgiving. Rivers of living water flow from you to other persons as a witness to Christ, who lives in you through the Spirit.

WHO ARE YOU?

Now evaluate your life.

- Are you a natural person whose spirit is dead? Do your bodily senses and your natural desires control you?
- Are you a worldly Christian who has allowed Christ to enter your life but is still being mastered by the desires of the flesh? Is the big *I* still in control?
- Are you a spiritual Christian who has been crucified with Christ and is being controlled by the Holy Spirit?

(Write *I Thessalonians 5:23-24* under *Galatians 2:20*.) First Thessalonians 5:23-24 says: *May God himself, the God of peace, sanctify you through and through. May your whole spirit, soul and body be kept blameless at the coming of our Lord Jesus Christ. The one who calls you is faithful and he will do it.*

Spiritual Christians are not perfect, but daily they crucify the flesh and consciously allow the Holy Spirit to fill them. When they are tempted, they invite Christ to fill their lives, and they close the door of the flesh. When they sin, they ask for God's forgiveness and strength to help them overcome the next temptation.

Remember these seven steps to Christlike character:

1. Ask God, through the Holy Spirit's guidance, to help you *will* to do the right thing.
2. Open the door of the *spirit* to the Spirit of God by asking Him to fill you.
3. Close the door of the *flesh* to Satan by confessing your sins and by claiming Christ's crucifixion of the flesh.
4. Renew your *mind* by saturating it with the Word of God.
5. Allow the Holy Spirit to master your *emotions* by producing the fruit of the Spirit in you.
6. Present your *body* to Christ as an instrument of righteousness.
7. Love the Lord your God with all your *heart*, with all your *soul*, with all your *mind*, and with all your *strength*.

____

[1]Some people believe that the soul and the spirit are the same rather than two distinct aspects of your personality. Their function is the same whether you think of your soul as having three parts (body, soul, and spirit) or two parts (body and soul, with the spirit being seen as the part of the soul). Although people who hold to each position believe they have a biblical basis for their position, your view of this matter does not affect the meaning of this presentation. It deals with the battle between the flesh and the spirit, not between the soul and the spirit.

The Spiritual Christian

Gal. 2:20
1 Thess. 5:23-24

GOD

Eph. 5:18

sight — S O U L — *taste*

SPIRIT

sound — mind (Rom. 12:2) · will (Phil. 2:13) · emotions (Gal. 5:22-23) — *touch*

smell — FLESH — CRUCIFIED

B O D Y

Rom. 6:12-13

1 Cor. 6:19-20   *Rom. 12:1*

SATAN

Applying the Disciple's Personality

James 4:1-8

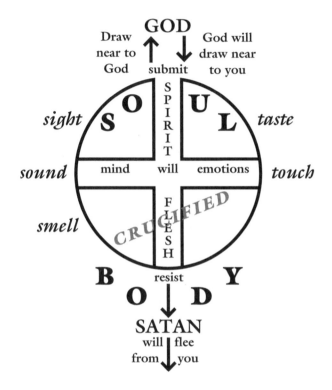

Galatians 5:16-25

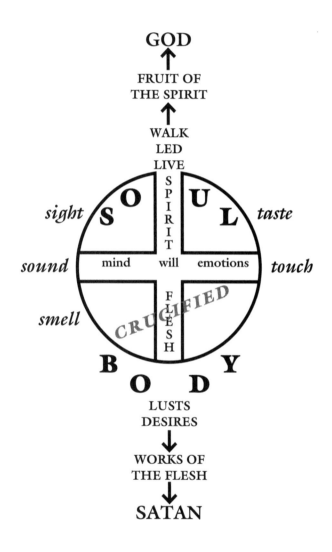

Hearing the Word

Date _____ **Place** _____

Speaker _____ **Text** _____

Title _____

Message
Points, explanation, illustrations, application:

_____

_____

_____

_____

_____

_____

_____

_____

_____

_____

_____

_____

_____

Summary

The main thing the speaker wants me to do, be, and/or feel as a result of this message:

_____

_____

_____

_____

Application to My Life

What did God say to me through this message?

_____

_____

_____

_____

How does my life measure up to this word?

_____

_____

_____

_____

What action(s) will I take to bring my life in line with this word?

_____

_____

_____

_____

What truth do I need to study further?

_____

_____

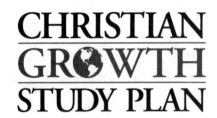

CHRISTIAN GROWTH STUDY PLAN

In the **Christian Growth Study Plan (formerly the Church Study Course)** *MasterLife, Student Edition,* is a resource for course credit in the subject area Personal Life in the Christian Growth Category of diploma plans. To receive credit, read the book; complete the learning activities; attend group sessions; show your work to your pastor, a staff member, or a church leader; and complete the following information. This page may be duplicated. Send the completed page to:

Christian Growth Study Plan
One LifeWay Plaza
Nashville, TN 37234-0117
FAX: (615) 251-5067
E-mail: cgspnet@lifeway.com

For information about the Christian Growth Study Plan, refer to the Christian Growth Study Plan Catalog. It is located online at *www.lifeway.com/cgsp.* If you do not have access to the Internet, contact the Christian Growth Study Plan office (1.800.968.5519) for the specific plan you need for your ministry.

MasterLife, Student Edition

COURSE NUMBER: CG-0438

PARTICIPANT INFORMATION

Social Security Number (USA ONLY-optional)	Personal CGSP Number*	Date of Birth (MONTH, DAY, YEAR)
Name (First, Middle, Last)		Home Phone
Address (Street, Route, or P.O. Box)	City, State, or Province	Zip/Postal Code
Email Address for CGSP use		

Please check appropriate box: ❏ Resource purchased by church ❏ Resource purchased by self ❏ Other

CHURCH INFORMATION

Church Name		
Address (Street, Route, or P.O. Box)	City, State, or Province	Zip/Postal Code

CHANGE REQUEST ONLY

☐ Former Name		
☐ Former Address	City, State, or Province	Zip/Postal Code
☐ Former Church	City, State, or Province	Zip/Postal Code

Signature of Pastor, Conference Leader, or Other Church Leader	Date

*New participants are requested but not required to give SS# and date of birth. Existing participants, please give CGSP# when using SS# for the first time. Thereafter, only one ID# is required. **Mail to:** Christian Growth Study Plan, One LifeWay Plaza, Nashville, TN 37234-0117. Fax: (615)251-5067.

Revised 4-05

Additional Discipleship Resources

David: Seeking God's Heart
by Beth Moore

Based on the Beth Moore study, A Heart Like His, this six-session interactive youth resource provides a real-life account of David's life in a way that allows students to discover God's heart and the relationship He desires to have with His children. By relating to David's triumph and tragedy, his agony and ecstasy, students can reflect upon and personally examine their own attitudes, motivations, actions, character and heart—and come away knowing that they can always find comfort and forgiveness in God's arms regardless of their failures or successes. (6 sessions)

Student Edition 0-6330-1734-5
Leader's Guide 0-6330-1735-3

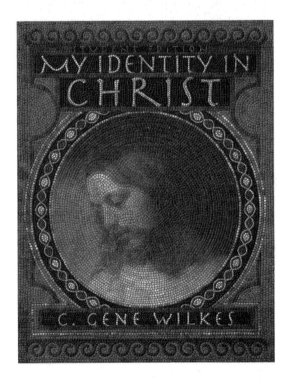

My Identity in Christ, Student Edition
by C. Gene Wilkes

It's easy for young Christians to get caught up in what their friends and classmates think about them—so it's easy for them to develop a self-identity based on peer pressure and the thousands of other pressures of the everyday world. Through this Transformational Discipleship resource, students can better understand who they are in Christ, which is the only identity that counts. It will encourage them to live a life that portrays Christ-likeness and will instill a sense of confidence about themselves as they mature into young adults. Student book also includes group sharing and activity ideas for those leading the group study. (6 sessions plus introductory session)

0-6330-2992-0

Additional Discipleship Resources

Experiencing God, Youth Edition, Revised
by Henry Blackaby and Claude V. King

With over 500,000 copies sold, *Experiencing God: Knowing and Doing the Will of God* is one of the most significant studies in which students and adults can participate.

This study guides students through a crucial understanding of knowing God and joining Him where He is at work. It is designed for teens to study and apply biblical principles to their daily lives. It is about helping them to experience God—day-by-day, moment-by-moment.

In this book teens will:
- Learn how to hear God when He is speaking to them.
- Find out where God is working and join Him.
- Discover that God pursues a love relationship with them that is real and personal.
- Faces crises of belief as they join God where He is working.
- Experience God doing through them what only God can do!

Experiencing God: Knowing and Doing the Will of God is a nine-week course designed for both individual and small group study. Students and their leaders will spend time with God every day using the student book (ISBN 141582603X) and then meet together in a small group once a week for group study (*Leader's Guide*: ISBN 1415828598). Also available is the *Experiencing God Youth DVD Pack* (ISBN 1415828660), which contains one leader's guide, one student book and a DVD to use in weekly group meetings. In this drama, teens will watch the story unfold each week and will discover parallels between the video and the principles in *Experiencing God.*